CONTENTS

1. **THE HEALTHY HORSE**
   Before You Can Recognize And Treat An Ill Horse, You Must
   Know *Equus Caballus* In His Healthy State 4

2. **PROPER GROOMING AND HOW TO**
   Cleanliness Is Part Of Good Stable Management And
   Brings Trouble Spots To Light Early 6

3. **DISEASES: CAUSE & TREATMENT**
   The Horse Is Plagued With Many Diseases, And Listed
   Here Are The Most Common, With Treatment For Each 14

4. **INTERNAL DISORDERS**
   The Inner Workings Of The Horse Are Complex And Finicky,
   Prone To Upset By These Conditions 26

5. **EXTERNAL PROBLEMS**
   Bruises, Cuts And More Serious Injuries Befall The
   Horse. Know How To Minimize The Danger And Pain 36

6. **PARASITISM: PREVENTION & TREATMENT**
   Research Continues To Show The Major Role Of Parasites
   In Other Equine Maladies 46

7. **PRACTICAL HORSE FEEDING**
   This Is A Complicated Subject, But One
   The Horseman Should Understand 62

8. **FOCUSING ON FEET**
   A Fact-Finding Expedition Inside The Hoof
   Details Its Complexities, Which You'll Need To Know 68

9. **SHOEING THE NORMAL FOOT**
   Few Horses Are Blessed With Perfect Feet And Legs,
   And All Need The Services Of A Good Farrier 75

10. **CORRECTIVE TRIMMING & SHOEING**
    See What The Experienced — And Only The Experienced —
    Farrier Can Do To Alleviate Or Minimize Foot Problems 87

CHAPTER 1
THE HEALTHY HORSE

Before You Can Recognize And Treat An Ill Horse, You Must Know Equus Caballus In His Healthy State

All horsemen should be able to distinguish between a horse in good health and one that isn't, confirming his suspicions with simple checks. Most people instinctively recognize something wrong with their animals when behavior alters considerably.

Healthy horses appear alert, interested in what's going on around them. Their eyes, which can tell a horseman so much, should be bright, clear and wide open, except when resting. Another good indication that a horse is healthy is his appetite — he'll eat the bottom out of a bucket! If he stands with his head down, ears drooping like a mule, eyes partly closed and dull in appearance, he favors one of his limbs or quits eating, something is wrong. Before calling the veterinarian, run these simple tests which may help with his diagnosis.

First, take the horse's temperature, which requires that a horseman have a good-quality rectal thermometer on hand. The normal temperature for a horse is between 99.8 and

Mighty Warrior, a champion Pinto gelding, reflects the healthful picture for which all horsemen should strive. He's in good flesh and immaculately groomed, a procedure that handler Beverly May relates in Chapter 2. Horseowners must recognize the responsibilities they assume upon purchasing a horse, the purpose for this book.

Top show jumpers like Rodney Jenkins carefully watch their chargers, since Number One Spy and others can't perform optimally if ill. Pleasure riders, as pictured below, should follow their lead.

101 degrees Fahrenheit (37.5 to 38.5 degrees Celsius) and, if the horse is over or under this mark, jot the results down for passing to the veterinarian.

The procedure for inserting the thermometer is first to shake it snappily to drive all the mercury to the bottom, just as performed on TV medical programs. The thermometer is coated with a lubricant such as petroleum jelly, then is inserted into the anus. After one to two minutes, the thermometer is removed and the results noted.

The horse's anus must be tightly contracted to take a correct reading. If it isn't, the recorded temperature will be lower than it actually is. And because the temperature in other parts of the body differ, the rectum is the only location in which the casual horseman can take a reading. If the anus is not contracted tightly, this fact also should be passed to the veterinarian.

Another function which bears examination is the breathing rate of the horse and this should be taken when he is resting, not active or excited. This can be determined most easily by watching the flanks as they swell outward with each inhalation. Count the number of breaths he takes in thirty seconds, then multiply this number by two to give the total for a minute. Horses at rest generally take between eight and sixteen breaths per minute. The rate of foal respiration is naturally higher. Note the rate for the vet.

The pulse rate is checked easily by gently pressing the large artery under either side of the horse's jaw. It should be measured with the second finger of either hand for fifteen seconds, the total being multiplied four times for one minute's total. The average rate of heartbeat is between thirty-six and forty beats per minute and, if the horse is ill, it may either be lower or higher than this group. As with the other readings, note the results for the veterinarian.

Much can be told about a horse's physical condition by his mucous membranes, specifically the eyes, nose and mouth. When the horse is healthy, the tissue around the eyes is moist and pink, denoting proper blood circulation. If the tissue is pallid, this could denote an anemic condition, hemorrhage in another part of the body or congestion of the abdominal organs, among others. If the membranes are yellowish in color, the horse may have liver problems; if red, they're inflamed. Should they be dry to the touch, the horse probably has a fever.

Examine the feces of the horse, along with his urine. If there is a change in consistency from normal, note the dif-

Karl Mikolka, a top dressage rider and trainer, was tutored in proper horse care at Spanish Riding School.

ference. If the urine changes color from normal, note that, too. The only exception to the latter is in some of the northern Midwest areas. Because of pigment in the urine, it assumes a reddish coloration when contacting snow on the ground which some horseowners claim resembles blood. If the animal does urinate blood, inform the veterinarian of the fact upon his arrival or when contacted by telephone.

No matter the ailment or its severity, always consult professional advice. The following diseases, their causes and symptoms are to be used solely as guiding and informative compilations and never do they supercede the advice of your veterinarian.

No matter the ailment or its severity, always seek professional advice. Many of the diseases and health problems discussed have similar symptoms. Your veterinarian can recognize the cause and diagnose correctly. The information in this book never supercedes the advice of your veterinarian.

CHAPTER 2

PROPER GROOMING AND HOW TO

Cleanliness Is Part Of Good Stable Management And Brings Trouble Spots To Light Early

As mundane as it sounds, grooming is of major importance in the horse health world. Not only does grooming improve the appearance of the animal, but also removes external parasites, aids in the control of internal parasites, removes sweat and other excretions, improves circulation, stimulates tissues and helps rid the horse of unneeded winter hair during the spring thaw. Also, frequent and proper grooming is much like regularly servicing an automobile; the owner can discover maladies early, before they do serious damage to his equine form of horsepower.

Grooming is a daily chore requiring at least a good half hour of the horseman's time and some specialized, inexpensive tools. These are a sweat scraper, a grooming or rub rag, towel, rubber comb, curry comb, body brush, dandy brush, soft-bristle brush, mane and tail comb, hoof pick and a set of electric clippers. By far the most important tool a horseman can bring to the task is old-fashioned elbow grease — plenty of it.

The type of grooming given to a horse daily will depend, to some extent, on the section of the country and time of year. Especially in cold climes, for example, a horse with heavy winter coat won't be bathed as often as during summer months, unless the horseman wants to spend extra time at his task to ensure thorough drying by hand to prevent chilling which can lead to respiratory problems, among others.

For the most part, a horse is groomed only slightly before working. Usually this calls only for brushing before tacking up. This removes any foreign matter on the coat which could irritate the skin under the saddle or cinches and ensures the hair is lying flat in the proper direction. Start at the neck near the head on the left side of the horse and brush away all dust and foreign matter, progressing backward to the croup and hind legs before moving to the right side and repeating the procedure. Pay careful attention to the withers and back, where a burr or thistle will gouge the skin after application of the saddle and a rider's weight.

After a work, it is essential that a horse be cooled thoroughly before beginning any grooming. The easiest way to accomplish this cooling out is to walk the horse back to the barn from the exercise area and, if the horse has worked hard, a twenty to forty-minute walking stint is required. If additional walking is required, remove the tack, go over the horse with a sweat scraper to whisk away excess moisture

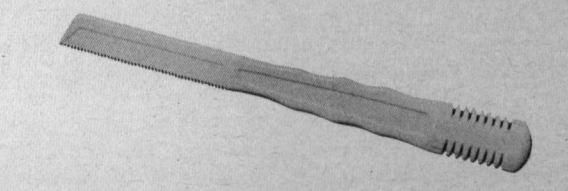

There are many styles of grooming implements on the market today, one of which is the shedder/scraper/trimmer shown here. Used properly, they help horses.

Beverly May puts elbow grease behind body brush when grooming Mighty Warrior, a Pinto champion (left). A curry comb was used previously, to loosen dirt (above).

from the coat, mop up the remaining moisture with a rub rag or grooming cloth, then blanket the animal if weather requires it and walk him until the chest is cool to the touch and his respiratory rate returns to normal. The chest is the last area to cool and, when no longer hot to the touch, the animal can be watered. If watered while hot the horse can founder, which will be explained in another chapter.

When cool, the groomer first should remove all excess dirt and mud with the rubber comb, metal curry comb or stiff dandy brush. The latter has stiff bristles some two inches long, attached to a wooden or plastic spine with some type of hollow middle for easy handling. Again starting on the left side directly behind the head, brush the hair toward the rear with firm strokes. If using a rubber comb, groom in circular fashion which will loosen deep dirt. Move from the neck down to the chest, shoulder, withers, down the foreleg to the knee, then over his back, croup, belly and hindquarter, going down to the hock. This is repeated on the right side of the horse with the same implements and, if dirt still remains on the coat, go over the horse again with the body brush, which has fairly stiff bristling with a loop of some type for solid hold.

Some horsemen feel the curry comb should be used only to clean the bristles of the body brush, which it does admirably. It shouldn't be used on the head or legs below the hocks. These areas have little fatty tissue or muscle between the skin and bone, making them extremely sensitive. Grooming these areas with the curry comb could lead to some interesting — and unwanted — rodeo-type action when the metal teeth dig in. Instead, use only a soft-bristle brush, rub rag or towel on these areas.

The mane and tail require attention next. It's hard to

Some larger stables make good use of vacuum cleaners, with fine results. This horse enjoys the belly-rub action! Simpler implements are available to horsemen with a more limited income, though, and do the job admirably.

Once tangles have been removed with a mane and tail comb, Beverly May favors a woman's hair brush for final separation of hair. The text gives more details.

believe the incredible tangles and snarls which can develop, often with burrs or foxtails thrown in for good measure. The metal mane and tail comb has been designed specifically for this task and, with a little patience, it doesn't take long to have the individual strands separated and hanging properly.

To avoid pulling hairs from the mane and tail, begin by applying the comb at the bottom of the mane or tail and work upwards. Sometimes a squirt of tangle remover or coat conditioner will help and, when finished, brush with the body brush. Use care when attending the forelock: hold it suspended above the poll when brushing because the poll is sensitive.

Because germs can accumulate on grooming implements, it's a good idea to disinfect them at regular intervals. This is especially important if more than one horse is groomed with the same tools, as often is the case in a stable. A mild disinfectant will kill the germs on your implements. The rub rags and towels should first be soaked in a disinfectant solution then washed, which also keeps their appearance pleasing. Like any professional craftsman, it's always more of a pleasure to work with the proper tools in good condition.

There are times, like directly prior to an upcoming show, when a bath is in order. There are several schools of thought regarding proper bathing procedures, but most

The wise horseman keeps all of his grooming tools and aids in a box like that pictured below. This saves time and money, as tools don't become lost and always are at hand. Prior to heading for a horse show, other items can be added to the box.

A hoof pick is inexpensive protection against hoof disorders like thrush. Used from heel to toe, it removes dead sole and built up materials. Daily use means a healthy hoof.

trainers rely on the garden hose with a sprayer nozzle and a bucket of suds. Others use a series of buckets and a sponge. Whatever the method, remember that a horse's hair differs little from a human's. Washing removes some of the natural oils — in horses, the sebum — which gives the coat its sheen and this should be replaced during washing, generally by the use of a lanolin-containing shampoo. Never use a harsh detergent for the chore; it could damage the skin or irritate the eyes. Stick to the shampoos specifically manufactured for equines, of which there are many.

Once the horse is wet, apply the shampoo with the hands, some type of sponge or a brush. Apply it all over the horse's body in much the same sequence as brushing, only start with the head. Work the shampoo into a rich lather, paying particular attention to the mane, tail and forelock, before rinsing. Wash all the suds from the body and remove the moisture with the sweat scraper. Complete drying with the rub rag or towel or, if it's a warm day, the horse can be placed on a walker to drip-dry after scraping. If the weather is cool, he should be blanketed with a cooler.

The feet need daily attention, also, and should be clean-

Depending upon the weather and time of year, horses should be bathed with regularity. The shampoo used should have some type of lanolin base, which replaces the coat's natural oils removed during shampooing.

ed with the hoof pick. Always work from heel to toe when cleaning, to prevent puncturing the frog. A good cleaning alleviates the possibility of thrush to a large extent and brings to light any other foot problems, such as dryness. Check the fit of the shoes when cleaning and whether the horse is due for a trim.

These are the basics of good grooming but, as in most other endeavors, there still are some extra steps which can be taken to improve the horse's appearance further, so vital when showing or selling the mount. The first of these involves clipping the unsightly hairs from the muzzle, eyes, ears and fetlocks, and functional trimming of the bridle path, or top of the mane at the poll across which a strap of a halter rests.

Trimming the hairs from the muzzle is an easy and straightforward procedure, less complicated than around the eyes. Most right-handed horsemen hold the mount's eyelid closed with the thumb of the left hand (vice versa for southpaws), which serves two important purposes. It keeps the horse from shying suddenly and perhaps damaging the eye with the clipper blades, and prevents him from blinking his eyelashes into the clippers, resulting in an unusual appearance.

There are several schools of thought relative to trimming the hair inside the horse's ears and center around the problem of insects. Trimming the hair growing inside the ear avails the ear canal to easy access by insects and horsemen favoring this look must keep the ears constantly protected with an insect repellent where insects are prevalent.

For the best fetlock appearance, clippers should be booted down, or used from the knee down to the fetlock and not vice versa. There should be no sign of the clippers having been used by this procedure. The only hair booted up is around the coronet band on the hoof — take care not to injure the pastern.

Clipping the bridle path is necessary but the length of the trim is disputable. On the average, most horsemen trim somewhere around three inches, which is wide enough to handle most halters and bridles. This is a matter of personal preference, as is roaching the horse's mane.

If the mane isn't roached — trimmed short its total length — most horsemen like to have it even; the same with

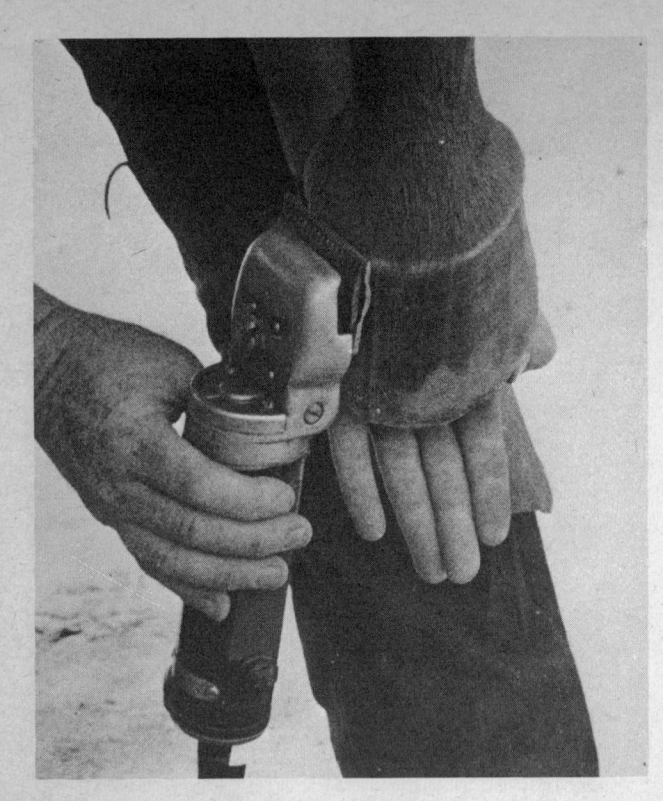

Some horsemen feel "booting" a horse's legs downward, using clippers from top to bottom, results in much more pleasing appearance. Boot up at pasterns, to avoid injury.

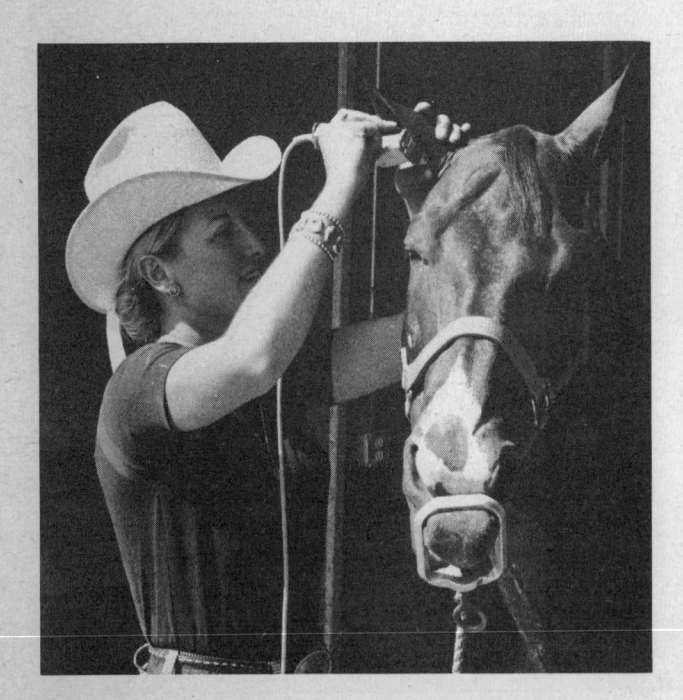

Blacking agents like Farnam's Hoof Black are employed mostly by show horsemen. This gives the hoofs a pleasing appearance — which can mean blue ribbons in the ring!

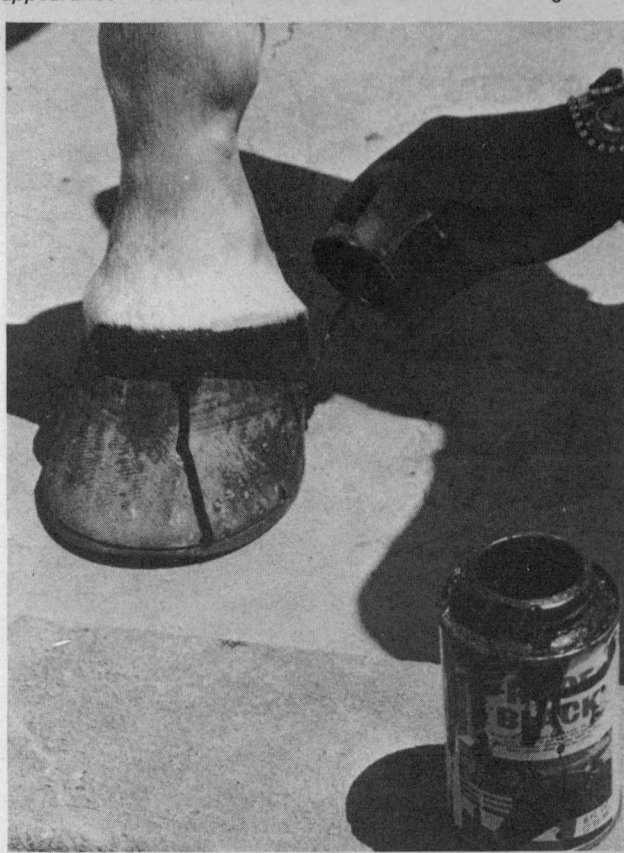

Clipping a horse's eyelashes must be done with caution, for a slip could result in eye injury. The lid should be held closed with the thumb during clipping procedure.

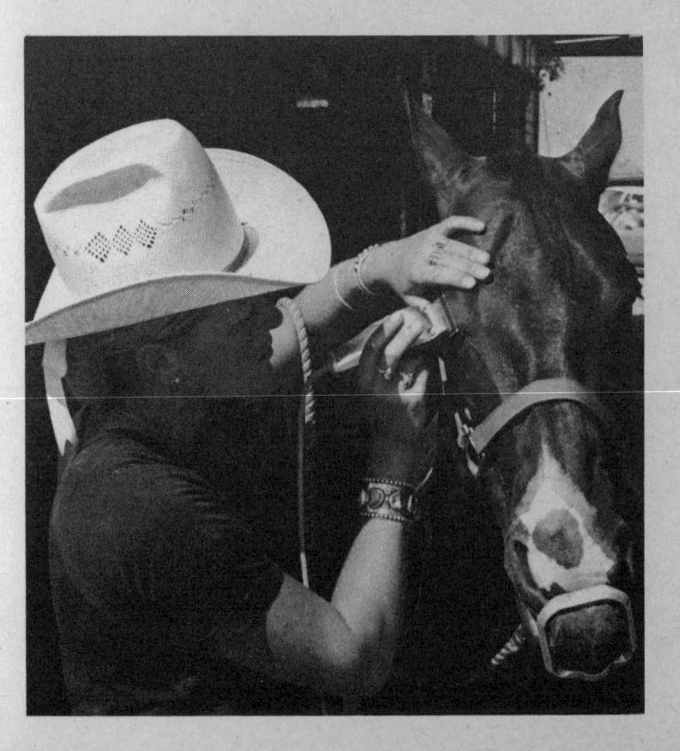

Some horseowners like the hair trimmed away from inside the ears, as Beverly May does (above). Once clipped, use insect repellent; ear canal now is open.

the tail. This is accomplished by pulling a few too-long hairs with the thumb and index finger of one hand, while pushing the surrounding hairs of the mane or tail toward the roots with the other. A short, snappy pull removes those too long or unsightly. Don't remove more than a few

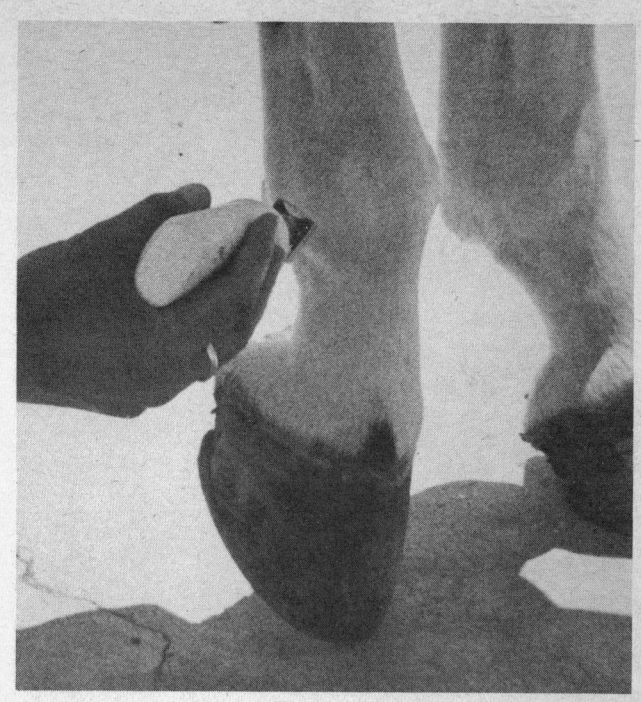

A horse sporting long muzzle hairs can be less than attractive and can be a fault in the show ring. It often takes time for a horse to become accustomed to vibration on his nose, but Mighty Warrior has no complaints (left). Any discolored or dark spots on this show horse's white stockings are touched-up with shoe polish. This extra step aids appearance.

strands with each pull, for the mane or tail will become sore. The tail usually reaches the hocks, seldom farther.

Sometimes a horse's mane won't lie properly. This can be rectified by braiding the mane on the side the horseowner desires it to hang, the weight ultimately training the hair. When unbraided or if the problem isn't too severe, the mane can be sponged with water on the side desired to aid in holding it properly. If the mane is really stubborn, some horsemen use dowels or broomsticks some two feet long, attaching them directly to the hair. The weight trains the mane.

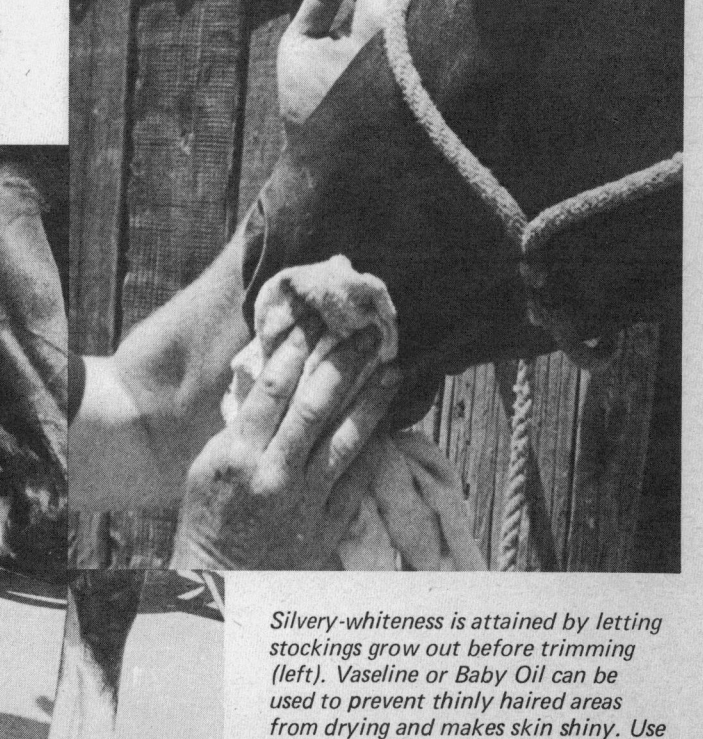

Silvery-whiteness is attained by letting stockings grow out before trimming (left). Vaseline or Baby Oil can be used to prevent thinly haired areas from drying and makes skin shiny. Use it around the eyes, muzzle, on rump, etc.

Natural sheen in manes and tails is enhanced through use of such products as Grand Champion spray (left). Most now favor the even mane when the hair isn't roached.

The clipped length of a horse's bridle path is a matter of personal preference, but should be long enough to accommodate horse's halter. Use sharp clipper blades.

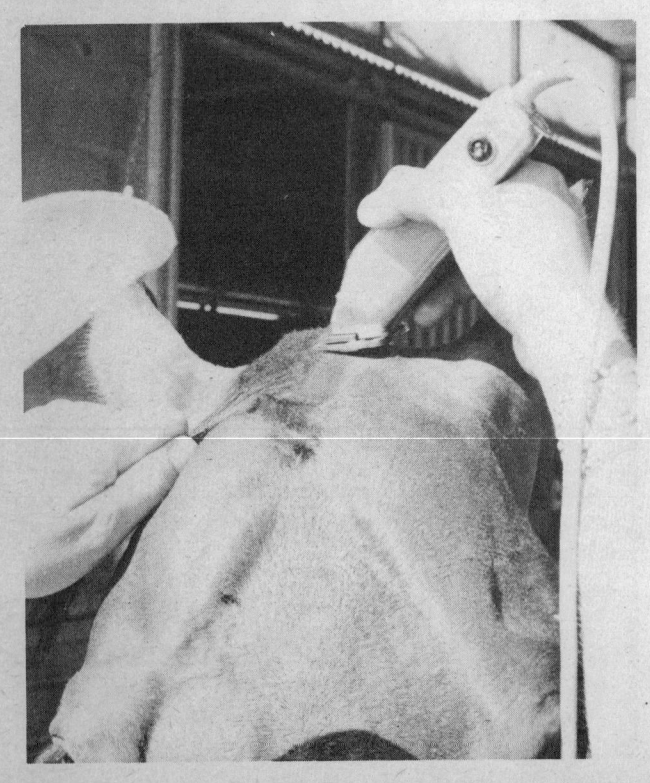

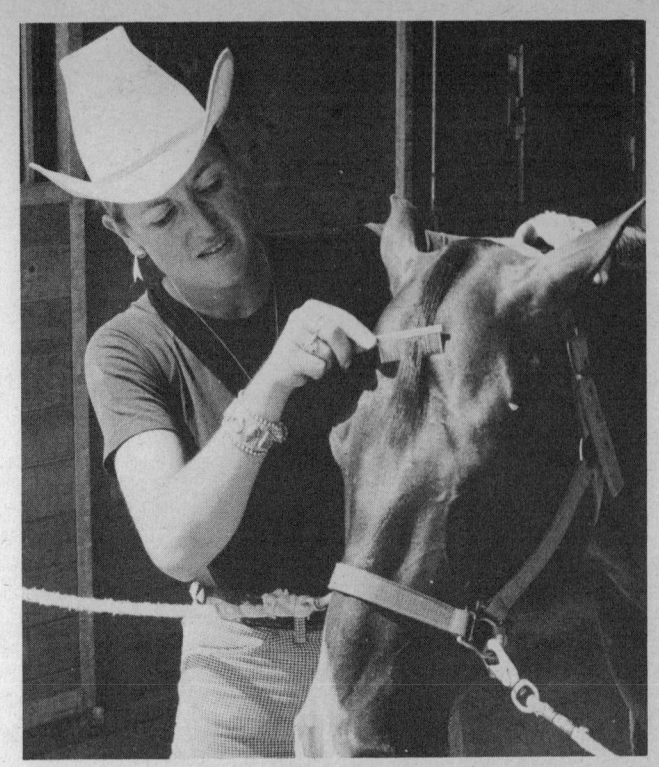

The amount of hair left in forelock is determined by the shape of the horse's head, specifically width. A thin forelock enhances the width of the head, what judges like.

Show horsemen frequently apply some type of coat conditioner to the hair, which brings up gloss. Ms. May here uses Dazzle, which is applied to wet horse.

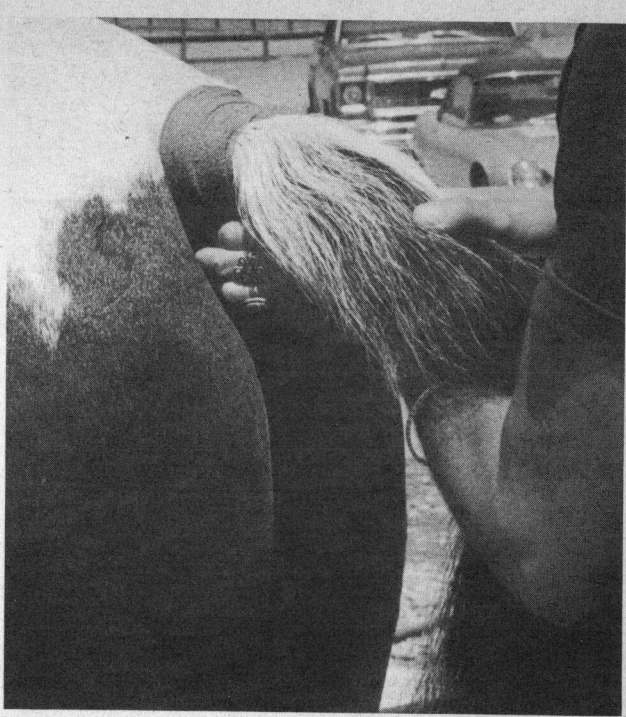

Wrapping a horse's tail is usual procedure prior to shipping or hauling, the proper way shown in the four photos on this page. After initial wrap, here using Velcro-backed Vetrap by 3M Company, is started at the base of the tail, it is wound progressively down the horse's tail. This serves to protect the tail's root, along with fending off any excrement stains.

The last chore in grooming is to sponge the eyes and nostrils with plain water. Grooming is an endless procedure but, as noted at the beginning of this chapter, is good for the horse in more ways than one!

The wrap should be overlapped slightly as it is affixed around the horse's tail and the end result should approach that seen below right. Care must be taken, however, to avoid wrapping the tail too tightly: this cuts off vital blood circulation to tail.

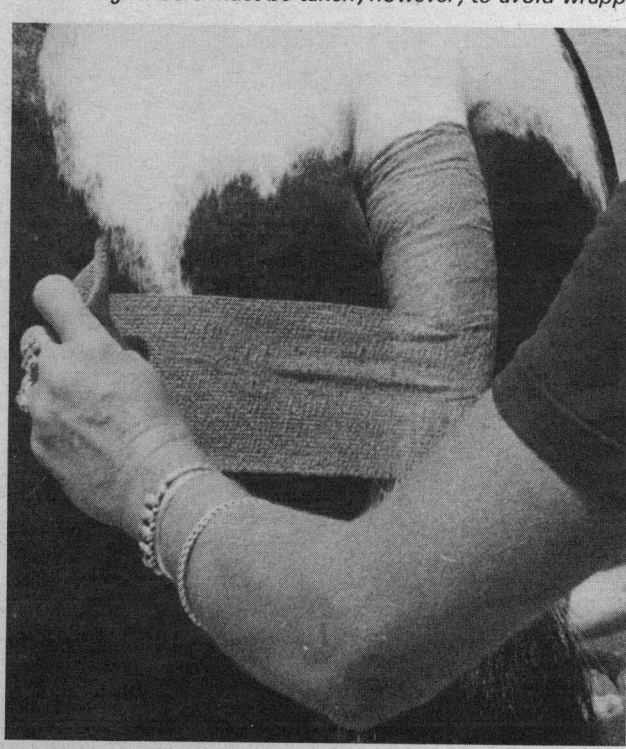

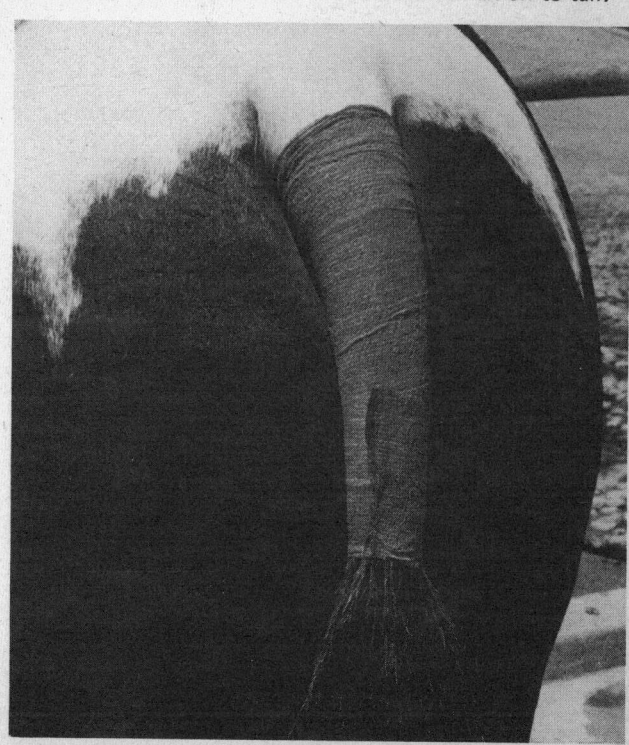

CHAPTER 3
DISEASES: CAUSE & TREATMENT

This happy mare/foal team have overcome the possibility of infection and death by numerous equine diseases up to this point. To keep this scene from assuming one of those on the following pages, the horseowner should follow instruction in text.

Unfortunately, despite all of science's efforts, diseases plague the American horse population. A surprising number of these diseases could be eradicated, since serums have been developed which guarantee immunity against them. However, there always remains a certain percentage of horseowners who fail to have their horses immunized, which leads to continued affliction.

The most common diseases encountered will be covered in this chapter. These include: distemper, equine infectious anemia, colds and influenza, equine viral arteritis, equine viral rhinopneumonitis, *Salmonella abortivoequina*, equine encephalomyelitis, leptospirosis and periodic ophthalmia, tetanus, malignant edema, piroplasmosis, chronic pulmonary emphysema, colitis X, neonatal pyosepticemia, viscosum infection and neonatal isoerythrolysis.

DISTEMPER
Equine distemper, also known as strangles, is a disease prevalent where horses gather in large numbers — at race tracks, big stables, showgrounds — and is caused by *Streptococcus equi*, a bacteria. It affects weanlings and yearlings as much as older horses, but most are exposed to and are immune by the time they are 5 years old.

Generally encountered in early Spring when the weather is wet and cold, strangles strikes horses with resistance lowered through fatigue, exposure to rapid changes in temperature or stabling in drafty, cold facilities. Strangles spreads rapidly by direct contact with the mucousal secretions of an infected horse, or indirectly through water troughs, grooming tools, blankets and feed boxes or mangers. There also is a possibility of transmission by the horseowner.

The symptoms of strangles usually appear five to six days after contracting the disease and initial signs are a fast-rising temperature which peaks at around 104 to 106 degrees, increased and/or difficult breathing, general depression and the horse goes off his feed. The nasal passages will become inflamed and dry, and a clear, watery discharge begins some two to three days later. After several days, the discharge thickens and the amount increases, which leads to breathing difficulty, coughing and snorting.

At the same time, the lymph glands at the base of the lower jaw at the neck begin to swell, which may cause the horse to hold his head abnormally high, the neck outstretched. The lymph glands will become abscessed and, as the swelling continues, eventually the skin surrounding the area will rupture, or be surgically opened, releasing large quantities of thick, creamy pus. Unless there are complications, the horse generally will begin improving as his temperature drops. The fatality rate for horses infected with strangles is only about two percent.

As noted, complications are infrequent. These include the formation of abscesses in the lymph glands of other areas, including nasal and abdominal regions. The secretions draining from the nose may progress into the throat, causing breathing difficulty but rarely requiring tracheotomy to prevent suffocation. Sometimes when the lymph glands rupture, small amounts of pus are inhaled into the bronchial tubes or lungs proper, which can lead to pneumonia or pleurisy.

To hasten recovery, the horse should be isolated and placed in a draft-free stall protected from the elements, and have complete rest. Fresh drinking water should be available at all times and he should be encouraged to eat by frequently offering small amounts of appetizing, easily swallowed feeds. The veterinarian will treat him with antibiotics such as penicillin, tetracycline and chlortetracycline, or various types of sulfa drugs.

To prevent reinfection or the spread of strangles, the horse's bedding should be removed and burned, his equipment thoroughly disinfected and the stable kept clean. When the horse has recovered, the stall should be completely disinfected. A good vaccine is available.

EQUINE INFECTIOUS ANEMIA

Equine Infectious Anemia (EIA), also known as swamp fever, once was found predominantly around swamps but now is found just about everywhere. It is a serious ailment and if the horse doesn't die, his usefulness may be at an end.

The EIA virus is present in the horse's blood consistently, although it has been isolated in milk, urine, semen, feces containing blood and nasal secretions. It is transmitted by biting horseflies, mosquitos and use of unsterilized instruments, especially hypodermic needles. Bad outbreaks have been caused by repeated usage of unsterilized needles.

Once contracted, the disease can take one of three forms, with symptoms usually developing from seven to twenty-one days after infection: acute, subacute or chronic. In acute cases, the horse's temperature skyrockets up as high as 108 degrees Fahrenheit, he sweats profusely, is depressed, won't eat, his head hangs low, he loses a great amount of weight, rests his weight on the hind legs, gets progressively weaker and dies. Subacute cases begin in the same manner, but for some reason the febrile attacks decrease in intensity and frequency after three to five days. The horse may suffer repeated attacks and, if spaced relatively close together, the animal dies.

Cases where the attacks are spaced far enough apart to keep the animal alive are termed chronic. The horse suffers intermittent fever, weight loss, lack of appetite, diarrhea and may be anemic, although in some cases the red blood cell count is normal. The average mortality rate is somewhere between thirty and seventy percent.

A problem with swamp fever is that it cannot be diagnosed readily by a veterinarian. An old way of testing was to inject blood from horses suspected of infection into test horses and observing the results. If the test animals showed symptoms of the disease, it then was assumed the horse was indeed infected; this procedure took approximately two months and was done only when numerous horses were involved.

The U.S. Department of Agriculture and many states now

The Horse Is Plagued With Many Diseases, And Listed Are The Most Common, With Treatment For Each

When infected with strangles, caused by a bacteria, horses are generally debilitated. The lymph glands at base of lower jaw (circled) swell and later rupture.

recognize the "agar-gel immunodiffusion" (AGID) test, often called the Coggins test. It now is official and widely used. A small blood sample is taken by a veterinarian and submitted to any of several USDA-operated laboratories for analysis.

It is safe to suspect Equine Infectious Anemia if some of these symptoms become apparent or, if for no apparent reason, several horses exhibit other-than-normal behavior after introduction of a new horse to the premises. Because there is no vaccination available or workable treatment, there is little a horseowner can do but have the test performed on the suspect horse. If the results are positive, have the animal destroyed, the carcass either burned or buried well below the surface. To do otherwise simply endangers the other horses around the infected animal, which remains an active carrier for years.

The best way to avoid the disease is to have all horses tested and require tests on all horses admitted to the farm. A good insect control program should be implemented, especially during Summertime when mosquitos and other biting insects are at peak numbers. Finally, a horseman who does his own doctoring should ensure his surgical instruments are sterilized after usage on each horse; boiling in water for at least fifteen minutes will kill any germs and bacteria. Also, since the virus may be contained in the body secretions and excretions, disinfect all equipment and facilities coming into contact with that horse.

COLDS & INFLUENZA

As with humans, horses suffer from these illnesses which cause more discomfort than serious problem. The cold is the least serious of the pair and usually makes its appearance in Autumn and Winter, or strikes foals within the first few months of their lives. The symptoms are markedly similar to human colds, with fever lasting a few days, watery nasal discharge which thickens later and an overall not-so-hot feeling. The cold, unless complications arise, generally runs its course in four to five days. Complications, especially in foals, usually affect the respiratory tract, setting the system up for pneumonic infection.

Equine Influenza, commonly called "the flu," is somewhat more serious, especially for younger horses which seem more susceptible to catching the *Myxovirus*-caused ailment. Basically, there are two types of flu present in the United States, dubbed A-1 and A-2, and older horses are affected usually by A-2. Young foals and older animals with low resistance levels are susceptible to both, however.

The symptoms of influenza, which spreads rapidly from horse to horse through direct contact or in the air, appear some two to ten days after infection. The horse's temperature rises rapidly to between 102 and 106 degrees and the fever will last up to a week. Accompanying the febrile reaction are nasal discharges, constricted nasal passages and, dependent upon the horse's usage, a cough. In working horses, the cough generally is frequent and loud, while it may not be apparent at all in brood mares or other non-working horses.

In common cases involving older horses, the treatment required is complete rest for a week to ten days, whereupon the malady disappears. Young foals which catch the virus will be treated by the veterinarian with various antibiotics and other supportive care. It's rare that horses expire because of influenza; those that do usually are young foals which develop pneumonia.

The best way of preventing the spread of disease is through sound, sanitary animal management. Horses shouldn't be kept in one large group on the same pasture. Rather, by segregating them into small groups spread over the premises, it often is possible to contain the respiratory disease should an outbreak occur. If a horse comes down with the ailment, isolate it from others and, when recovered, clean and disinfect all equipment and surroundings.

The horses, too, can be protected from *Myxovirus* influenza through innoculations currently available. Two shots are administered over a two-week period. Annual boosters then are required and should be given before the approach of Autumn. It's true that the horse will become immunized to the respiratory disease after infection, but why have him suffer through it?

Vaccines have been produced and are effective against nearly every disease mentioned in this chapter and conceivably could one day result in total eradiction. However, not all horsemen follow the example of the young horseowner shown below.

This sketch illustrates a horse exhibiting symptoms of equine viral arteritis. Head hangs low, he's oblivious to his surroundings, there's swelling in legs, elsewhere.

Veterinarian Bob Hunt takes a horse's temperature with a rectal thermometer. Each horseman should have and know how to use a thermometer for early warning signs.

EQUINE VIRAL ARTERITIS

When this respiratory disease first made its appearance, it was confused with equine influenza and some of the symptoms are markedly similar. But through research, it was discovered that viral arteritis — also called pinkeye, shipping fever, stable pneumonia and epizootic cellulitis — is caused by a virus different from *Myxovirus*, the cause of influenza.

In most cases, equine viral arteritis isn't fatal, although it has caused abortion in pregnant mares, which makes outbreaks of this disease a real threat to breeding operations. It usually is noticed after introduction of a new horse to the premises and is highly contagious through direct contact.

Generally, an infected horse shows visible signs of the disease some two days to a week after contracting it, ushered in by a fever between 102 and 107 degrees. The white blood cell count drops and the horse becomes depressed, head hangs low and some swelling is encountered in the legs, tendon sheaths or teats. The horse is completely oblivious to his surroundings and the membranes around the eye become inflamed, hence the colloquial term pinkeye. The cornea may become clouded and insensitive to light, and these symptoms usually appear two to five days after the onset of fever.

In all but severe cases, these symptoms persist for ten days to two weeks, whereupon the animal recovers. In severe cases — which usually lead to death — the horse may have persistent signs of colic, diarrhea and respiratory difficulty. As noted, however, mortality is relatively low and most deaths occur as the result of abortion.

As there is no vaccine currently available to guarantee protection against viral arteritis, protection lies in proper stable management. This includes the isolation of any new horses for at least three weeks. If a horse does exhibit symptoms of the disease, he should be isolated in a draft-free stall and given complete rest until symptoms abate, then for another two weeks or so. When completely recovered, the horse should be brought back to usefulness gradually. The stall and equipment used on the animal should be thoroughly disinfected. A program of insect eradication should be implemented.

RHINOPNEUMONITIS

A far more serious threat to breeding establishments is Equine Viral Rhinopneumonitis (pronounced rye-no-new-mon-itis), often called rhino or EVR. Each year during late Fall, Winter and Spring, this killer takes its toll on the foal crops in breeding farms and it appears rhino will be with us for an indefinite period.

Essentially, it is a disease that attacks the respiratory tract of young animals and pregnant mares, transferred through direct contact with carriers or their airborne respiratory secretions. It also can be transferred through contact with a fetus aborted because of the disease.

Young horses in their first exposure to the disease generally show a temperature of between 102 and 107 degrees some one to seven days after contraction. He will appear run down, go off his feed, have a cough and suffer constipation which sometimes is followed by diarrhea. The disease usually will run its course, barring secondary infections of the respiratory tract.

In the case of pregnant mares, however, usually these symptoms aren't present and the horseowner won't know his mare is infected. It's possible for the mare to abort from three weeks to five months after contraction, but most abortions occur between the eighth and eleventh months of

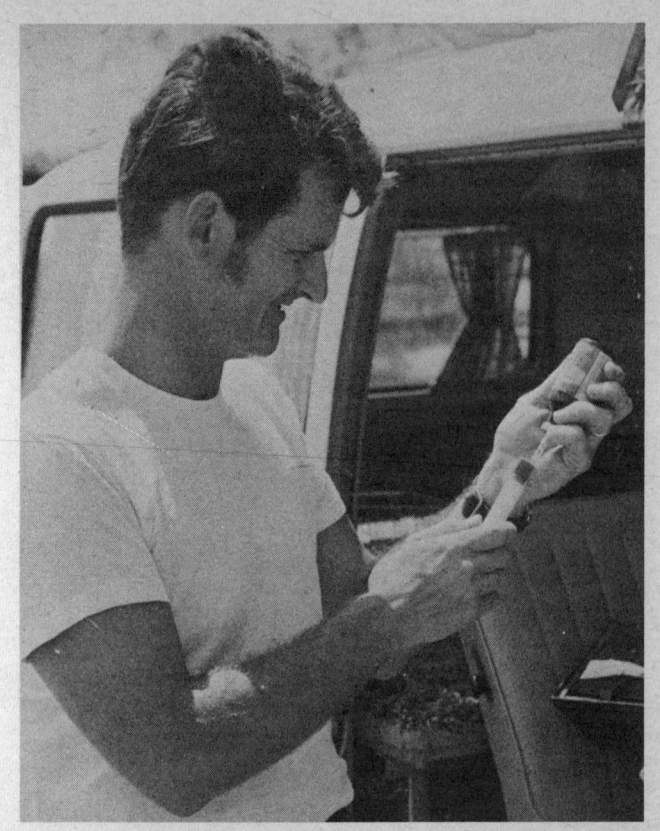

When measured against the costs of post-infection care and supportive treatment, inoculations are dirt cheap! Veterinarian Bob Hunt prepares an injection for tetanus.

The "Rhinomune" vaccine developed by Norden has been a blessing to breeders and farm managers. It provides long-sought protection against deadly rhinopneumonitis.

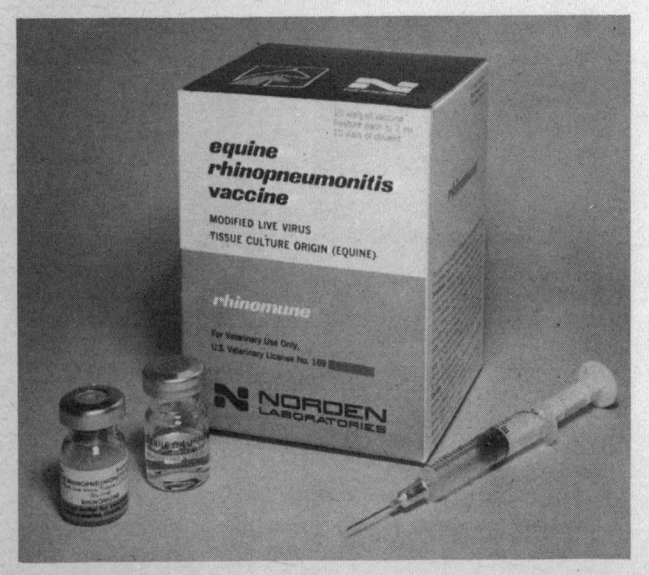

pregnancy. The only way a horseowner can positively identify the cause of abortion is to have a veterinarian examine the aborted fetus; the blood of the mare after abortion shows no signs of EVR.

Though infrequent, diseased foals sometimes are born following full-term gestation, but generally they die hours or a few days after foaling. They are weak and often have pneumonia. Sometimes a veterinarian can save the foal provided diligent care is provided.

A mare which has aborted is not affected in producing other foals, although it is possible to become reinfected with EVR. It is true that horses contracting and recovering from the disease have a high immunity rate to rhino during the next several months but, after this period wanes, it is possible to contract the disease again. It appears that older horses, which have been infected several times, have higher antibody counts.

As noted, there isn't much that can be done once the horse has contracted rhino. But a new vaccine developed by Norden Laboratories, dubbed "Rhinomune," now is available. Very effective, it is entirely safe to use at any time; there's no danger of it starting an outbreak.

Another abortion-causing disease that rates only passing mention — since no cases have been diagnosed in the United States in the last twenty-five years — has the scientific handle of *Salmonella abortivoequina*.

This disease is contracted through ingestion of pasture or other feed materials which have been contaminated by contact with the aborted fetus, afterbirth or fluids. Also, a mare following abortion may have a vaginal discharge which contains the *S. abortivoequina* bacteria. Therefore, following abortion and positive identification of *S. abortivoequina* by a veterinarian, the mare should be isolated until all signs of vaginal discharge have disappeared.

This disease is found in Canada, South America and other countries. It is plausible to assume it could be reintroduced into the United States, an event we hope doesn't materialize.

EQUINE ENCEPHALOMYELITIS

Often called sleeping sickness, there are three types of encephalomyelitis which can affect U.S. horses: Eastern equine encephalomyelitis (EEE), Western equine encephalomyelitis (WEE) and Venezuelan equine encephalomyelitis (VEE). EEE and WEE get their names from geographical prevalence: EEE in Eastern, Atlantic Seaboard and Gulf Coast states, and WEE in Midwest, Southwest and Western states. VEE is so named because it first was recognized along the Venezuelan/Colombian border.

VEE really made only one strong showing in the United States, back in 1971. Until that time, few cases had been reported in Florida and Louisiana. But a combination of excessive flooding, a bumper crop of mosquitos and constantly northward movement of the disease from Central America provided the needed factors for a bad epizootic, in which thousands of horses in the Southwest died. The Department of Agriculture released a supply of vaccine to the stricken states — which were quarantined — and the spread of VEE was checked. Since early 1972, no cases of VEE have been reported within our boundaries.

Despite all the attention VEE gained through nationwide media exposure, its cousin killers are responsible for more deaths *each year* than VEE caused throughout its outbreak. EEE and WEE epizootics appear each Summer, as wild birds migrate northward. The infected birds then are bitten by one of several strains of mosquito, which spread it to horses upon biting the latter. In no way can EEE or WEE be spread from horse to horse or from horse to man; the horse is not a carrier or a threat to health. VEE can be spread by mosquitos from horse to horse and from horse to man, however.

Of the two, grim horse-harvesters, Eastern equine encephalomyelitis is the more deadly. Nearly ninety percent of horses contracting the disease — which also affects man — die within a short period. The mortality rate for WEE is substantially lower: between twenty and fifty percent.

Symptoms of both diseases include fever, incoordination, a depressed condition with little appetite, drowsiness (hence the name sleeping sickness), reduced reflexes and impaired vision, among others. Horses exhibiting mild symptoms usually recover; the acute cases die.

There isn't much a veterinarian can do once a horse contracts the disease, other than provide supportive treatment. In mild cases, the horse generally will recover after several weeks of complete rest. Since the mosquito is the prime vector of transmission, the horseowner should implement a program of insect eradication during the late spring months. And, like so many other diseases still prevalent, there are vaccines which can guarantee immunity from infection — if the horseowner has them given. There is a combination vaccine, given initially in two doses one week to ten days apart, which is highly effective. After initial

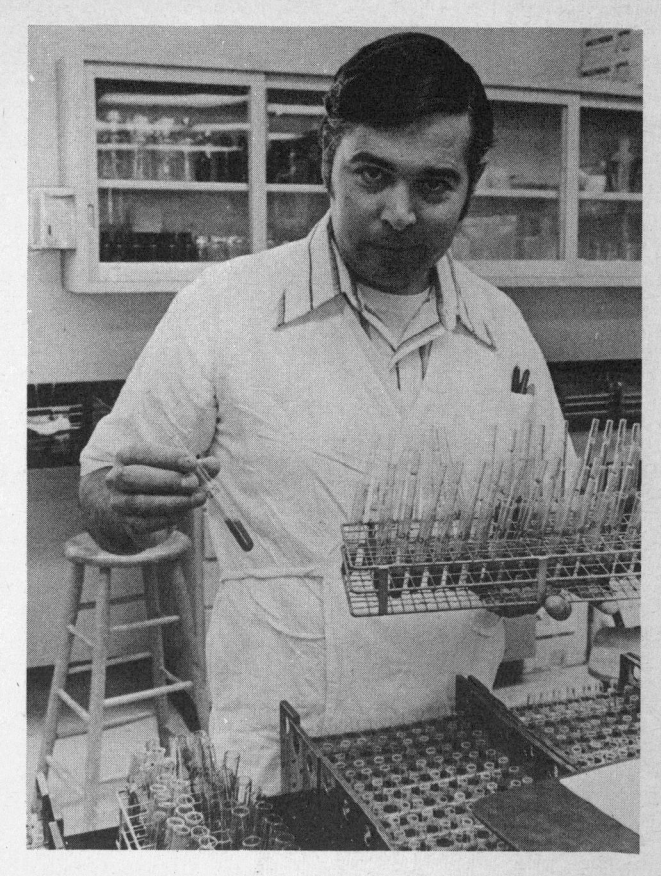

Bob Morris, Serology Laboratory manager at University of California, Davis, holds blood checked for brood stock. USDA veterinarian Lloyd C. Weldon takes blood sample from colt suspected of infection with VEE during late 1971.

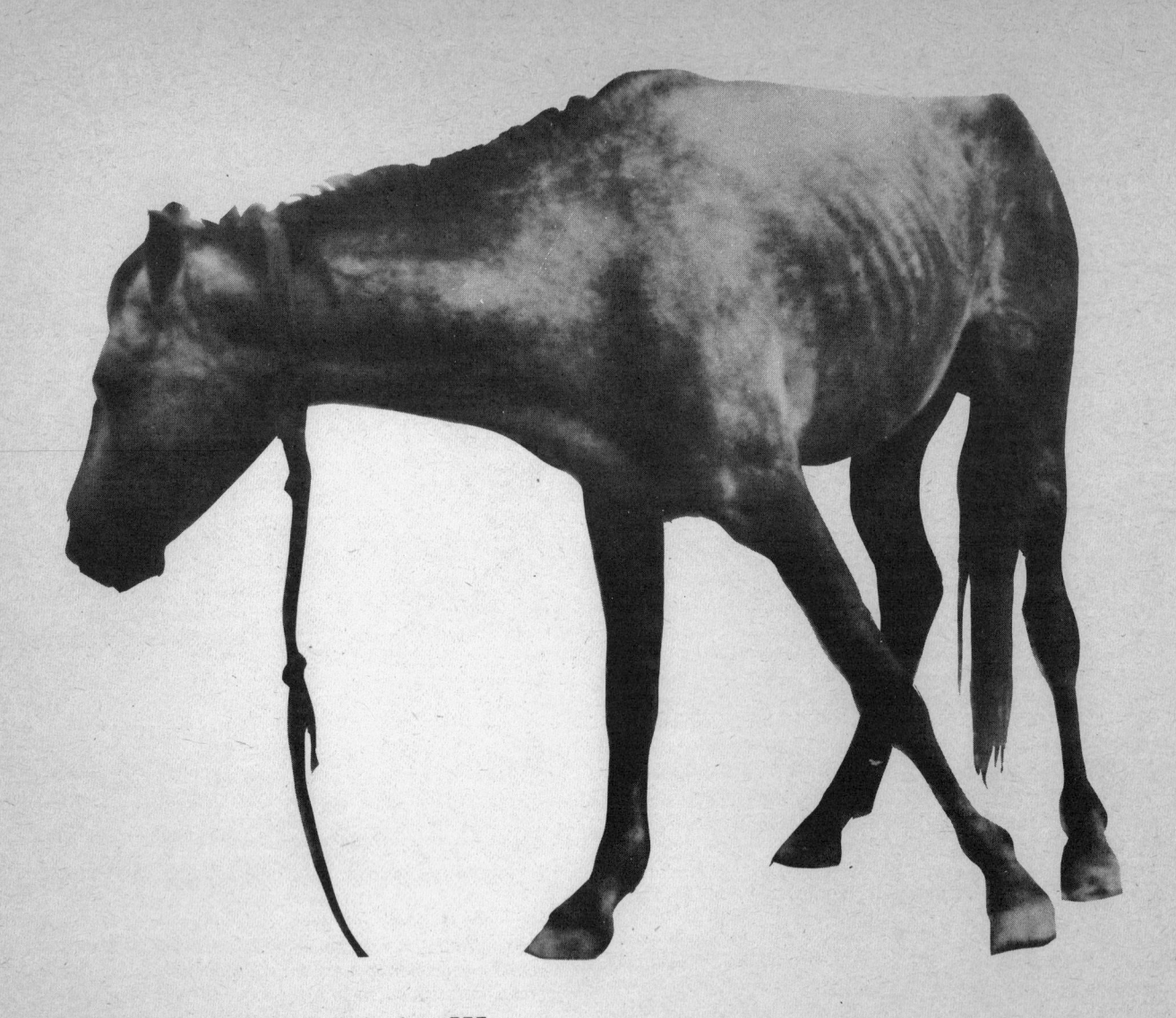

This is classic example of horse suffering from EEE (above). Check the text for symptoms of the disease.

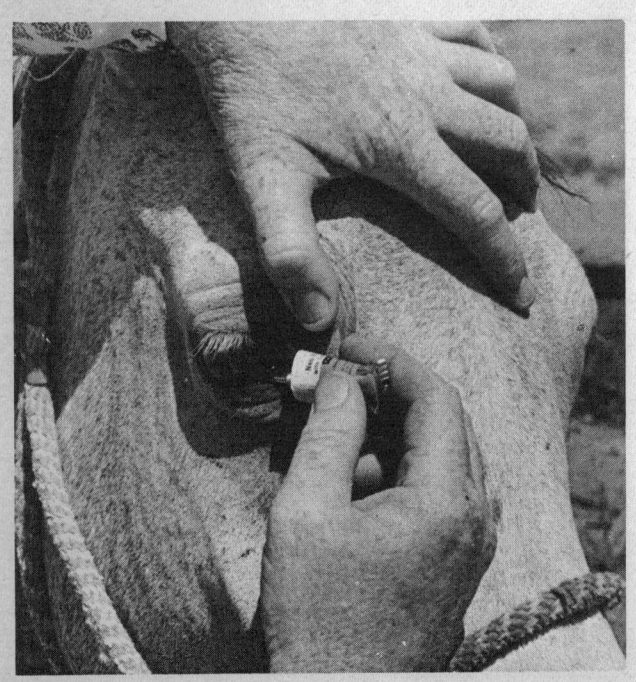

application, the horses need only annual boosters to ensure their protection.

LEPTOSPIROSIS

"Lepto" in horses generally is not a serious disease. Some horses will suffer fever, depression, loss of appetite, lethargy or jaundice, while others will exhibit none of these. It can cause pregnant mares to abort or lead to periodic ophthalmia, the most common cause of blindness in horses.

The ailment is caused by spiral-shaped bacteria known as spirochetes, of which more than fifty strains have been detected, broken into nonpathogenic and pathogenic categories; the latter cause the problems mentioned earlier. It is transmitted to susceptible horses through contact with secretions or excretions from infected animals and the bacteria can live for many days in damp or saturated soil. The bacteria is rather fragile and cannot survive on dry soil or in direct sunlight. It can survive up to a month in a warm, stagnant pond.

Most horses are able to fight lepto on their own, but it

The cause of tetanus is found nearly in all soil, just waiting to be introduced to a horse by some type of wound. The result, as shown here can be fatal.

Leptospirosis is caused by spiral-shaped bacteria and cattle are also susceptible. It can reduce a working ranch horse into a helpless animal.

can lead to abortion or blindness. A vaccine is available to guarantee protection, which should be administered as necessary.

Periodic ophthalmia, often erroneously called moon blindness, is a serious matter. The first symptoms are watering of one or both eyes. The pupil constricts, the eye is sensitive to light and the eye membrane may be inflamed. The cornea may become cloudy and the horse may keep his eye closed during attacks, which are recurrent in history. Each attack, which occurs at regular intervals, further damages the eye and blindness is the result unless carefully treated.

A horse suffering the aforementioned symptoms should be placed in a dark barn or stall until the attack subsides to rest the eye and help relieve pain caused by bright sunlight. A veterinarian will prescribe a treatment schedule that should be followed rigorously.

TETANUS

Tetanus, often called lockjaw, is a disease to which both horse and horseman are susceptible. It is caused by a bac-

Leptospirosis usually is not serious on its own, but can lead to periodic ophthalmia, main cause of blindness. A veterinarian may prescribe use of eye drops.

teria called *Clostridium tetani*. This bacteria, which survives without oxygen, is found in the soil and the feces of horses. Deep punctures from nails or slivers is usually how the bacteria enters the skin, where it begins to grow and multiply, producing a poison that affects the motor nerves or central nervous system.

Anywhere from a week to four months after infection, the symptoms begin to appear. This usually will first be a stiffness of the area surrounding the puncture, or perhaps stiffness of the hind legs. About a day later, the horse may begin having tonic spasms, where he continually contracts his muscles involuntarily. It's the tonic spasm of the head muscles, which makes opening the mouth difficult, that leads to the "lockjaw" term.

As the disease progresses, movement of the limbs becomes difficult, due to muscular contraction. The involuntary muscles — those that work independently, like the heart, liver, kidneys, etc. — are upset by this behavior and often work at increased rates, especially in fatal cases, accompanied by a fever that sometimes hits 110 degrees. In mild cases of tetanus, both pulse and temperature may remain nearly normal.

If a horse has received a deep wound with the possibility of tetanus high, a veterinarian usually will inject tetanus antitoxin into the animal to be safe. If the animal is exhibiting signs of the disease, the veterinarian will administer a massive dose of the antitoxin, along with tranquilizers, which have proved effective in the past. He then will clean and thoroughly disinfect the wound site and, if the horse is going to survive, it will recover fully after some six weeks of supportive treatment. During that time, the horse should be placed in a quiet, darkened box stall since, when infected, sudden movements send the animal into panic. A constant source of feed and water should be available and high enough that the animal suffers no discomfort when trying to take either.

As in man's case, there is a vaccine which can be administered to prevent tetanus. Annual vaccination with tetanus toxoid is widely done and recommended.

Horseowners should take great care to remove sharp objects which horses can contact. Periodic inspection of all stalls, paddocks, fences, mangers and water troughs — or any other possible source of injury — with appropriate corrective action taken will reduce the chances of lockjaw visiting your spread.

MALIGNANT EDEMA

Clostridium septicum, the cause of malignant edema, is a cousin of the tetanus producer. And like its cousin, *C. septicum* grows in an oxygen-free environment, usually entering

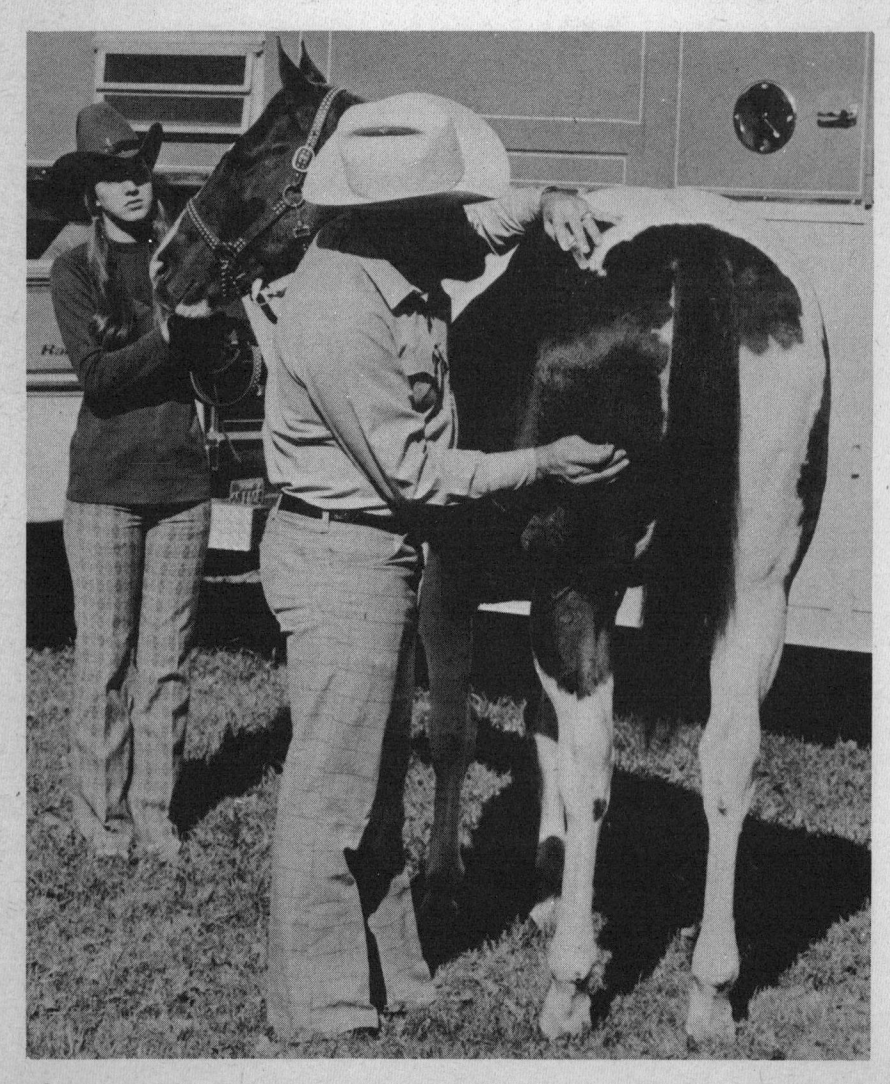

After initial inoculation, only annual boosters are required to protect against tetanus. It's foolish to forego shots!

the body through a puncture or similar injury and is found in most pasture soil. It's as deadly as *Clostridium tetani*, if not more so.

Usually within hours after picking up the bacteria, a horse's temperature starts rising and there is swelling directly around the puncture site. The skin is hot and touching the wound causes great pain. The horse also goes off his feed, is depressed and exhibits signs of respiratory difficulty. From the wound site a thin, reddish secretion will run and, as the disease progresses, the horse will suffer convulsions.

If caught early enough, there may be something the veterinarian can do in the way of administering antibiotics such as penicillin. But once the disease gets a firm hold on the animal, death is inevitable.

When the symptoms become noticed, isolate the horse from others and, because the horseman is susceptible to infection, only handle the horse when suitably protected with rubber gloves. After the horse has expired or been put down by the veterinarian, either cremate the carcass or bury it deeply; the causative spores will live on after the host has died and this will prevent the possible spread to other mounts.

There is a vaccine available which protects horses from malignant edema and this should be included in any regular inoculation program. It's better to pay now than later.

PIROPLASMOSIS

Equine piroplasmosis, also known as *babesiasis*, is common in most tropical countries and was introduced into the United States over a decade ago. Now restricted to southern Florida, piroplasmosis is transmitted by tropical horse ticks only. The disease manifests itself as a blood disorder following initial sickness accompanied by fever and anemia. It can be treated by a veterinarian and rarely results in death.

CHRONIC PULMONARY EMPHYSEMA

More usually called heaves or broken wind, this is a serious respiratory ailment, the specific cause of which is unknown, that reduces a horse into a useless boarder.

Heaves occurs principally in stables and scientists feel it is contracted through ingestion of dusty, moldy hay, which causes bronchitis that leads to this strange disorder, although the cause of chronic pulmonary emphysema is unknown. The first symptoms, which are usually overlooked, include a shortness of breath after moderate working. As the disease progresses, however, the symptoms become readily apparent: Respiratory rate is increased and, upon expiration, the abdominal muscles contract in an extra expiratory effort. Try it a couple of times and the painful effect of this disease is readily apparent.

After a short period, a horse with heaves develops a barrel chest and a "heave line" behind the rib cage. A chronic cough may develop, along with a nasal discharge. He begins losing weight.

If the disorder is a by-product of bronchitis, a change of diet to pasture grass or pelleted feeds sometimes brings about normal respiratory function. This diet change can be supplemented with medication to treat the bronchial condition. But if the disease is caused by chronic pulmonary emphysema, no known cure is available. Sometimes the diet change will provide relief.

Since scientists feel the bronchitis condition which often causes heaves comes from eating moldy or dusty hay, the horseowner should take pains to avoid feeding this to the animal. If the feed is merely dusty, it should be wetted prior to feeding, which cuts down the dust. The stable also should be adequately ventilated, since perhaps the mixture of stable dust with that from the roughage may help bring on the disorder.

COLITIS X

Colitis X is a noncontagious, usually fatal disease affecting the intestinal tract that is brought about mostly through exposing a horse to stress too soon after having been sick with some infection, such as a racehorse being put into a

Veterinarians are equipped with about everything except an operating room. The diseases and injuries to which a horse can fall victim are enormous.

race before he has completely recovered from a bout with the flu. Because of the suspected cause, it sometimes is called exhaustion shock.

The symptoms of the disease progress rapidly and the first to appear usually is severe diarrhea or flatulent colic (explained later in this chapter). The horse begins breathing rapidly, breaks out in patchy sweating, dehydrates, the pulse may be weak and he may exhibit colic-like pain. Death usually occurs within three to twenty-four hours after onset of the symptoms.

Veterinarians can and do save many cases if they get to them early. Large quantities of fluids and electrolytes are given both intravenously and by stomach tube. The solutions must be given before the case gets well advanced,

hence the need for the owner to be observant and call his veterinarian at once. Time is of the essence.

NEONATAL PYOSEPTICEMIA

Better known as Navel-Ill, this disease is caused by any of several bacterial strains, usually with the same result: death. In fact, the mortality rate is up around ninety percent.

This disease can be passed to the foal either prenatally or after foaling, in the former through the umbilical cord. The stump of the umbilical cord also can be the entrance after foaling, although researchers feel it is more often picked up through other means, principally ingestion or inhalation.

Symptoms vary according to age of the foal, but general-

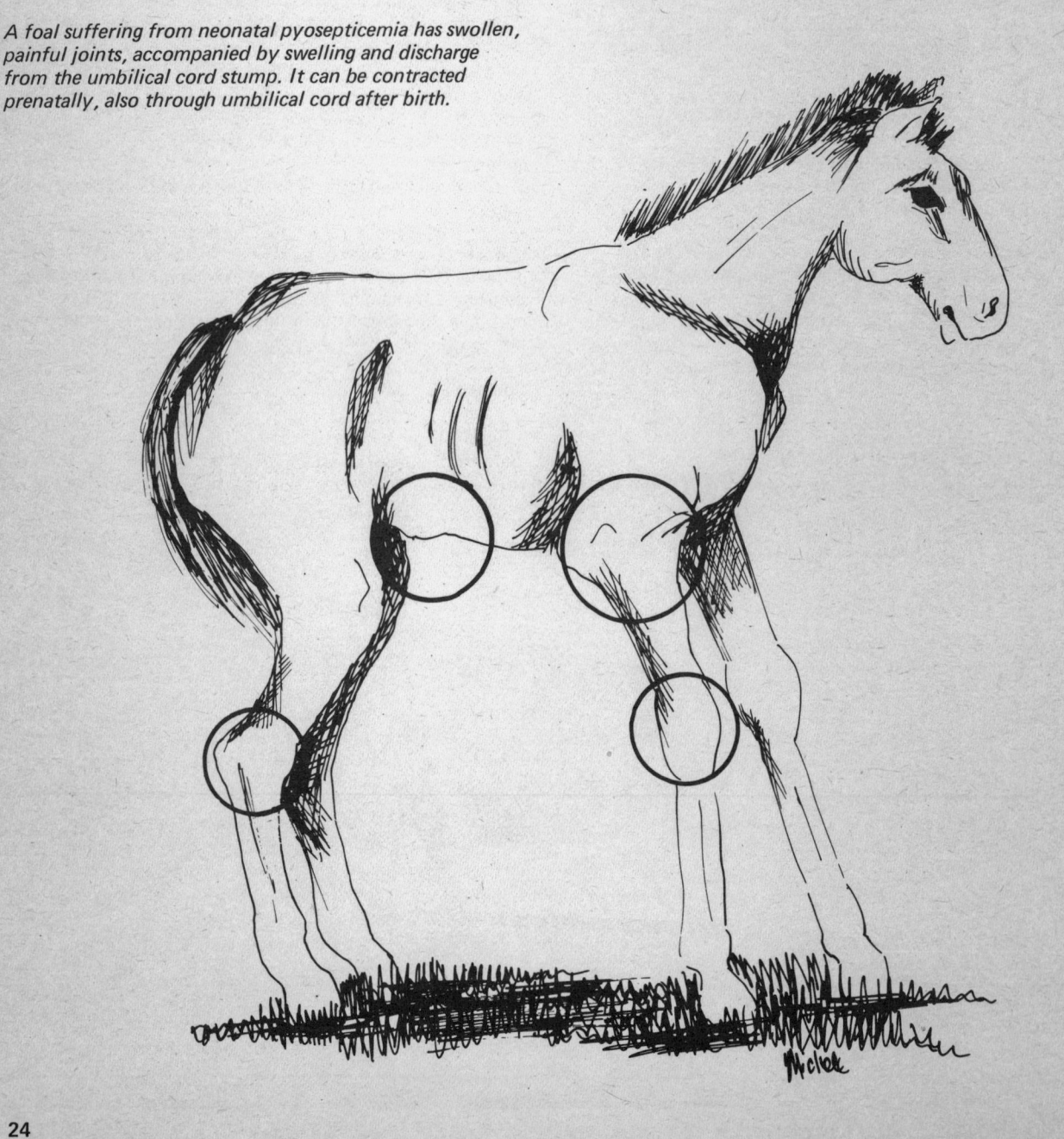

A foal suffering from neonatal pyosepticemia has swollen, painful joints, accompanied by swelling and discharge from the umbilical cord stump. It can be contracted prenatally, also through umbilical cord after birth.

ly the horse's temperature will be high, he suffers lack of appetite, is generally depressed and the joints will become swollen and sore. There often is swelling and discharge at the umbilical cord stump.

The survival rate of the foal is in direct proportion to his age: the older he is, the better his chances. When infected prenatally, death usually comes between one to three days after foaling and there's nothing the veterinarian can do. If the foal is a couple of weeks old when symptoms develop, the veterinarian will treat the animal and the chances of recovery are good.

If the foal already has the disease through prenatal infection, there is little the horseowner can do at foaling time. However, he should always paint the stump of the umbilical cord with iodine as quickly as possible.

VISCOSUM INFECTION

This foal disease is generally fatal if not discovered and quickly treated. It has been known by horsemen for years as the "sleeper" or "dummy" foal and is caused by *Actinobacillus equuli*, not by *Shigella equirulis* as was previously thought.

This illness, rarely prenatally contracted, is characterized by a listlessness, he's dull and little concerned with his surroundings. Temperature, pulse and respiration rates increase dramatically and, as the disease progresses, the foal becomes weaker until finally it cannot stand at all. During this course, the foal will not nurse. There is a mortality rate of approximately thirty percent within twenty-four hours of the first symptom's appearance.

As quickly as possible after detection, the veterinarian will begin administration of dihydrostreptomycin, following this with proper supportive treatment. If caught in time, the foal's chances of survival increase fifty percent.

NEONATAL ISOERYTHROLYSIS

Usually called Hemolytic disease or the jaundiced foal syndrome, this condition is not a disease in the communicable, virus or bacterial-caused sense. Rather, it is a problem which occurs because of differences in the blood of a foal and his dam and, if not properly handled, it leads to certain death for the foal.

During fetal development, the jaundiced foal's blood develops a genetic incompatibility with the mare's and her blood begins building antibodies against the foal's. Upon birth, these antibodies are collected in the colostrum found in mother's milk. Consequently, upon nursing the foal takes in antibodies against his own blood which destroys the red blood cells and causes death.

The jaundiced foal's mucous membranes take on a yellowish color and, should this be noted during foaling, the new arrival should be muzzled to prevent him from nursing. He should be bottle-fed for the next forty-eight hours and, at the same time, the mare should be milked until the potentially dangerous antibodies have disappeared. The foal then can begin nursing.

While there are many other communicable diseases a horse can suffer, these are the bulk the American horseman may expect to contact. As mentioned, most can be avoided by simple vaccinations, usually just once a year. When the cost of the shot is measured against the expense incurred with a sick horse, it's easy to see that it doesn't pay to be "penny-wise and pound-foolish."

This is the life a foal is supposed to lead: carefree, happy, inquisitive. Exposure to one of these diseases can change all that, so prevent them!

CHAPTER 4
INTERNAL DISORDERS

Using tractor tires as feed troughs for rental horses appeared a fine idea, until horses began dying from colic at this stable in California. Autopsy disclosed intestinal blockage with rubber as cause of death — horses had been cribbing on the tires.

There are internal disorders a horse may suffer which comprise a separate classification in our look at the complex world of veterinary medicine. The most common are: azoturia (paralytic myoglobinuria); colic (flatulent, spasmodic and impaction); exhaustion; fractures; roaring (laryngeal hemiplegia); sprains (sore shins, carpitis, bog spavin, capped hock, capped elbow and tendinitis); sunstroke (heatstroke, heat cramps and heat exhaustion); teeth problems; thumps; and tying up (myositis).

As with the chapter on diseases, consult professional advice immediately if your horse exhibits any of the ailment symptoms outlined in the following chapter. Pay strict attention to the therapy recommended by your veterinarian.

AZOTURIA

The scientific name, paralytic myoglobinuria — which basically means paralysis accompanied by iron-containing, muscle-protein pigment in the urine — is much more fitting in describing this serious ailment than azoturia, which translated roughly means nitrogen in the urine.

While the scientific reason of *why* it happens is unknown, researchers have discovered *how* azoturia develops. A horse has been working hard and his owner has been feeding him accordingly. Then the horse will get a few days' rest, still being fed the increased ration. When the horseowner attempts to put the horse back into service, problems arise.

Usually within a few moments, often within sight of the barn, the horse begins to sweat profusely and stiffness in one or both back legs begins; rarely are all four legs involved. Unless halted, the horse becomes extremely nervous, stiffness continues until he cannot extend his legs fully, respiratory and pulse rate increase and the horse usually goes down. The muscles of the croup and hindquarters are swollen and rock-hard. If the horse urinates, it usually is a dark red or even coffee color, caused by the myoglobin in the urine.

26

The Inner Workings Of The Horse Are Complex And Finicky, Prone To Upset By These Conditions

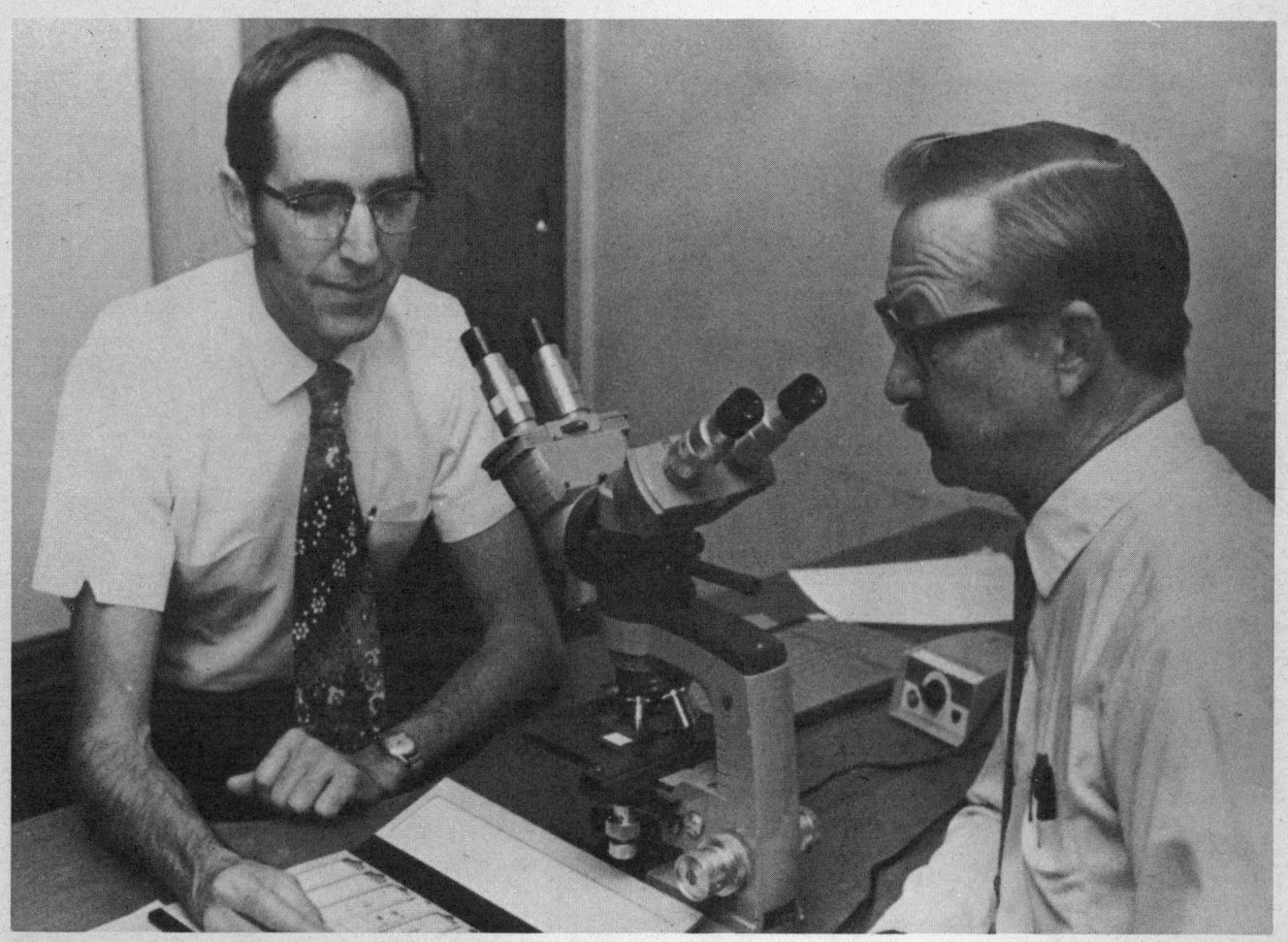

It's in the laboratory where such noted veterinarians as Dr. Albert E. McChesney (left) and Dr. Jerry L. Adcock hunt for cures, that knowledge relative to internal disorders is gathered. Much has yet to be learned of equine inner workings.

If the horse is stopped upon first indication of stiffness and sweating, usually he will remain standing and, if not moved for several hours, the attack usually subsides to the point that he can be returned to the barn. He then should be given complete rest for up to two weeks and brought back to work gradually.

If the animal goes down his chances of recovery aren't as good, unless he remains relatively calm. If nervous, the veterinarian can administer tranquilizers and, after a twenty-four-hour period, the horse usually recovers control of the muscles and can be moved to the barn. During the time he's down, the veterinarian may change his position to avoid bedsores and remove the urine with a catheter, if muscle stiffness precludes normal bodily function. During recovery, mild laxatives often are given and horses appear to respond favorably to vitamin E and selenium therapy.

The simplest way to avoid this disorder is through sound animal management. If the horse is rested several days, his feed — especially grain — should be cut back accordingly. Daily exercise, even if of relatively short duration, is better than none.

COLIC

One of the most common yet serious maladies to befall horses, colic is divided into two basic categories: true and false. True colic can be categorized even further, into flatulent, spasmodic and impaction colic. None are any fun, either for horse or horseman.

Looking first at false colic, this is a term given for colic-like symptoms that aren't caused by colic in its true form. Rather, false colic sometimes is caused by inflammation of the intestinal organs. When discussing spasmodic colic, the distinguishing characteristics will be noted for accurate preliminary diagnosis by the horseman.

Generally, colic is believed caused by eating feed spoiled through mold or containing indigestible elements like oat husks; by rapid consumption of feed; overeating; sudden changes in feed; poor chewing; feeding or watering when extremely fatigued; watering too soon after working; using the horse for hard work too soon after feeding; irregular feeding schedules; fermentation of feed in the stomach; windsucking (inhaling great quantities of air); and the presence of foreign matter like dirt or sand in the stomach.

There recently has been another theory advanced for the cause of colic: parasitism; specifically, infestation by *Strongylus vulgaris* – the bloodworm. A group of researchers estimate that ninety percent of all colic cases result from damage done by bloodworm larvae migrations in the horse's bloodstream. A respected authority, Dr. James Rooney, performed autopsies on over ten thousand horses and claims eighty-five to ninety percent of those cases diagnosed as colic were directly or indirectly caused by the bloodworm.

To understand why the bloodworm is so dangerous and how he does his damage, one must understand his life cycle and how he lives. We have long known that the adult worm attaches to the inside wall of the horse's intestine where it lives and produces eggs which pass out with the droppings. In a few days larvae emerge from these eggs on the ground, attach to blades of grass and are ready to be consumed by a horse.

Eggs may lay dormant on the ground for months. The adult egg-laying worm may live in the intestine for many months where it does very little damage. From the time a larvae is swallowed, it may be eight to nine months before it ceases migrating in the body tissues and matures in the intestines.

In an attempt to determine the migrating route of *Strongylus vulgaris* larvae, Dr. J.L. Duncan in Scotland infected each of nine work-free pony foals with a pure culture of 750 infective larvae (such as a horse might consume in an infected pasture). Ponies then were killed and examined at intervals over a period of nine months. Results clearly showed that the larvae penetrate the intestine wall within a few days where they moult. They then penetrate the very small arteries which supply the intestine and migrate up the lumina of these vessels to the anterior mesenteric site in about fourteen days (this is the site where mass thromboses and damage is most commonly found).

In this site – or other site of choice – the larvae further develop for three to four months and, after a fourth moult is completed, the young adults migrate back down the arteries, penetrate the wall and enter the inside of the intestines where they mature. The total migration within the horse's body is complete within six or seven months after infection. Other research workers have confirmed this damaging migratory pattern of the bloodworm.

It is these larvae migrations that cause the damage to blood vessels – inflammation, swelling, debris, stoppage. Mass migrations produce sufficient damage to cause a horse to die in shock. The cause is obvious when it happens.

Less obvious and much more common are problems that result later from the damage left behind by the larvae. Blood vessels are restricted, clogged, damaged, scarred so that an adequate blood supply cannot reach various portions of the intestine. Thus, areas of the digestive tract are weakened to where only a minor stress causes it to improperly function – and the resultant colic.

These stresses or insults to the system in most instances are the immediate triggering cause of the colic. However, the real cause may be a deficient blood supply to some portions of the intestine due to previous damage done by the bloodworm which makes it unable to function normally and withstand stress.

Looking first at flatulent colic and keeping in mind the bloodworm theory, this results usually from the fermentation of spoiled feed in the stomach, which gives off large quantities of gas but can result from windsucking or ingestion of large amounts of green feed at one time. There is no mistaking flatulent colic for other intestinal disorders, for the stomach is bloated and distended. Tapped with a finger, it gives off a resonant sound not unlike tapping a drum.

As the amount of gas builds, it puts pressure on the internal organs, causing pain and leading to respiratory difficulty; internal organs pressing upon the lungs makes breaths short and rapid. He may sweat profusely, paw the ground, kick at his stomach or lie down and, if the pressure isn't relieved, death is probable through ruptured intestines, twisted bowels or shock.

When the veterinarian arrives, he will attempt to rid the gas without resorting to work inside. But under threat of imminent death, the veterinarian will puncture the bowel or colon, freeing the gas.

In cases of spasmodic colic, the horse suddenly shows signs of abdominal pain through groaning, anxious facial expression, straining to urinate or defecate, kicking at the belly (which isn't distended as in flatulent colic), turning the muzzle to look at the stomach, pawing the ground, sweating, rolling and may even throw himself down as if

Dr. Willard D. Ommert removed these concretements from small colon of 8-year-old gelding. Similar to gallstones, these form in small intestine. They fitted so tightly together they blocked intestine, causing colic.

pole-axed. Then, just as suddenly, the pain diminishes and the horse acts normally by eating or drinking until the next and usually stronger spasm begins. These will increase in intensity until the animal dies or gradually decrease in intensity, thus effecting recovery.

The difference between flatulent colic and inflammation of the inner organs is readily apparent through distention of the belly in the former. But accurately diagnosing spasmodic colic is somewhat more difficult and takes a sharp eye on behalf of the horseowner.

Probably the biggest difference is that inflammation affords no periods of relief, as does spasmodic colic; the pain in the former is continuous. Also, horses suffering from spasmodic colic generally have a normal temperature and pulse rate, unlike inflammation which causes increases in both. Another important difference is that inflammation usually leads to tautness of the belly, which causes pain when touched. This same procedure seems to cause relief when the horse suffers from spasmodic colic.

Impaction colic is still another serious category of this malady, a blockage of the intestines which, if not removed, causes death. This is the result of ingestion of foreign matter like sand or dirt from eating roughage thrown on the ground, but also can be caused by insufficient mastication of feed, overeating or bad feed, among others outlined earlier.

A horse suffering from impaction colic, often called simply impaction, usually resembles a horse with spasmodic colic except that feces will be passed for a time before the animal becomes constipated. If mild, the horse will recover upon passage of the obstacle. If severe, death through ruptured intestines may be the result.

When the veterinarian arrives, he will try administering enemas or other purgatives to break the blockage and, if he begins within the first day of the condition, results usually are satisfactory.

The proper way to handle all types of colic is through prevention, which is only sound stable management. Feed only what the horse needs relative to his service and make sure the hays and grains are of good quality, free from spoilage or dust. Don't offer forage that is highly fermentable or grains that can combine in lumpy masses. Make any

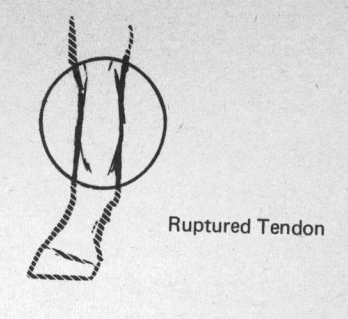

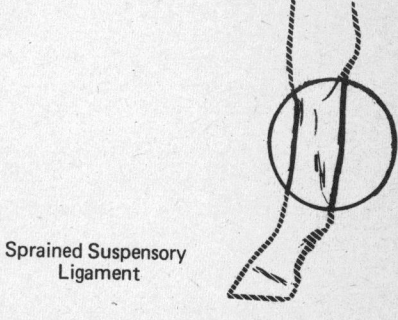

Ruptured tendons and sprained suspensory ligaments can cause lay-up at best, lameness at worst. See comments under sprains for treatment routine.

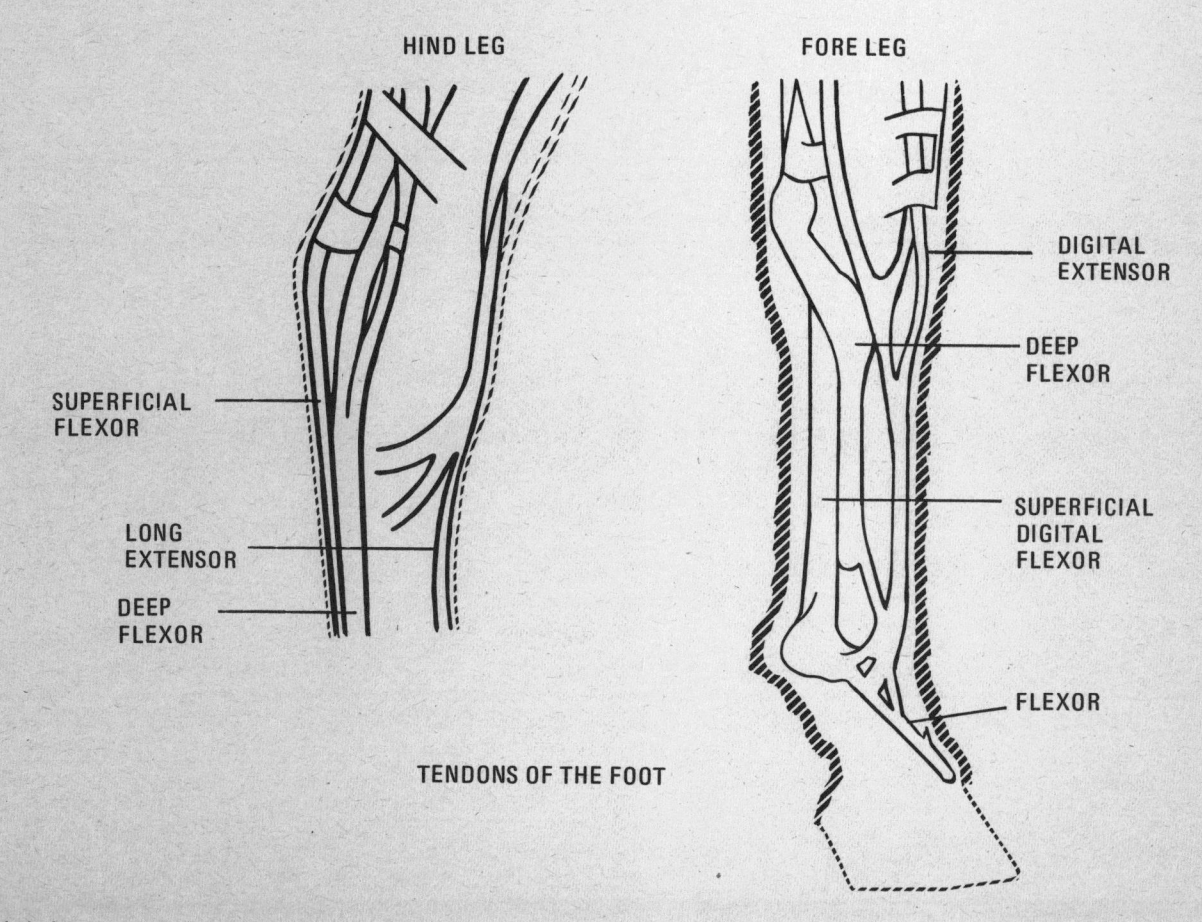

TENDONS OF THE FOOT

It behooves each horseman to know the physical makeup of his horse. This aids in proper early diagnosis of ailments which can save having the condition turn into a permanent disability. A horse provides indications when injured, so watch for them.

ration changes slowly and keep the horse on a regular feeding schedule. Remember, horses are used to eating more than one meal per day so two or more feedings are best. This keeps the level of bacteria in the intestines — which break down the ingested feeds — high enough to preclude problems. Use a feeder box or a manger; never feed on the ground.

Keep the horse fit through adequate exercise and never work the horse immediately after eating. Assure that fresh water is available at all times. Have the horse's teeth checked regularly and floated as necessary. Teeth problems will be covered later in this chapter. Initiate a regular program of parasite control. This also will be covered later in this chapter.

EXHAUSTION

Exhaustion or extreme fatigue usually is brought about through overwork or strenuous working of an out-of-condition horse. The horse will be visibly tired upon arrival back at the barn, then may shun any food offerings made, even grain. At the same time, the animal will be extraordinarily thirsty and may lie down between waterings.

The best treatment is to cover the horse with a cooler to prevent chilling and the legs should be massaged vigorously to increase circulation. Small amounts of water should be given frequently and, if rested completely for two or three days, the horse should be fine.

Horseowners should take pains to keep their horses in condition, not overly fat or thin. The work schedule should revolve around the horse's condition and environmental factors. Don't try accomplishing too much work in one day, as you may end up losing the animal's services for several.

There is a great difference in severity between simple exhaustion and sunstroke, which is covered later in this section. It behooves the horseowner to recognize the differences and know how to treat accordingly.

FRACTURES

Fractures are divided into two categories, simple and compound, and neither is good news for the horse. Simple fractures denote a clean separation of a bone, while compound means a bone broken in more than one place, shattered, or with part of the bone sticking through the surface of the skin.

During the time when cowboys rode the range, it was the normal and unwelcome practice to put down any horse which broke a leg. This is the usual prognosis for the average horse today. Nearly the only exceptions are expensive racehorses with impressive records; while their racing careers may be over, they still can make money in the stud.

Until 1971, fractures of the legs were, after being set, encased in plaster casts for the healing period. Plaster casts are heavy, break fairly easily and preclude much free movement of a horse. Most fractures still are treated in this manner, although a new fiberglass cast seems to be finding favor with top orthopedic veterinarians around the world.

It's termed the Lightcast and lives up to its name, being light of weight, much more resistant to breakage than plaster, is thinner, lasts longer and sheds moisture. It is responsible for the continued existence of such top-name racehorses as England's Mill Reef and America's Gaelic Dancer, Hoist the Flag and Sham, among others.

After the affected area of the limb is protected with a cushioning gauze, a web-like wrap is applied, then a fiberglass tape. After the tape is bound around the protective

Wrapping the injured limb of a horse is an art in itself: too tight and circulation is impaired; too loose and no good will result. The wraps shown, with Velcro backing, are made by 3M Company and can aid in immobilizing an injured joint.

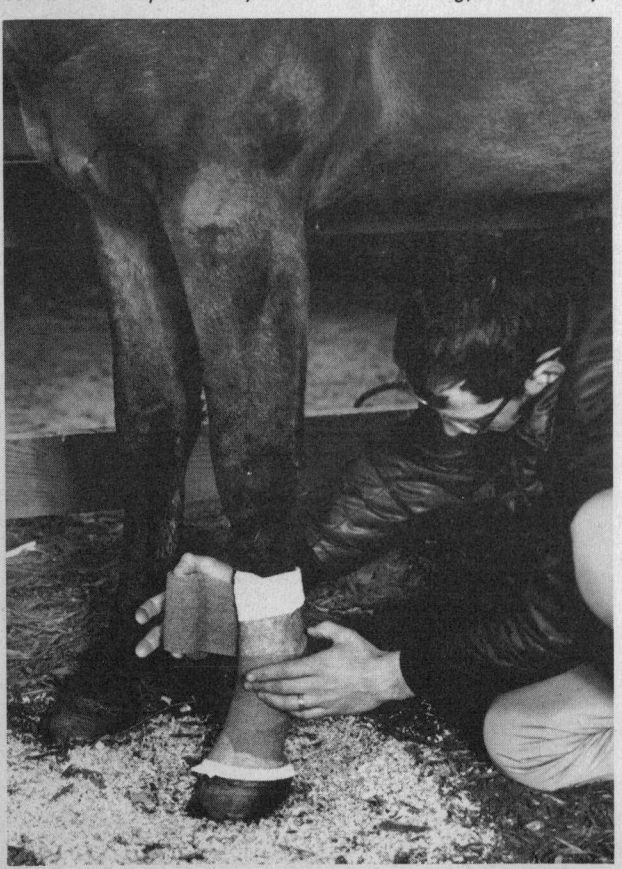

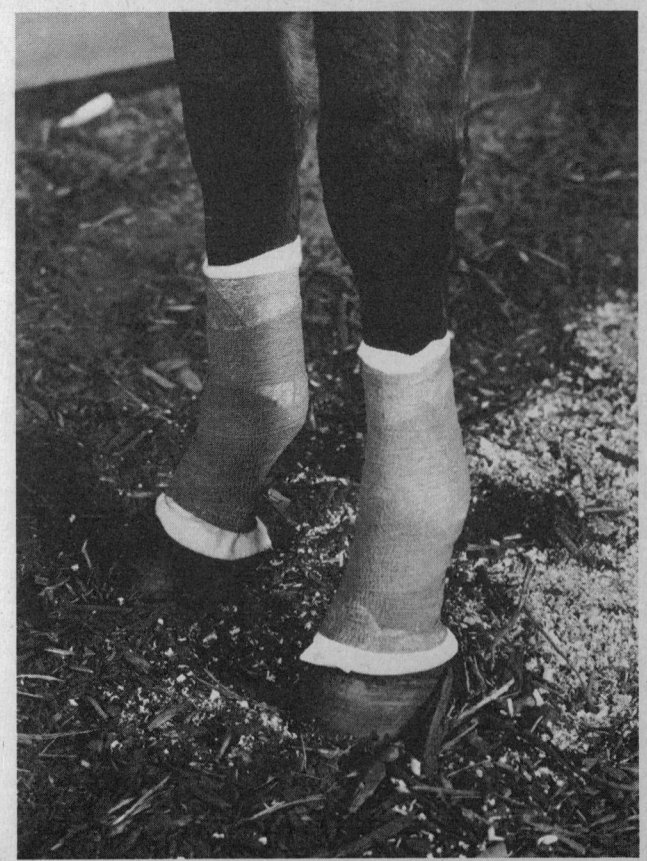

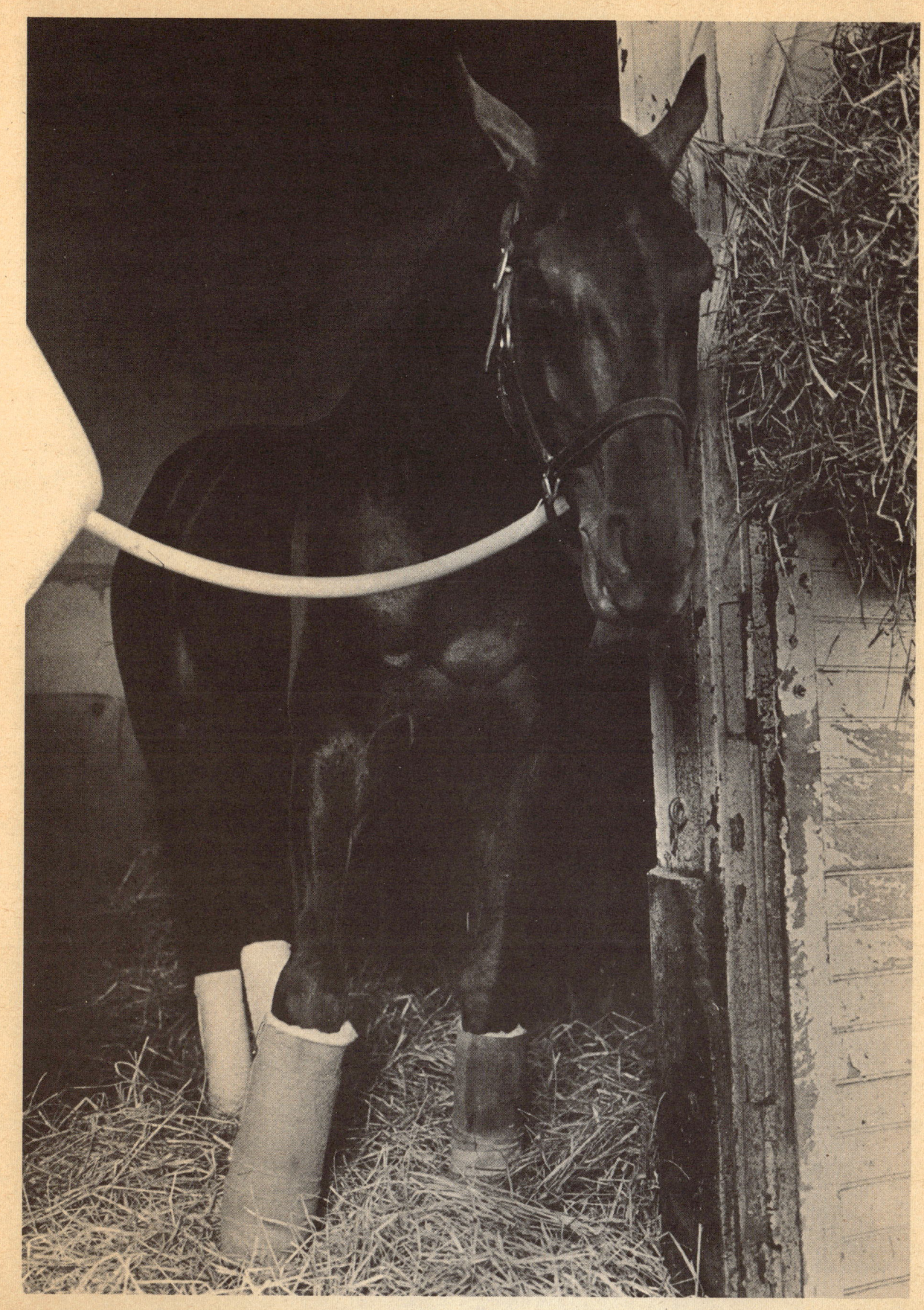

Sham, the famous 3-year-old that so gallantly raced in Secretariat's shadow, broke a bone in his foreleg during his last race and was fitted with a Lightcast II fiberglass cast following surgery and implantation of screws in the right foreleg. Much lighter in weight, much better at shedding moisture — and much more expensive — than plaster, it saved his life.

plastic wraps, a "black light" is used to harden the cast, which takes three minutes. There is no heat and it's the light's energy that cures the cast. Another advantage is that it's possible to take X-rays through the cast.

The main disadvantages to the Lightcast are that not many veterinarians are yet able to apply it, local anesthetic needs to be used for roughly one and one-half hours (compared to one-half hour for plaster casts), it's around twice as expensive as plaster and immediate veterinary attention is needed to confine animal movement.

Because of the disadvantages of cost, inexperienced practitioners and immediate attention needs, the Lightcast treatment isn't used often. In fact, the prognosis for a horse with a broken leg receiving any kind of treatment isn't good. Consider, too, that even if the bone is set, most horses' active usefulness will be over after recovery. This is why most pleasure horses with broken legs are put down even today.

Other bones break occasionally. A horse's fondness for rolling in the dirt sometimes results in a fractured point of the hip. When so incapacitated, a horse will show visible signs of lameness on that leg and the point of the hip may be tender and swollen. This malady usually will heal, if the horse is given complete rest for a month to six weeks or until a veterinarian deems him sound again.

Broken leg bones usually are the result of either a blow from another horse or by stepping into a prairie dog's burrow. Nearly all a horseman can do to prevent this occurrence is to watch his animals and separate warring horses, and institute a good rodent control program. Pay attention when riding and avoid areas that can result in animal injury.

ROARING

Roaring, or laryngeal hemiplegia, is characterized by audible inspiration of each breath and, when so afflicted, there is little that may be done to correct the problem.

While scientists aren't definitely certain, there seems evidence to believe roaring is caused by an irritation of the larynx — the voice box — or as a result of another disease, an overextension of the head, or it may even be hereditary. In nearly all cases, the laryngeal nerves on the left side of the larynx become paralyzed, which leads to the roaring sound. The sound usually is evident during or immediately after exercise. A test which can often give indication of a roarer is a quick jab in the ribs of an unsuspecting horse. If the horse grunts, there is reason to believe it has laryngeal hemiplegia.

Roaring robs a horse of its usefulness and about the only correction comes from surgery on the larynx. Some seventy percent of the horses going under the veterinary surgeon's knife are restored to usefulness.

As there is speculation that roaring can be hereditary, it is wise to refrain from using such animals in the stud or brood mare band, at least until a causative element has been isolated.

SPRAINS

Technically, a sprain is a wrenching or twisting of a joint or muscle that results in torn or stretched ligaments, without breaking the overlying skin. There is soreness, swelling and heat at the location.

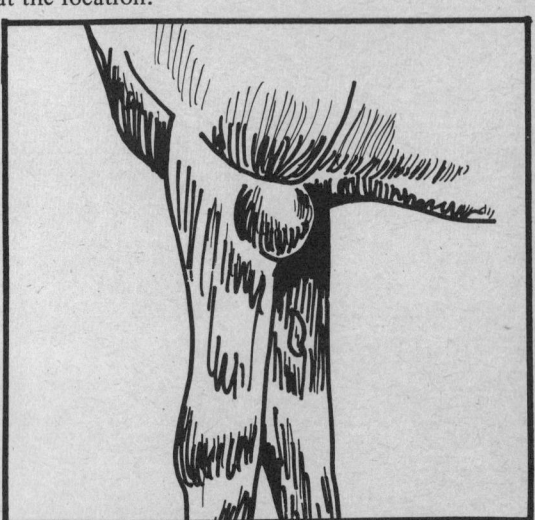

Horse (above) is suffering from heat exhaustion, a condition brought about through continued exposure to hot, muggy temperatures. The heat causes blood vessels to dilate and, if blood volume doesn't likewise increase, veins may collapse. A capped elbow is depicted at right, a swelling caused by horse bumping his elbow with a rear foot. See text for remedy.

Before understanding the treatment for sprains and strains, one first must comprehend the anatomical processes which occur in sequence immediately following injury. The first thing that happens is the animal feels pain, which serves two vital purposes: it keeps the horse from manipulating and perhaps further injuring the muscle/joint, and increases the amount of blood flowing to the affected area.

Blood flows to the injury faster than it leaves, resulting in a surplus that builds, producing two other recognizable signs: heat and swelling. If the sprain is minor, often these natural processes of forced rest, heat and increased circulation — bringing white blood cells to the site — will cure the injury after a few days. There are steps a horseman can take, however, to make the horse's convalescence more tolerable.

The first of these is to reduce the flow of blood to the injury. This requires constriction of the blood vessels, brought about through application of cold. If out on the trail when the sprain occurs, bathe the affected area in a stream or cool pond. If back at the barn, run cold water over the area from a hose, or apply ice wrapped in a towel or other cloth material. This action, by reducing the blood flow, keeps swelling down and relieves pain.

After an appropriate period of cold therapy, it's wise to take the opposite tack: applying heat and massage to the area. Heat, in the form of liniment, will open the blood vessels and allow more blood to reach the affected part. Massage aids in increasing circulation, thus speeding flow of the blood's necessary ingredients to and from the site. Make sure the three to five-minute massage isn't too vigorous; the horse will react adversely from pain!

Sometimes bandaging helps to immobilize the joint further. Most horsemen use two long strips of absorbent cotton wadding, applied separately, followed by bedsheet strips or one of the commercially available bandages. Apply the first layer of cotton loosely, the second with just light pressure, then the outer bandage just snugly. Don't tighten too much or not enough blood will reach the site to promote rapid healing.

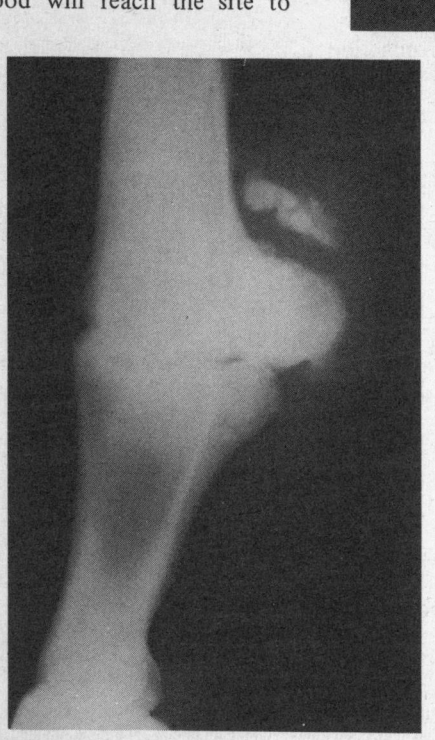

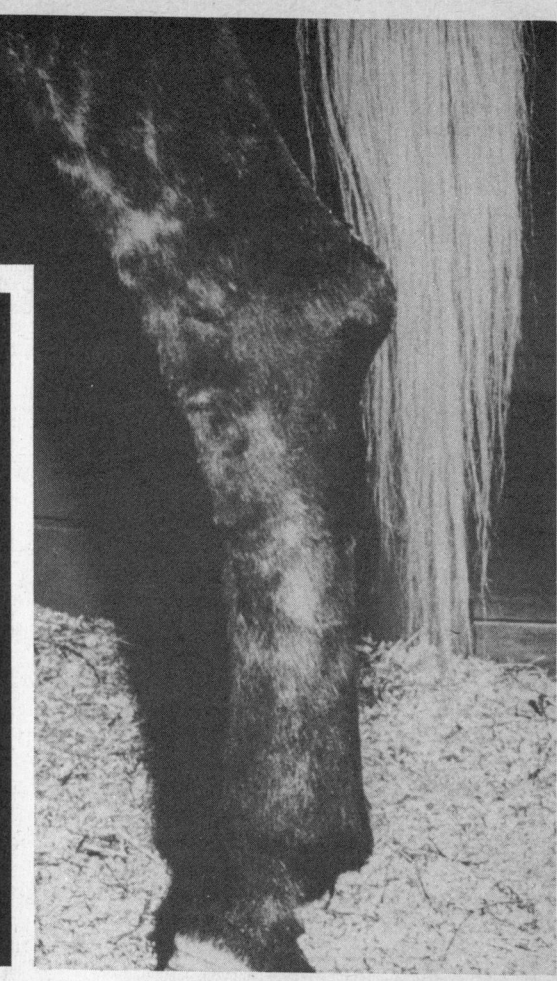

Fractured sesamoid, shown clearly in X-ray photo, much resembles the capped hock at far right. The proper diagnosis is of utmost importance.

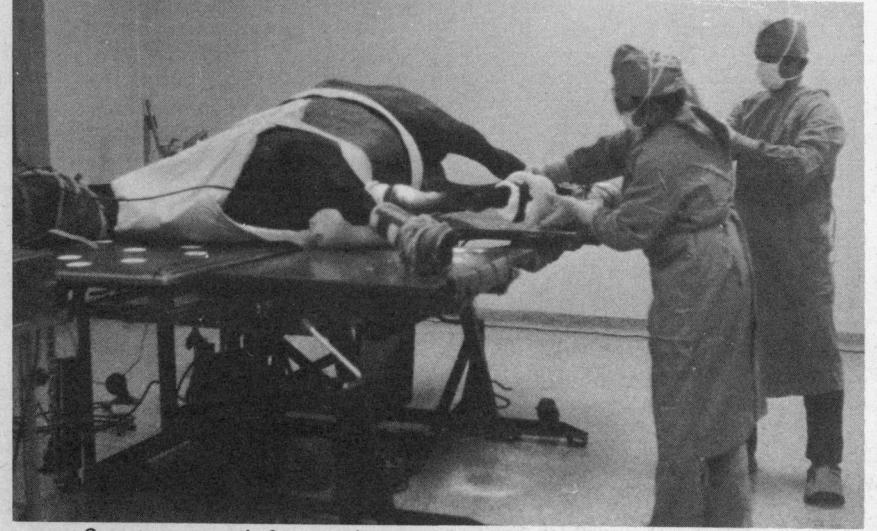

Surgery to repair fracture is expensive and usually limited to horses of great value (above). Following surgical repair, most are limited to work in the stud or brood mare band. Enlargement of fetlock denotes trouble, here osselets (right).

In extreme cases, a plaster or fiberglass cast may be required to totally immobilize the joint or muscle. Application of such a cast requires skills normally beyond the casual horseman and are best left to a veterinary surgeon.

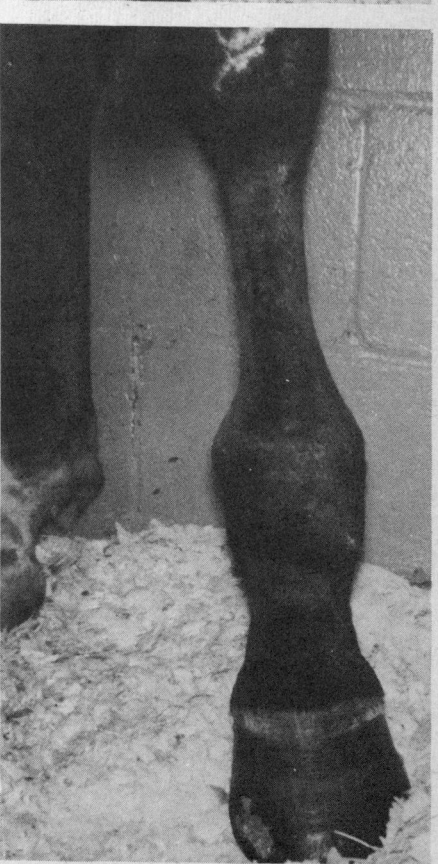

The types of strains or sprains to be discussed herewith include sore shins (bucked shins), carpitis (sore or popped knee), bog spavin, capped hock, capped elbow and tendinitis. It will be helpful to refer to the sketches showing internal configurations of bones and muscles making up the horse's legs.

Looking first at sore shins, this malady doesn't often befall pleasure or work horses used for Western equitation, striking mostly young thoroughbred or quarter horses used for racing.

Most common in the front legs, sore or bucked shins is an inflammation of the connective tissue at the front of the large metacarpal (cannon) bone, marked by swelling, pain and lameness. It is caused by concussion of leg striking the ground in racing, although the connective tissue, called the periosteum, can be stretched or torn by other strenuous activity not confined to the flat tracks.

When a horse shows the signs of sore shins, there is no recourse but to remove him from training or work. Application of cold packs may reduce the swelling and relieve pain. The horse should remain laid up until all signs of lameness have disappeared, then be brought back to work gradually. The rest period, depending upon severity of the condition, may sometimes last several months.

Carpitis, better known as sore or popped knee, is a common physical ailment around racetracks. It takes the form of an acute or chronic inflammation of the joint capsule of the knee and, in old cases, there sometimes is a spur or bony outgrowth present.

The cause appears to be concussion during hard training and horses not in peak condition sometimes break down with the malady. The horse will exhibit immediate signs of lameness and the knee swells. A veterinarian has to check for fractures in the knee, as often the symptoms are identical.

Rest is essential for a horse with carpitis. Like football players who develop water on the knee, removal of excess fluids in the joint may reduce the pain and this generally is followed by injection of cortisone or phenylbutazone, both procedures best left to a veterinary surgeon. He can't undo all the damage, however, and the knee never will be totally sound again.

Bog spavins are found on the hocks of a horse, being caused by faulty conformation, rickets or strain. It is characterized by distention of the capsule at the front of the hock joint, although the sides of the joint may also be involved. Unless the bones of the hock are affected, there usually is no hindrance on performance, although the bump remains visible. A veterinarian, depending upon the size of the spavin and its effect on the hock, may aspirate the accumulated fluids and inject muscle relaxants into the joint.

A capped hock is another injury-caused disability, affecting the rear of the horse's hock and characterized by a bulbous protrusion which normally is the result of reclining on hard floors, a kick, bumping the tailgate of a horse trailer, or a fall. It rarely causes lameness. If untreated, the bump may become fibrous and hard, to remain forever as a blemish which would detract from sale value.

Treatment of a capped hock is comprised of applications of a paint or liniment, which a veterinarian will prescribe. It's far better to remove the cause of capped hocks, though, through proper bedding, separation of horses showing physical dislike for one another, assuring adequate distance between the rump chain in a trailer and the tailgate, and removing obstacles which could lead to a fall in the barn area.

A capped elbow is much the same as a capped hock, the distinguishing feature being the area involved. Often called a shoe boil because it resembles a boil and is caused sometimes by brushing the elbow with a horseshoe when the horse is reclining, a capped elbow has a bulbous swelling which is more unsightly than serious. In fact, many veterinarians prefer not to treat a capped elbow, since the majority heal themselves in time.

Other causes of capped elbow are the horse assuming an unnatural position while resting in a stall, caused by the stall being too narrow, or having let the heels grow too long. A deep bed is the best prevention for capped elbow. Other corrective measures should be undertaken.

If a horse develops tendinitis, or bowed tendons, the horseowner has just lost a riding companion for about a year. Tendinitis is caused by exceptionally hard work on muddy, rough or hard ground, by beginning work too early with an immature horse, poor shoeing or, in some cases, conformation defects.

Tendinitis is an inflammation of the flexor tendons, the suspensory ligament or the check ligament, usually occurring in the foreleg, which generally shows up during hard work. The horse will be severely lame and stand pointing his toe to relieve pressure on the affected tendons. The affected area will be hot, swells rapidly and be painful to the touch. If caught in time, the ailment can be treated with good results before the tendon becomes fibrous or thick — the true bowed tendon.

The first step of treatment is to give the horse absolute rest and the inflammation should be treated with ice packs to reduce the swelling and pain. The affected tendons may be injected with a pain killer and the veterinary surgeon may opt to cast the limb in plaster or fiberglass.

When the cast is removed, bandages are applied for another month. When removed, the horse is rested for at least a year, after which time he is brought back to work with the utmost care. If the injury tends to be chronic in nature, it's doubtful the horse ever will be useful for hard work again.

The best prevention method is removal of the cause, that of working a horse too hard under adverse conditions or starting a horse working at too early an age. Naturally, if bowed tendons are apparent upon inspection of a horse prior to purchase, the animal should be overlooked.

SUNSTROKE

Actually, sunstroke is broken down into three separate categories including heatstroke, heat exhaustion and heat cramps, all of which are serious to the welfare of the horse. Similar to the afflictions of man, all three disrupt the heat-regulating mechanism inside the body.

Heatstroke is probably the most serious of the three and requires fast action to stave off death. Symptoms are abnormally rapid or deep breathing, the eyes may become glassy and staring, the rectal temperature hits nearly 110 degrees and the horse may collapse.

The best treatment is to immediately attempt to bring body temperature down, although not too fast. Cold water should be applied to the body, cold water enemas may be given and ice packs may be used around the brain. Temperature at the rectum should be taken at least once every five minutes and, if the temperature is dropping quickly, suspend ice pack and cold water therapy temporarily, then resume. If treatment isn't begun immediately, death results quickly.

Heat exhaustion, often called heat prostration, generally occurs following long periods of exposure to extremely hot, humid conditions, which causes the blood vessels to dilate or expand. Unless this dilation is followed by an appropriate increase in the volume of blood passing through the veins, the veins may collapse. Activity only aggravates this already serious condition.

Signs of heat exhaustion are characterized by rapid pulse, increased respiratory rate and/or deep breathing, muscular tremors and weakness. The horse doesn't usually have an increased body temperature at the outset, but it will rise if treatment isn't begun.

Just as with human heat-exhaustion victims, a horse should be moved to a shady spot and cold water should be given, if the horse will take it, in small amounts frequently offered. If a veterinarian is close-by, he may attempt intravenous introduction of a physiological saline solution. Because the circulatory system already is functioning abnormally or is impaired, he may opt to forego this procedure, however.

Heat cramps usually are the result of extended working periods in hot weather, which cause an electrolyte imbalance from the loss of too much salt through perspiration.

Generally the first sign of something amiss is the horse will stop sweating. He may then suffer muscle spasms. The horseman should immediately stop working, remove tack from the animal and try to replace the lost salt through offerings of cool water mixed with salt. It sometimes is given via stomach tube and, unless salt loss is overt, the horse usually will recover with rest.

As a horseman can't as yet control the environmental conditions of humidity and heat — unless he invests in an air-conditioned barn — there is little he can do to prevent heat exhaustion. As heatstroke seems partially tied to ventilation, he should assure the latter is adequate for his stable. Heat cramps can be avoided by using common sense when working in extremely hot, muggy weather; frequent rest stops are in order, as is the offering of salt and limited amounts of water during such breaks.

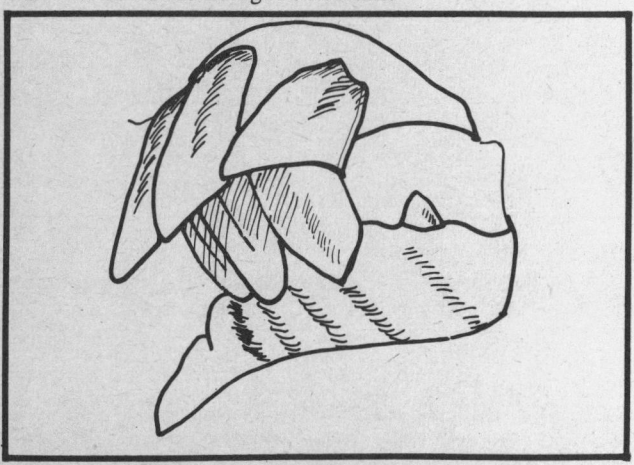

A parrot-mouthed horse should be avoided whenever possible, since it's a serious defect. They have great difficulty in grazing, nutrition problems, too.

TEETH CARE

It's not surprising that a horse's teeth play an important part in his overall health and his teeth should be examined at least once per year for abnormalities and/or corrective dentistry.

Except under rare circumstances, horses don't suffer from cavities, although they may have toothaches. In such cases, the tooth generally is extracted. But a much more common malady comes from sharp protrusions forming on the teeth through regular chewing which requires "floating" the teeth.

As a horse chews, or masticates, he gradually wears the surface of his teeth away. Unless the teeth grate perfectly atop one another during this process, not all of the teeth surfaces will be worn down uniformly, resulting in ridges on the inside portions of the teeth, next to the tongue. This causes discomfort and even injury to the tongue or gums, which can make a horse go off his feed or bolt it without thorough mastication, sometimes leading to impaction colic.

Teeth problems can be suspected when a horse will shun hard grain or, when munching grain, tends to open his mouth and let the granules drop out. While it also can be indicative of a greedy eater, horses with teeth problems sometimes bolt their grain, which will show by examination of the droppings. Too, if he eats exceptionally slowly he may suffer from teeth problems that need correction.

When eating roughage, horses needing dental attention sometimes will "quid" their feed, or partially masticate it then let it fall to the ground. Other horses sometimes will pack it in the side of the mouth instead of swallowing.

Floating a horse's teeth is an easy procedure for a veterinarian, who uses a special rasp and files down the protrusions. If a tooth is bad, it usually is pulled.

Teeth problems of a more serious nature are caused by conformation defects, two of which are parrot or salmon-mouthed horses. In the former, the upper jaw doesn't align with the lower in front — the horse has an overbite — which makes grazing difficult if not impossible. In the case of the salmon-mouthed horse, the lower jaw protrudes beyond the upper, resulting in underbite. As these defects can be inherited, it's wise to refrain from breeding animals with such defects.

THUMPS

Thumps are characterized by spasms of the diaphragm, which are regarded as the equine form of hiccoughs by some horsemen. Sometimes a distinct thumping sound will be heard, hence the name, and thumps are caused by strenuous exertion by unfit horses during hot weather.

If a horse develops thumps, the best treatment is through immediate rest. The horseman can sponge the body with cool water and, when the thumping subsides, the horse is returned to the barn. Water should be offered frequently, given in small amounts to avoid the possibility of founder, until all thumping ceases.

The best way to avoid thumps is to have a horse in proper condition before subjecting him to strenuous exercise. Also, use common sense when working under extreme temperatures: Horses don't like hard work in the hot sun anymore than does the horseman.

TYING UP

Myositis in horses often is confused with azoturia because many of the symptoms are the same. However, this muscular disorder generally strikes horses that are in service every day, without the rest period/full feeding which causes azoturia.

The initial signs of myositis are the same as for azoturia: increased respiratory rate, sweating, dark-colored urine and muscle stiffness in the hindquarters. But unlike azoturia, it is recommended to keep the animal moving, even if pain is apparent. Converse to azoturia, in which continued movement results in the horse going down, forced movement when afflicted by myositis seems to clear the condition. He should be removed to the barn and rested. Administration of vitamin E and selenium seems to produce favorable results. Bring the horse back to work cautiously.

There are other internal disorders a horse can suffer, but this has been an attempt to cover some of the most frequently encountered ailments. As outlined at the beginning of this section and elsewhere, always structure therapy around the instructions of your veterinarian. He is familiar with specific conditions as they exist relative to your horse, which can lead to a different diagnosis and necessitate treatment alteration.

CHAPTER 5
EXTERNAL PROBLEMS

Bruises, Cuts And More Serious Injuries Befall The Horse. Know How To Minimize The Danger And Pain.

On the average, more damage occurs to the outside of a horse than the inside and in this section will be described various physical maladies incurred externally by horses. As mentioned at the outset of this chapter, there is much cross-over of disorders into more than one category and, with this in mind, this chapter will deal with fistula of the withers; poll evil; allergies (photosensitization, nettle rash); wounds; acne (pyoderma); hidebound; dandruff; burns; saddle sores; and warts.

SADDLE SORES

Saddle sores can lead to a myriad of serious problems, including internal tissue destruction, unless treated early.

Saddle sores are caused by an ill-fitting saddle, which irritates one or both sides of the backbone. Unless the ailment is treated and the cause of injury removed, saddle sores progress in severity and finally require lay-up of the horse for an extended period.

Prospective saddle sores should be detected when grooming after a ride. The site is tender and the horse usually will exhibit signs of pain when the region is brushed or massaged. The hair follicles may be inflamed, although this is difficult to observe on most horses.

If a saddle sore is noticed early, applications of ice and

Saddle sores, as noted in the text, are caused usually by an ill-fitting saddle and should be detected upon after-ride grooming. Begin treatment immediately.

There is some feeling that fistula and brucellosis syndromes/may be related, the latter striking cattle. Horses should be segregated from cattle with disease.

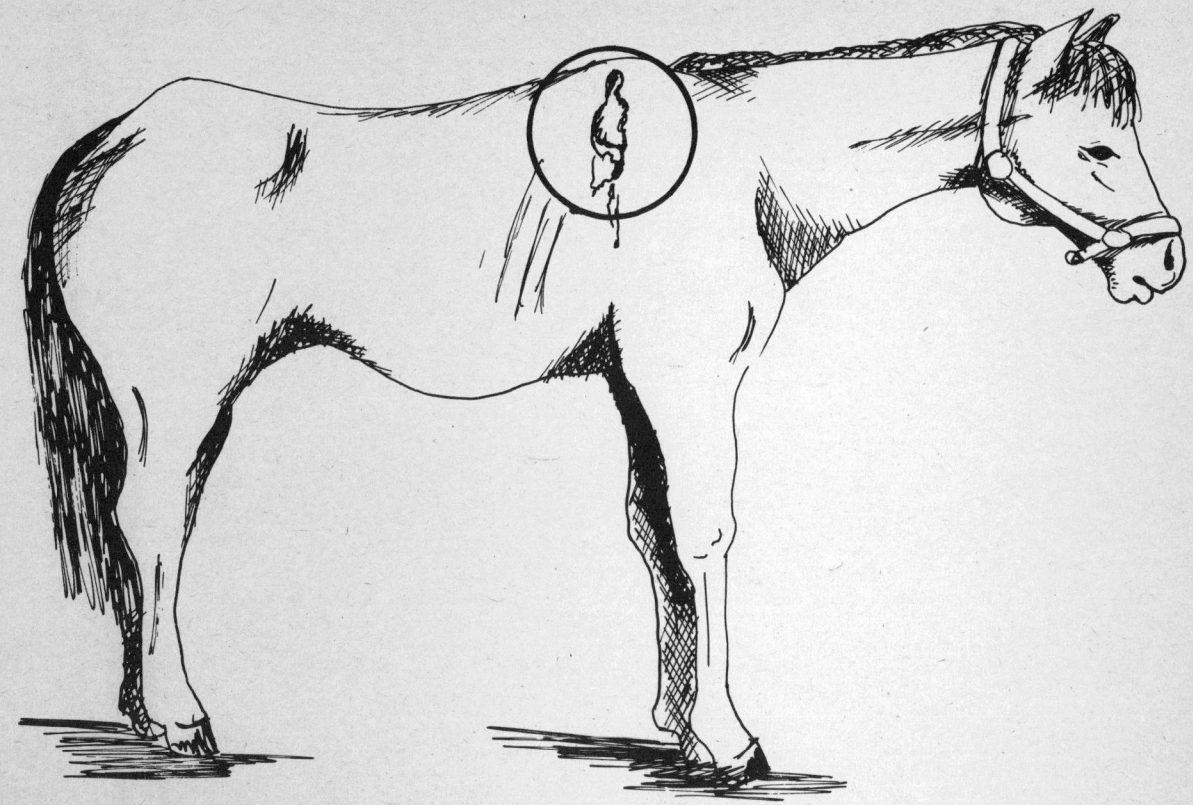

Fistula of the withers results from a variety of causes, most of which horsemen can remove. The wither area swells and later ruptures, then drains as tissues die.

later warm packs usually will relieve the irritation, provided the horse is rested during the process. If the sore is ignored, it will worsen and become a "gall" — a raw, open lesion. If the sore isn't treated at this stage, oftentimes hemorrhage occurs beneath the skin, causing swelling, heat and obvious pain. The skin sometimes will rupture and fluids will drain, which leaves the horse open to secondary infection. Untreated, the tissue may begin to die beneath the area or a scar will develop. And if the wound becomes infected, the condition could terminate in death through tetanus or other bacteria.

There is no excuse for failing to notice a saddle sore, as the horse will give all the clues necessary. He will exhibit pain when the horseman touches the sore, even if not yet visible. As the condition worsens the horse will perform erratically when ridden, because of the pain. The lesion then will become hairless and can't be overlooked.

Treatment calls for complete rest, daily applications of antiseptic ointment following cleansing of the wound with physiological saline solution. If the sore is a gall, daily treatment with saline solution will aid in hardening the surface. Keep insects away from the horse during recovery.

It is essential that each horseman match his tack to the animal to avoid this problem and others yet to be discussed. Only by so doing can he expect the maximum performance from his mount and the pleasurable experience horseback riding is supposed to be.

FISTULA OF THE WITHERS

This serious condition incapacitates a horse for extended periods, sometimes causing death. Its origin is disputable; some veterinary surgeons feel it arises from a bump or bite at the withers, while others are exploring the possibility it might be caused by bacteria or an internal parasite.

Let's first examine the plausible explanation that fistulous withers is caused through a bump, bite or fall. It's understandable that the withers are affected more than any other part of the body because of its unique structure. It's here where the vertebrae of the spine reach their highest level, forming a hump that can contact a low roof, corral fence or rocks when the horse rolls.

Fistula of the withers begins when the tissue bruises, causing inflammation. Because the tissue is of relatively low order on the healing scale, it sometimes breaks down and a hollow cavity filled with pus forms. Swelling occurs on both sides of the withers and, in rapidly developing cases, the withers will be hot and cause the horse pain when touched.

Eventually, this swelling terminates in an eruption at the withers, whereupon pus or other exudate drains. The destruction process continues, involving other interior areas, with tendon sheaths or membranes acting as "pipes" for the transfer of fluids to the surface for draining. This arrangement of pipes is where fistula gets its name: defined, fistula means an abnormal passage, hollow like a reed or pipe, from one abscess or hollow organ to the body surface.

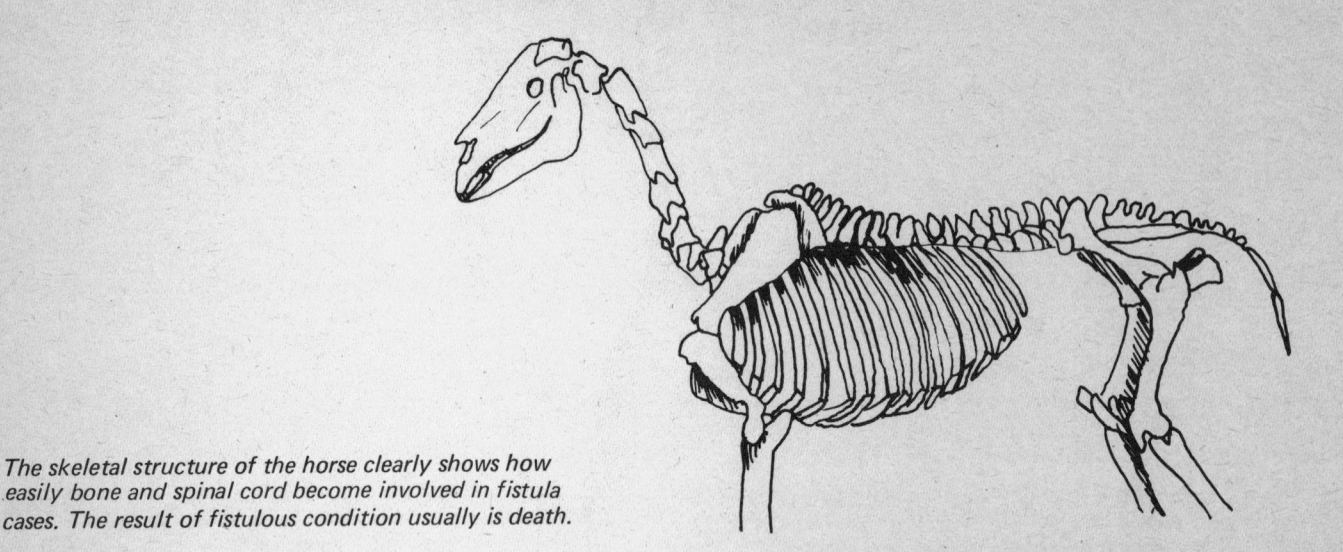

The skeletal structure of the horse clearly shows how easily bone and spinal cord become involved in fistula cases. The result of fistulous condition usually is death.

As the situation deteriorates, bone may become affected in the destructive process with death as a consequence. Blood poisoning also causes its share of deaths in these cases, as does paralysis if the tissue and bone destruction reaches the spinal cord. Horses deeply involved generally are put down humanely by the veterinarian.

A theory advanced by other veterinary scholars is that fistulous withers may be caused by a bacteria, *Brucella abortus,* or an internal parasite, *Actinomyces bovis.* This theory is based upon the positive reactions to brucellosis agglutination tests of horses with fistulous withers, and isolation of *Br. abortus* in fluid aspirated from the withers prior to rupture. Also, *A. bovis* has been regularly discovered in the infected connective-tissue wall. In tests, injection of only one member of this team has failed to produce the fistulous symptoms, although simultaneous injection of both has resulted in the characteristic signs.

Adding strength to the theory of bacterial or parasitic passage of fistula are findings that cattle infections both with *Br. abortus* and *A. bovis* occurred concurrently with the condition in horses, and outbreaks of brucellosis in cattle followed contact with horses having open fistulous lesions.

However it is contracted, it's not good news for horse or horseman. If noticed early in development, the horseowner can cool the withers with water or ice packs three times daily, which tends to reduce the swelling and heat. If this fails to check continuation, the only hope is surgery; remission is virtually nil.

Several days before operating, the veterinary surgeon

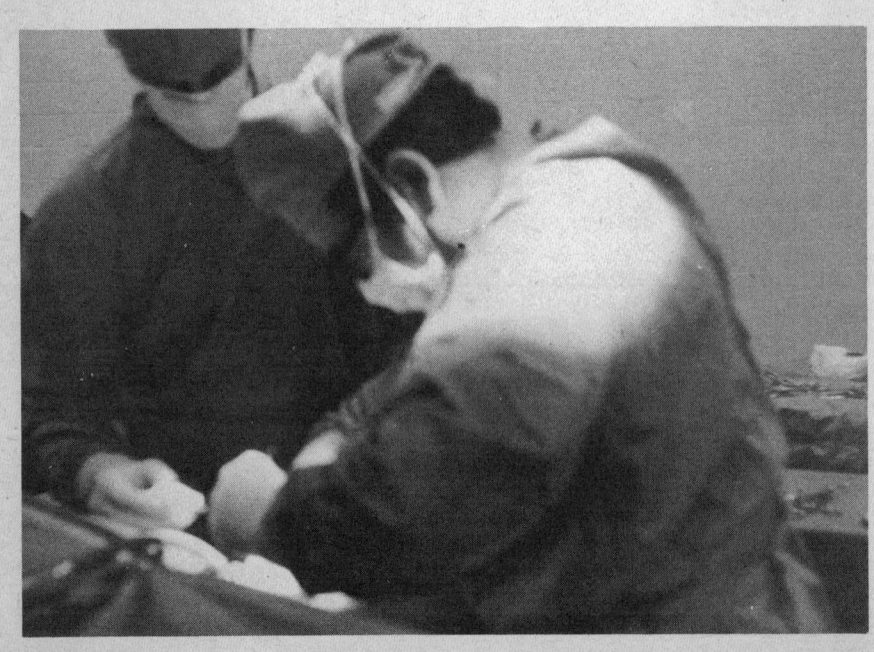

Surgery to remove any dead bone and necrotic tissue can be disappointing. It's much sounder to remove the cause!

Poll evil differs from fistula of the withers only in how fast a horse dies; closer proximity to brain and the spinal cord speeds the conclusion of the disorder.

will begin antibiotic therapy with streptomycin or the like. On the operating table, he will remove all dead and diseased tissue and bone, then continue treating the area with sulfa-based drugs. If lucky, the destruction will be halted.

One big problem with treating fistula of the withers is expense: Even if caught early, the veterinary attention required over the long course will exceed the horse's value. Too, results of surgery can be disappointing; such a horse generally has little further working value.

POLL EVIL

The poll is the second region most often affected by fistula, perhaps caused by a blow, bacteria/internal parasite, or a tight-fitting halter. The only great distinguishing feature between poll evil and fistula of the withers is that the former usually leads to a quicker termination in death through close proximity to the brain and spinal cord.

If the true cause of this fistulous syndrome is an internal parasite or bacteria, only sound stable management can prevent it. This includes keeping the horse away from cattle suffering from either infection. If the cause is a blow of some type, eliminate all likely causes of such. This should be extended to horses, also. One particular animal in the herd may be biting others on the withers or poll.

Remove all likely structures which could result in a blow to the withers or poll, and assure proper halter fit. It can save a great deal in the long run.

ALLERGIES

Horses seem more fortunate than other four-legged critters in that they aren't affected too often by allergies. The most frequently reported type — which isn't seen often — is a condition called photosensitization: allergy to sunlight.

This condition isn't a natural phenomenon. Rather, it affects horses that have impaired liver function, perhaps caused by the ingestion of plants like St. John's wart or buckwheat. It generally affects only nonpigmented areas of the body and at first resembles sunburn. If the horse remains in sunlight, the white areas of the body will swell, then become cracked and dry. Continued exposure to the sun's rays will lead to necrosis of the tissues involved; these will be sloughed off.

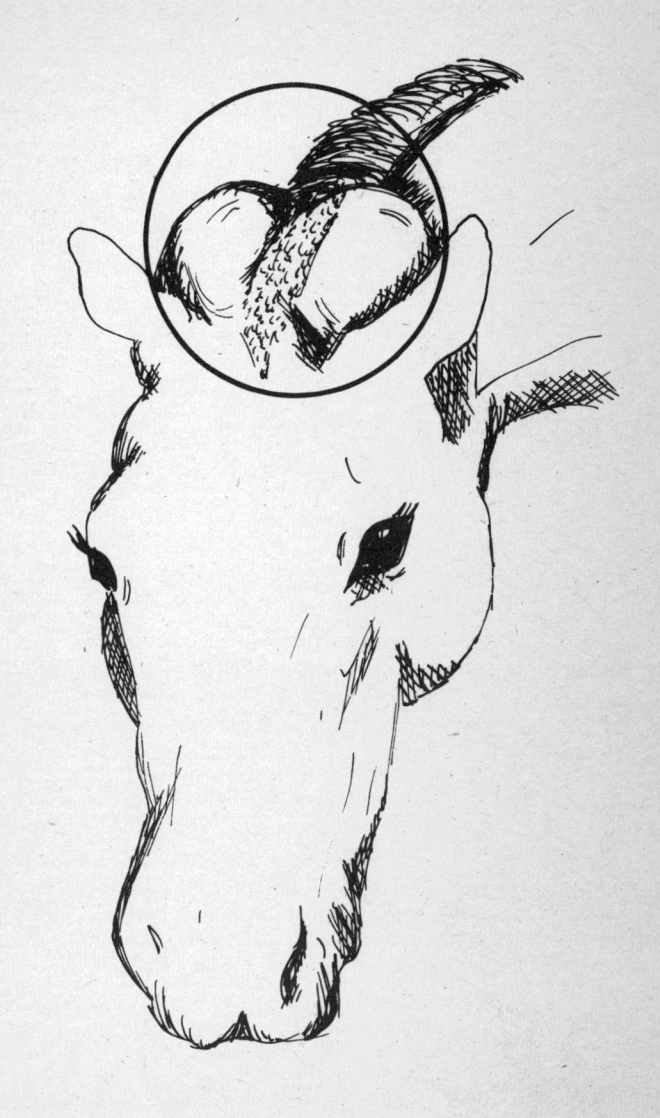

If the condition is noted early, the nonpigmented areas should be cleaned and a salve administered. The horse should be kept out of the sunlight. A veterinarian will treat advanced cases with antihistamines, which seem to clear the liver condition and the horse will recover, if kept in the shade. Once total recovery is effected, keep horses off pasture containing St. John's wart or buckwheat and chance of recurrence is slight.

Nettle rash or hives, scientifically tagged as urticaria, is an allergy caused by a substance to which the horse is allergic, or perhaps by insect bites. It is characterized by welts or plateau-shaped swellings measuring from one-half to as large as eight inches in diameter, appearing on the neck, flanks, back, legs and eyelids. They appear suddenly,

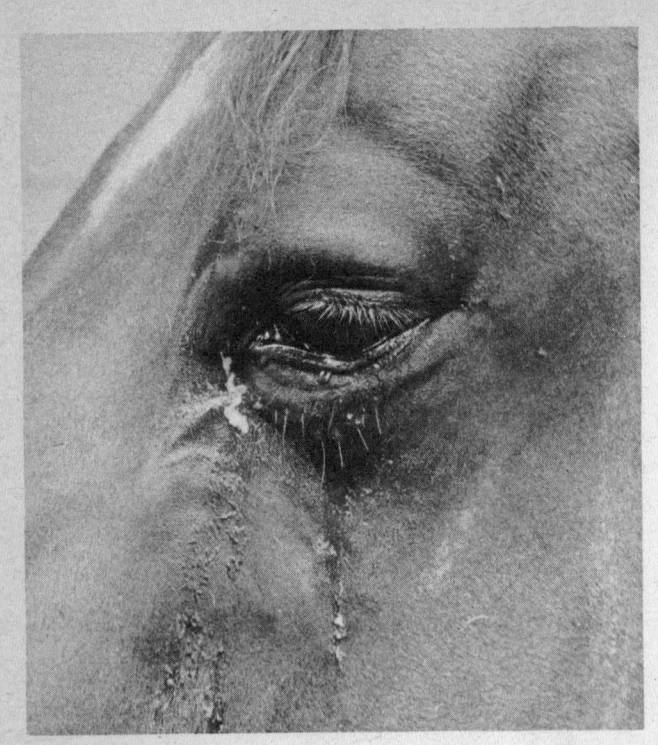

A horse's eyes can tell so much about what's happening on the inside that every horseman should be able to "read" them. In this case, the eye clearly denotes a sick animal.

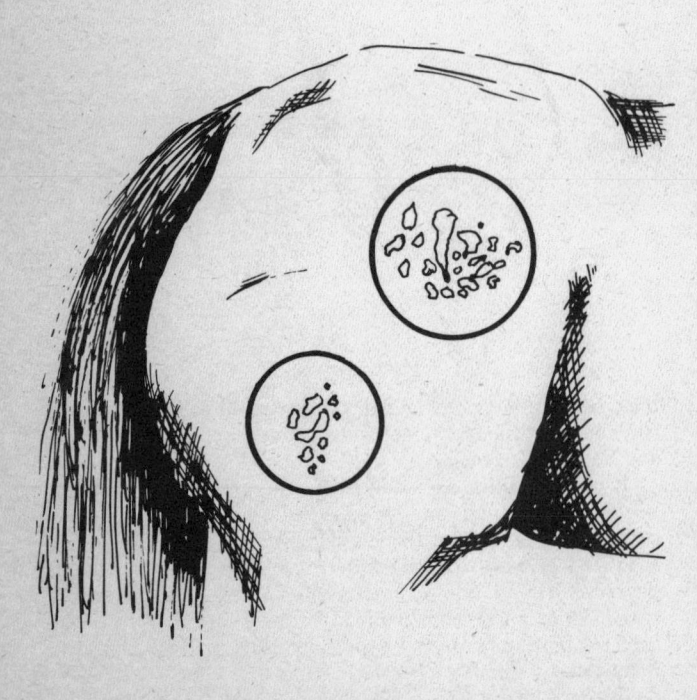

Symptoms of allergic reaction to the environment or parts thereof take differing shapes, such as nettle rash (above). Photosensitization generally affects unpigmented areas.

accompanied by lack of appetite, listlessness and temperature slightly above normal.

After several minutes or hours, the welts disappear just as suddenly as they appeared. Usually no treatment is needed, unless the horse literally is covered with the rash, whereupon antihistamines or the like are given. The symptoms will recur if the cause of this reaction isn't isolated and removed, and there is no simple way of doing this. Just as with a child too young to talk showing an allergic reaction, the horseman must begin a systematic elimination of all items with which the horse came in contact. Start with anything new around the stable which could have led to onset of the symptoms. Initiate a good program of insect control.

WOUNDS

Wounds can be divided into five different categories, depending upon severity: bruise, abrasion, incised, laceration and puncture.

A veterinarian follows a regular course of action when treating a wound, which is sound practice for individual horseowners. This sequence, from beginning to end, is: control the bleeding; relieve pain; prevent shock; control infection; control the patient; and provide supportive care.

A bruise is caused by a bump, fall, kick or other contact that doesn't break the skin. In humans, a bruise is easily recognized by discoloration of the skin, caused by excess accumulation of blood. Many times the bruise is indistinguishable in horses because of his coat or coloration.

If a bruise is minor in scope, no treatment is necessary; the excess blood will be reabsorbed into the surrounding tissues in time. If the horse has a bad bruise that has resulted in the formation of a blood blister, recovery often is slower. In fact, many times a veterinarian will puncture the blister and let the excess blood drain off. The horse then recovers with no ill effects, providing some type of germ-killing agent has been added to the lanced spot.

The second least-serious wound is an abrasion. This occurs when a horse scrapes against a rough surface, usually causing slight bleeding from the capillaries and it's painful. Because the skin has been opened, it should be cleaned gently with a mild disinfectant like physiological saline solution or soap and some type of antiseptic ointment applied. If infection develops, a veterinarian should be consulted as soon as possible.

An incised wound is more serious than either a bruise or abrasion because it constitutes a clean cut into the tissue. The first concern is bleeding, since severing a major artery could cause death if bleeding isn't stopped.

The best way to treat an incised wound bleeding slightly is through application of direct pressure to the wound site. If back at the barn where the first-aid kit is kept, a pressure bandage is best used for this task, pressed firmly over the wound until all bleeding ceases; this takes several minutes. If in the country, the palm of the hand will suffice, applied in the same manner as a pressure bandage.

If a major artery is severed by an incised wound, the situation is more grim. Such occurrence is easily recognized by blood squirting from the wound each time the heart beats. If the blood is bright red, an artery carrying blood from the heart has been cut; if dark red a vein carrying blood back to the heart has been severed.

In either case, immediate attention is required to keep the animal from bleeding to death. Dr. Wayne O. Kester, executive director of the American Association of Equine

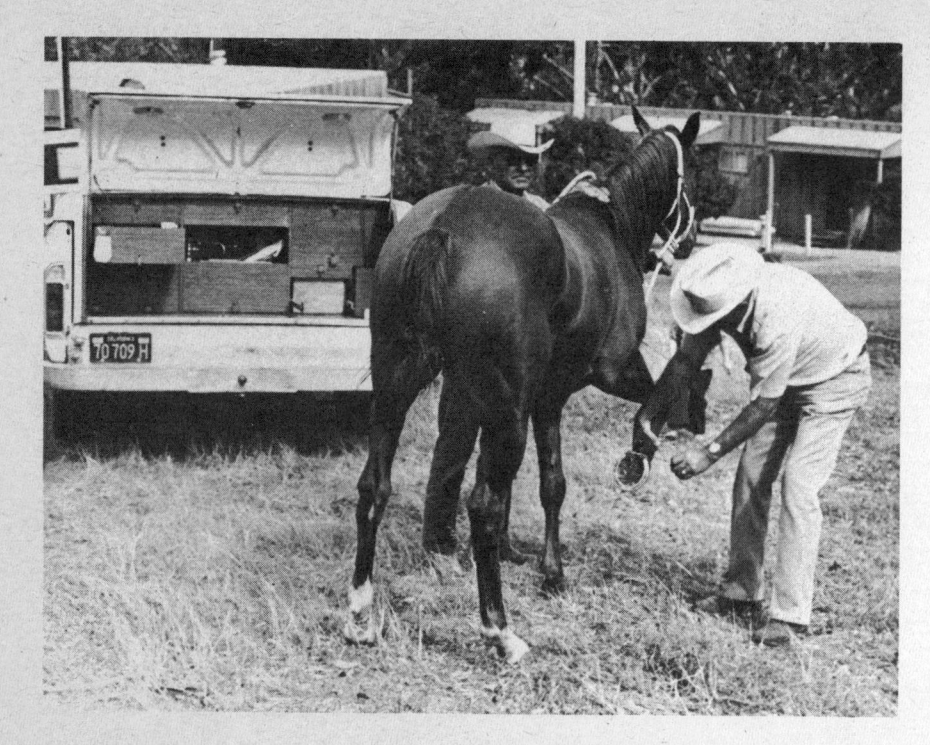

The frog is particularly susceptible to puncture wounds from glass, nails, wire and the like. Here, a veterinarian examines a foot of horse showing signs of lameness in his right foreleg.

Practitioners and one of the most respected veterinary surgeons in the world, never recommends use of a tourniquet in these cases. "There are several reasons for this," says Dr. Kester. "First, the arteries are so placed in a horse's leg that it is difficult to constrict them without extreme pressure. Second, damage to the tendons, ligaments and other underlying tissue is unavoidable, even if the tourniquet is released every five to ten minutes. And third, a tourniquet is painful and a horse will fight it, thus stimulating circulation.

"The best procedure is to place an absorbent patch or wad of gauze, cotton, a bath towel — even a dirty shirt — over the wound and bind it down snugly with some kind of bandage over the wound," continues this eminent authority. "Any absorbent pack bound firmly over the wound and around the leg soon will saturate and cause the blood to clot and back up into the wound for rather prompt control of bleeding. It can be removed in an hour or so and the wound treated properly."

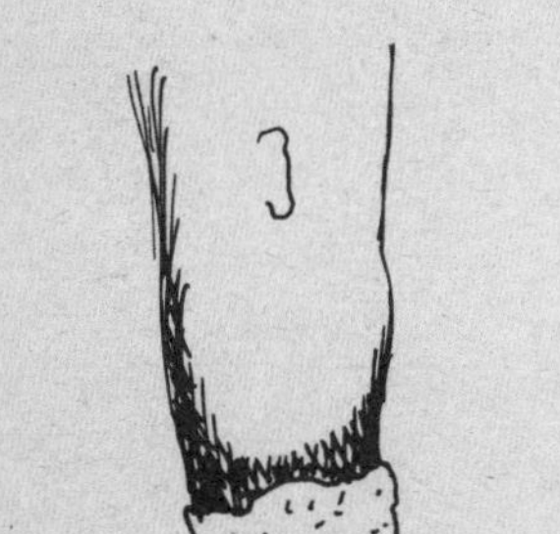

After bleeding has stopped, the injured area should be bandaged properly. Old sheets torn into strips work well, but in emergency any material can be used.

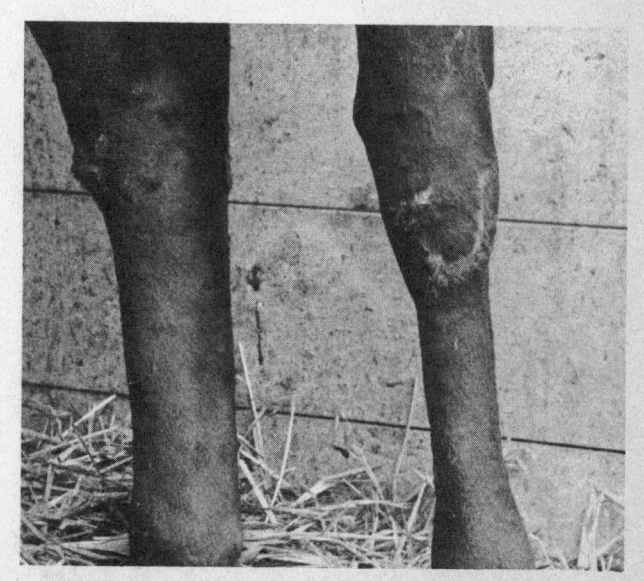

This horse's back legs have been so scarred he no longer can be used in show classes or performance events. The equine nemesis, barbed wire, did the damage here.

Friday Jacobs and Sal Llamas examine a blunt pipe that injured horse shown on these two pages. The pipe entered right at the throatlatch in freak accident, cutting a jagged hole in horse's windpipe, almost killing him.

When the bleeding has stopped, the wound site should be cleaned if dirty, foreign matter removed if present and an antiseptic ointment daubbed generously on the wound. A bandage then can be used to keep it clean if in a tenable position.

The major difference between incised wounds and lacerations is the nature of the cut; the latter is jagged, a tearing of the tissues rather than sharp separation. The chance for permanent scarring — development of proud flesh — is greater with lacerations, which makes proper treatment important.

The first step is to control the bleeding, using the same practices for incised wounds. The wound then should be cleaned thoroughly and rinsed with a saline solution, then a mild antiseptic ointment is applied. The hair surrounding the wound should be shaved and coated with a substance like petroleum jelly, which keeps draining fluids from sticking to the hair, irritating the skin. Reapply ointment as needed, which will repel insects and keep germs from penetrating. If the laceration is severe, consult professional advice. He may decide to stitch the wound closed.

The last category of wounds is punctures, most often caused by a nail or stiff splinter penetrating the body surface or the foot. A veterinarian should be called immediately and he will administer a tetanus antitoxin to guard against the growth of *Clostridium tetani* bacteria. He will shave the site and enlarge the opening to promote better drainage during recovery.

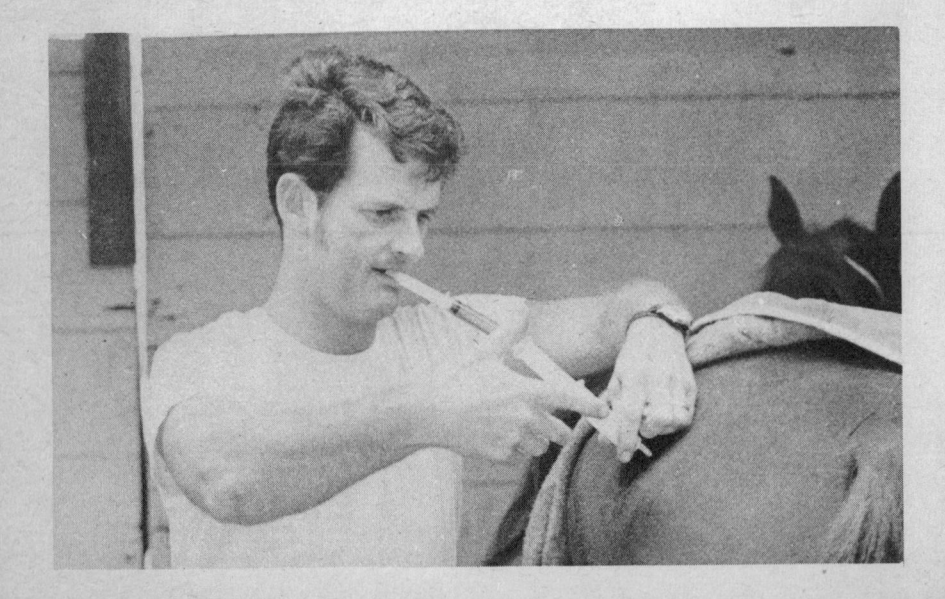

Dr. Bob Hunt gives Windy's King a tetanus injection after suturing the wound closed. Upon closure, because of clogged nasal cavity, horse began suffocating and required tracheotomy.

Terri Lester gently comforts the injured horse, which required twenty-eight stitches. One jugular vein was severed but the horse is mending. Note the garden hose used for emergency tracheotomy that's taped to neck.

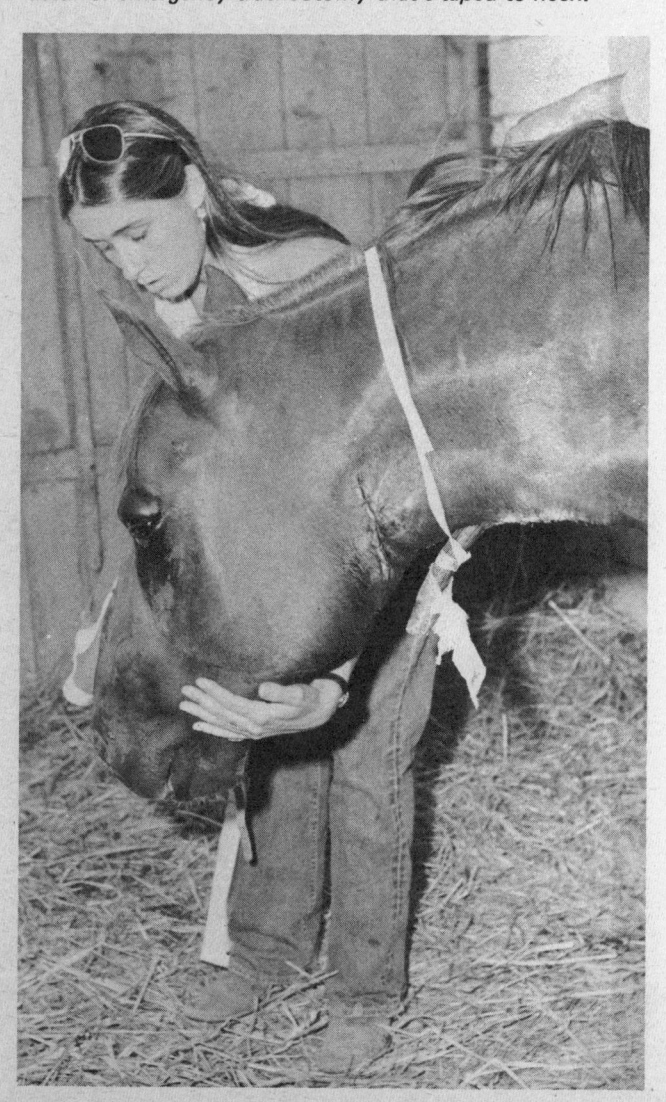

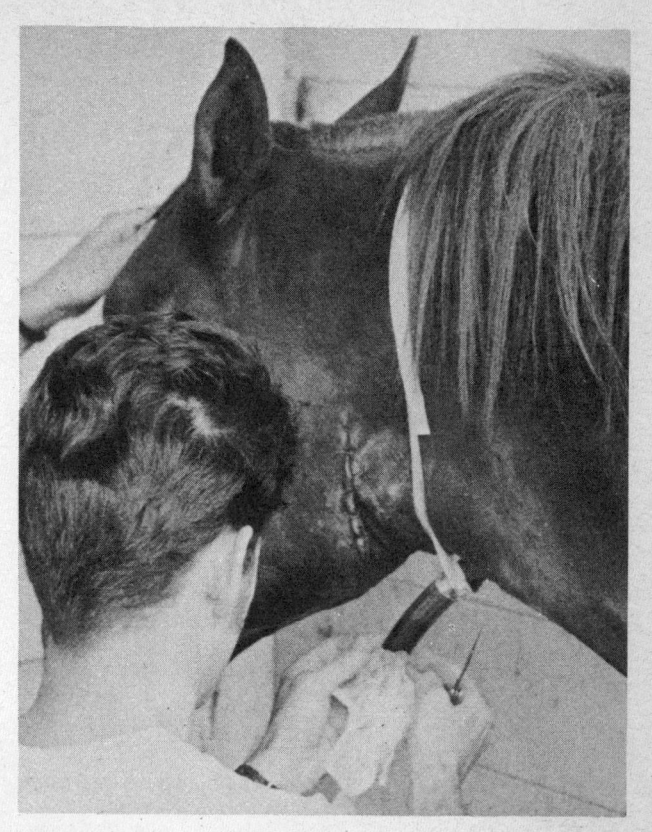

The end of the makeshift tracheotomy tube is covered with a gauze wrapping, to keep the horse from inhaling insects or dirt directly into the lungs for more trouble.

Puncture wounds of the feet can lead to lameness. The nail or splinter shouldn't be removed until the hole can easily be seen. This wound then is packed with iodine or an antiseptic paste, following a thorough cleaning with a disinfectant like hydrogen peroxide to kill existing germs. The affected foot then should be bandaged to keep foreign matter from the wound and a veterinarian will administer a tetanus antitoxin. Other steps may be necessary to prevent lameness, depending upon depth of the puncture.

ACNE

More accurately called pyoderma, this skin disorder usually is caused by the entry of *Staphylococcus aureus*, *Staphylococcus epidermidis* or *Streptococcus* into the skin, seen initially as inflammation of the hair follicles.

Most often seen around the saddle area of the back, pyoderma manifests itself initially as swelling and extreme sensitivity, followed by the appearance of what look like pimples (hence the colloquial term acne). These pimples may fill with pus and after two or three days rupture and become small cysts, or they may merge into raised welts. If untreated, this condition can worsen until nearly all of the surface skin is involved or underlying tissues become inflamed.

Sometimes, however, this condition will disappear spontaneously after several weeks. If it doesn't and leads to inflammation of other skin layers, treatment is difficult and best left to a veterinarian, who should have been called upon first notice of the disorder.

HIDEBOUND

When healthy, it is possible to pull a horse's skin and it will stretch, as with a dog. When a horse is hidebound, the skin is taut.

A hidebound condition usually is the result of improper feeding, lack of nutrients, a digestive disorder or lack of condition, characterized by tightly drawn skin over all portions of the body. The ribs usually will be visible because fatty tissue between bone and skin isn't present.

The first course of action is determination of the cause. Once isolated and corrected, the horse will return to normal, aided through addition of high protein supplements to his feed.

DANDRUFF

This condition usually is the result of improper grooming or poor diet, but also can indicate high parasite load or digestive upset. It is characterized by flaky, scaly skin, similar to the human condition.

The best treatment for dandruff, which is more unsightly than serious, is through elimination of the cause. Proper diet, good grooming and efficient parasite control are important. Clearing the condition can be hastened through addition of generous amounts of linseed meal to the feed.

BURNS

Though infrequent, horses do suffer from burns and these command the attention of a veterinarian. They can be caused by chemicals, steam, flames or contact with hot

When riding through brushy terrain, keep on the lookout for partially hidden obstacles like downed logs or sharp tree limbs (below left). The horse could stumble and fall or receive a nasty wound, the last thing desired when away from the barn! Upon completion of the ride, the horse is groomed thoroughly (below right). At this time, check for sores or any injuries.

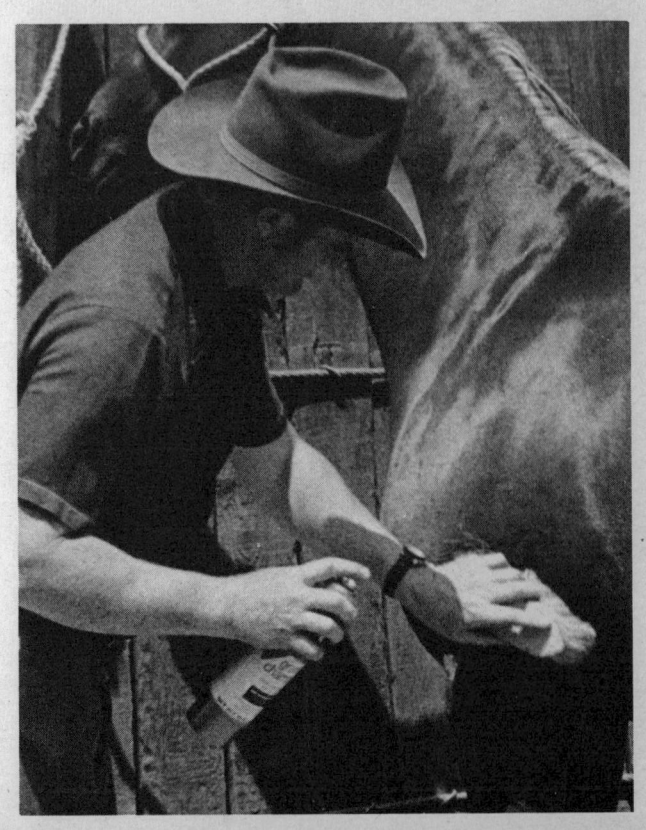

surfaces and the prognosis depends upon severity of the burns.

Since there is constantly changing thought on the part of veterinary surgeons regarding treatment of even minor burns, we won't offer suggestions which could be outdated as new treatment practices become known. Rather, we suggest contacting a veterinarian at the earliest opportunity and leaving the burn alone. More damage can be done by people with good intentions than had they done nothing. Simply attempt to keep the horse quiet and free from insects until the vet's arrival.

WARTS

These unsightly blemishes, which generally show on the face and nose of the horse, don't usually cause trouble unless they appear at a spot over which tack fits, causing irritation. They are caused by a virus and can spread through a herd in short order.

As with humans, horses sometimes rid themselves of warts in time. If there is more than one horse present, the horse with warts should be isolated to prevent spread. A veterinarian can treat warts, sometimes with good success, with vaccines or external medications.

It's true that horses sometimes suffer from other external disorders not outlined here. In such cases, it is the common and advised practice to call a veterinarian, which should be done when the disorder first is noticed. Oftentimes this can preclude advancement of a minor ailment into a serious, expensive problem.

Besides being a cribber's delight, this wooden barrier poses still another possible source of injury. Like, what happens if something spooks this horse right now? He could possibly slam his chin or jaw on the wood!

Horses, just like humans, are susceptible to warts. In nearly all cases, they disappear on their own. Isolate affected horse to prevent spread of warts.

CHAPTER 6
PARASITISM:

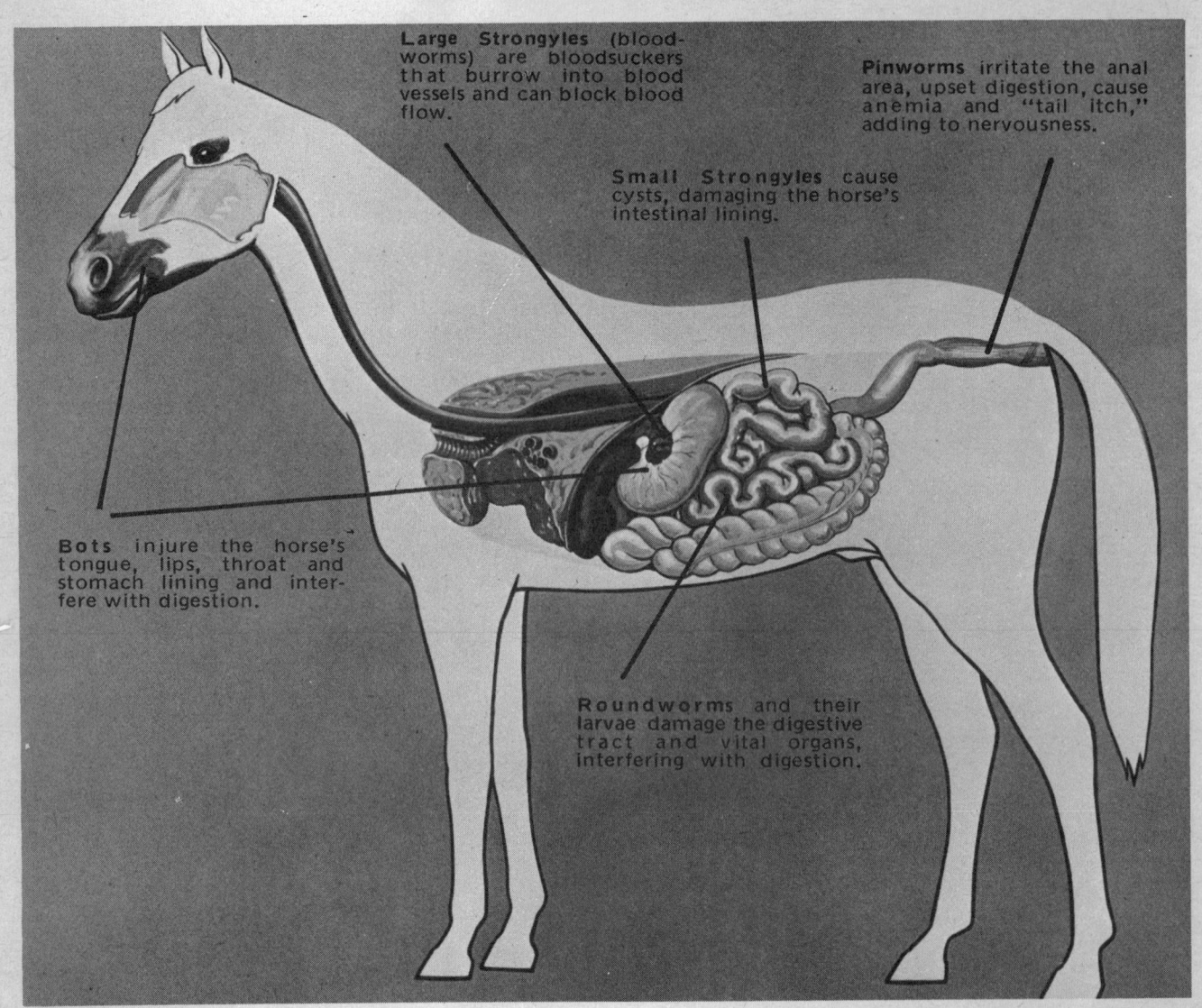

Large Strongyles (bloodworms) are bloodsuckers that burrow into blood vessels and can block blood flow.

Pinworms irritate the anal area, upset digestion, cause anemia and "tail itch," adding to nervousness.

Small Strongyles cause cysts, damaging the horse's intestinal lining.

Bots injure the horse's tongue, lips, throat and stomach lining and interfere with digestion.

Roundworms and their larvae damage the digestive tract and vital organs, interfering with digestion.

The five most common types of internal parasites found in horses, and the area inside the body they favor, are shown in the illustration above. All cause problems, though some of a less severe nature than others, but none are beneficial.

Parasites by their very natures, are freeloaders. They depend upon a host — in this case, the horse — for survival, but contribute nothing to the horse's welfare. Indeed, the more than 150 different types of parasites which can infect horses do nothing but cause problems, varying in scope from mild annoyance to death.

For ease of classification, parasites are divided into either external or internal types, dependent upon their specific area of involvement. External parasites usually are easier to spot. In fact, many times a horse will appear normal when carrying a high load of the internal "bad names."

Some of the symptoms which can denote internal parasitism are: colic; tail rubbing; anemia; rough coat; lameness; weakness; wasting feed; enlarged, distended abdomen; cough; and emaciation. Since these symptoms also can be indicative of other ailments, a veterinarian will examine feces samples under a microscope, although many internal parasites will be plainly visible in the droppings.

Of the 150-plus parasites which can infect horses, only a handful are seen with any degree of regularity. Internally, these are bots, pinworms, ascarids, large and small strongyles, large and small stomach worms, and tapeworms. Externally, the pests include mites, fleas, mosquitos, lice, gnats, ticks, ringworm, houseflies, stable flies, horseflies and blowflies. Treatment procedures for both will be covered at the end of each respective section.

PREVENTION AND TREATMENT

Research Continues To Show The Major Role Of Parasites In Equine Maladies

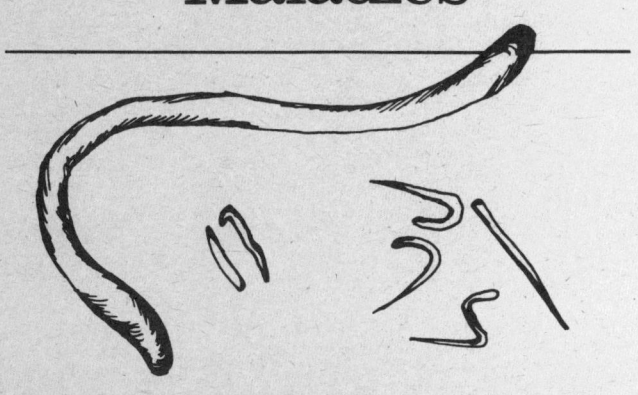

This artist illustration shows three types of worms: roundworm (left), large strongyles (center) and itchy pinworms (right). Keep after them!

Internal

LARGE STRONGYLES

As outlined in the chapter dealing with colic, strongyles are perhaps the most serious of all internal parasites — they can cause death of the host. Often called bloodworms or redworms, there are three major groupings of strongyles: *Strongylus vulgaris, Strongylus edentatus* and *Strongylus equinus. S. vulgaris* is the most troublesome.

To recap the history of this parasite which grows from one-half to two inches long at maturity, a host defecates manure containing eggs in a pasture. Under favorable conditions, the eggs hatch some seven days later and the worms feed on the manure. If the surrounding grass is wet, the worms slither up blades of grass and gain entry to the horse's digestive system as the horse grazes on the contaminated pasture.

Inside, the immature worms migrate extensively throughout the horse's system, to the lungs, heart, liver and pancreas, among others, causing severe damage by burrowing into the wall of the small arteries, or disrupting the flow of blood through large arteries to the intestines. When nearing maturity the worms migrate back to the large intestine, cecum or colon, where the female lays thousands of eggs. These are passed with the feces and the life cycle begins anew.

It's safe to suspect large strongyle infestation if a horse is anemic, performs poorly, is weak or emaciated and has diarrhea. Strongyle infestation can set up a horse for colic, due to impaired blood flow to the intestinal area. If sufficient blockage of arterial blood flow to the intestines or other organs is attained, a horse can die quickly from shock. Heavy infestation in a young horse can lead to stunted growth. Lameness has been encountered through interference of the circulatory system.

SMALL STRONGYLES

Small strongyles, of which there are many types, don't provoke the problems of their larger relative, apparently because they don't migrate but collect in the colon and cecum after maturing in the intestine. They don't suck blood, but one species, *Triodontophorus tenuicollis*, can produce severe ulcers in the colon wall.

PINWORMS

Oxyuris equi causes severe discomfort, more than serious damage. These are small, whitish-colored worms that concentrate in the colon, cecum and rectum of a horse. The females lay eggs that are passed with the feces, but sometimes crawl out of the anus and deposit their eggs near the rectum. The latter causes intense itching, which a horse tries to relieve by rubbing on fence posts or the like. The eggs fall to the ground whereupon they again are ingested

As noted in the text, the various types of botflies have specific areas they favor for egg-laying, circled at left.

by the horse before they hatch and the cycle starts over again.

Pinworms often can be seen in the droppings of a horse heavily infested, but more often the signs are constant rubbing of the buttocks on stationary objects. This leads to poor hair growth or, if rubbing is frequent, secondary infection may develop. There are medications which can control pinworms which will be discussed later.

ASCARIDS

Parascaris equorum has a gruesome-sounding life cycle, affecting young horses from foal age to nearly 4 or 5 years of age. A young horse ingests the roundworm eggs, which can survive for several months on contaminated soil, whereupon the eggs hatch in the small intestine. Roundworms, which measure up to fifteen inches at maturity, nearly half an inch thick, then penetrate the intestinal wall and migrate to the liver, heart, then the lungs.

They remain at this location for a week or so, whereupon they migrate in the bloodstream to the windpipe. They either crawl or are coughed up the esophagus to the pharnyx, then are reswallowed. They develop to maturity in the small intestine, where the female lays eggs that are passed with feces, completing the cycle and starting it again.

Migration of these large worms can cause damage to the liver, heart and lungs, even impairing circulation or causing impaction of a foal's small intestine. They can be suspected in young horses showing respiratory difficulty, lack of energy, digestive disturbance or unthriftiness.

BOTS

Bots are not worms, but are the larvae of the botfly. There are three types of bots to which the horse is susceptible: *Gasterophilus intestinalis,* the common bot; *Gasterophilus nasalis,* the throat bot; and *Gasterophilus haemorrhoidalis,* the nose or lip bot.

Rotational pasture system is beneficial in reducing quantity of parasites in a horse's system. This kills eggs, larvae.

The botfly much resembles a bee (above) and is most persistent in laying eggs. Since they don't feed, usage of poison baits or repellents generally is ineffective.

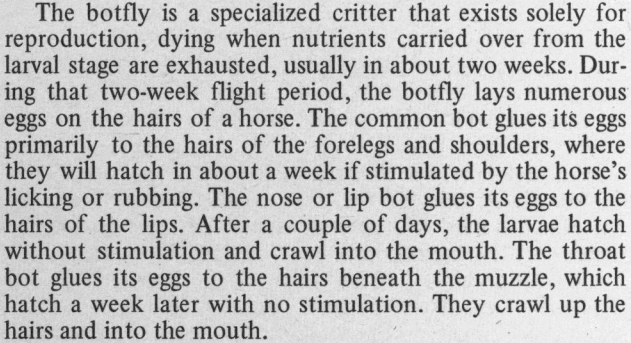

After the eggs hatch and make way into horse's mouth, the bot larvae remain until passing to the stomach and attaching to intestinal wall (above). Pits lead to infection.

The botfly is a specialized critter that exists solely for reproduction, dying when nutrients carried over from the larval stage are exhausted, usually in about two weeks. During that two-week flight period, the botfly lays numerous eggs on the hairs of a horse. The common bot glues its eggs primarily to the hairs of the forelegs and shoulders, where they will hatch in about a week if stimulated by the horse's licking or rubbing. The nose or lip bot glues its eggs to the hairs of the lips. After a couple of days, the larvae hatch without stimulation and crawl into the mouth. The throat bot glues its eggs to the hairs beneath the muzzle, which hatch a week later with no stimulation. They crawl up the hairs and into the mouth.

Once the larvae enter the mouth, they attach to the mucous membranes or around the molars and remain for about a month. They then are swallowed and attach to the stomach lining where they remain for eight to ten months before passing out in the feces. They pupate in the soil for approximately a month and emerge as the botfly to start the whole procedure again.

Botflies are most prevalent during late Summer or early Fall in most areas of the country before the first frost kills the flies. In some arid regions, botfly activity subsides during hot summer months, appearing in early Spring and again in the Fall.

While the botfly doesn't sting a horse when laying eggs, the perennial buzzing has been known to cause horses to run blindly in an effort to escape the pests. Internally, bots create digestive disturbance, robbing a horse of nutritional value and scar or pit the lining of the stomach. This pitting can lead to bacterial invasion, creating other problems.

LARGE STOMACH WORMS

This *Habronema* family of worms can cause both internal and external damage. The three main types which infect a horse internally are *Habronema muscae, Habronema microstoma* and *Draschia megastoma,* the latter causing the most severe problems, including swelling of the stomach wall and colic.

Eggs are passed in the manure of an infected horse, which then are ingested by stable or houseflies feeding on the feces. The eggs then are passed to horses when the flies feed on the horse's lips, or from ingestion of an unwary fly by the horse. They then hatch and attack the mucous membranes of the intestines or, as noted, the stomach wall. Reaching maturity, females lay eggs which are passed in the feces and here we go again!

When the worms have hatched, their affection for mucosal linings leads to inflammation which causes digestive upset and even colic. The *Draschia megastoma* worm infects the stomach wall and tumor-like enlargements, filled with worms and dead tissue, result. This naturally leads to digestive upset.

The *D. megastoma* culprit also is guilty of causing external trouble, often called summer sores. A horse has some type of skin abrasion or cut. Stable or houseflies which have ingested large stomach worm eggs while feeding on contaminated manure feed at the wound site, in the process re-depositing the worm eggs. When the eggs hatch, the larvae burrow into the open sore, irritating the wound and protracting healing. Small, round granules appear in the

One species of large stomach worm infests open sores and causes condition known as summer sores. This can lead to more servere problems so cover all open sores.

A foal wormer such as this offering from Top Form can be effective in controlling ascarids and other parasites. Use only as directed, or the poison could kill the foal.

wound, which resemble scar tissue. Treatment to date has not been too effective; granulations usually require cauterization following surgery for removal.

SMALL STOMACH WORMS

Not much study has yet been devoted to this *Trichostrongylus axei* worm, or to the damage it does. However, enough is known to recommend that horses don't get them!

The small stomach worm causes a chronic inflammation of the intestinal mucous membranes which leads to digestive upset, pain and lack of condition. It can cause congestion of the stomach, as the afflicted mucous membranes exude a variable amount of mucus.

TAPEWORM

Scientists know that three different types of tapeworms affect horses, but little else about them. The guilty species are *Anoplocephala magna, Anoplocephala perfoliata* and *Paranoplocephala mamillana. A. perfoliata* usually is found in the cecum and only occasionally in the small intestine, home of the other two parasites.

If infestation with tapeworms is light, the horseowner may not even suspect anything is out of whack. But if the horse is heavily infested, there can be digestive disturbance, anemia and even emaciation as the worms rob the horse of needed nutrients.

This is about the extent of knowledge of tapeworms in horses, but research is continuing. Hopefully, treatment methods will be isolated that prove totally effective in dealing with this parasite.

TREATMENT

Since man has so long equated solutions to problems in terms of what it will cost in dollars and cents, it's a wonder there still are internal parasites to hinder horses. Destroying worms through the methods to be outlined here, everywhere in the world, at first glance seems monetarily and logistically impossible. However, when the cost of this global effort is measured against what the average horseowner spends for veterinary treatment, dollar loss through waste of food, purchase of worming compounds, dollar loss through worm-caused equine fatalities, and cost of compounds for post-worming treatment, it would be cheaper in the long run. A world-wide effort of this nature shouldn't meet opposition from pharmaceutical houses. While their long-range business would be gone, they would make enough money during the course of the program to make even the Arabian oil sheiks look like paupers!

However, a program of this nature never will be contemplated, let alone initiated, so it will remain the horseman's chore to control his horses' individual worm problems. Toward that end, researchers have developed compounds

Wormers designed for addition to horse's feed must be tasty or the animal won't eat it. Apple-flavored wormer has had good equine results.

which kill internal parasites and these are called anthelmintics. The better-known compounds are piperazine, dichlorvos, trichlorfon, phenothiazine, thiabendazole, carbon disulfide, pyrantel tartrate and combinations of these.

The term, "broad spectrum," often is associated with various brands of horse wormers, which means the ingredients are active against more than one species of parasite. This saves time and money for the horseman, not having to purchase several wormers to administer at different times.

There are several ways of administering anthelmintics and it is imperative the horseowner follow manufacturer's directions explicitly. One of the most effective ways of worming a horse is through use of a stomach tube, a long, rubber, hose-like implement that is inserted into the throat through the nasal cavity, where the solution is deposited. This ensures all of the medicine reaching the stomach at one time, which leads to improved efficacy.

Another popular administration method is a dose syringe, which usually is filled with the proper amount of worming compound to doctor a horse needing attention. This is placed in the corner of the horse's mouth and the contents are discharged on the animals' tongue, which he swallows (hopefully!). This method demands that the compound be palatable to horses, usually through some type of molasses-flavored base. It's safe and effective, providing the proper amount is administered.

Sometimes capsules, called tabs or boluses, are used for worming. These resemble large pills which are inserted into the horse's mouth and passed to the stomach by swallowing. The bolus has a pre-measured dose of anthelmintic which gets right down to work.

The final worming method is perhaps the easiest, but also requires a great deal of care. This entails sprinkling the worming compound on the feed, which the horse ingests when eating. Using packaged wormers of this type is by far the easiest and cleanest method of administration, but a wormer of this type has possible flaws: It must taste good or the horse isn't going to eat it. Too, it must have a wide safety margin in the event a horse takes in too much of the compound.

Which brings us back to label directions: Worming compounds contain some type of poison which, if taken in great quantities, can kill the horse along with the worms! Most are administered according to body weight; the heavier a horse, the more wormer he's given.

In addition to describing how much of the compound to use, package instructions will also inform the horseowner under what conditions he should not use that product. For example, many anthelmintic manufacturers flatly state a wormer shouldn't be administered if a horse is suffering from diarrhea, severe constipation, shows symptoms of colic, shows symptoms of heaves or other respiratory ailments, has blood poisoning, has an infectious disease of some type, is severely debilitated or under veterinary treatment with tranquilizers, muscle relaxants, medications for the central nervous system or insecticides. Take time to thoroughly read and understand all label directions, then follow them!

Looking at the parasites involved, we will list the individual compounds which have proven effective in killing them. Therefore, when a horseman has determined the types of parasites infecting his horse, he should check for the appropriate compounds within the wormers on a dealer's shelf.

Large and small strongyles are knocked by thiabendazole, pyrantel tartrate, dichlorvos, phenothiazine (when combined with other drugs), dyrex, neguvon, dizan and parvex plus. Because of the migrating habit of strongyles, the horse should be wormed every two months.

Pinworms, the itch in the rear, meet their demise through use of dyrex, pyrantel tartrate, trichlorfon, dichlorvos, thiabendazole, dizan and piperazine/phenothiazine combinations. As horses can be reinfected with pinworms at any time, constant vigilance, accompanied by further anthelmintic administration, may be required to keep the parasite in check.

Ascarids, better known as roundworms, usually are found only in immature horses. Once a horse hits 4 or 5 years of age, he develops some type of immunity to the damaging parasite and rarely requires treatment.

Young horses which contract ascarids are treated with trichlorfon, dichlorvos, dyrex, dizan, parvex, piperazine/phenothiazine combinations, piperazine and pyrantel tartrate. Interestingly, thiabendazole therapy nets poor results against roundworms. Because of the migrating nature of ascarids, it is necessary to worm infected horses regularly, starting at two and one-half to three months of age.

Bots, the larvae of the botfly, aren't wiped out by the majority of anthelmintics heretofore mentioned. A combination of carbon disulfide and piperazine is effective, as is trichlorfon, dyrex and dichlorvos.

As noted in the treatment section on these and following pages, trichlorfon is effective in controlling pesky bots. Since no horse is ever free of worms, repeat as needed.

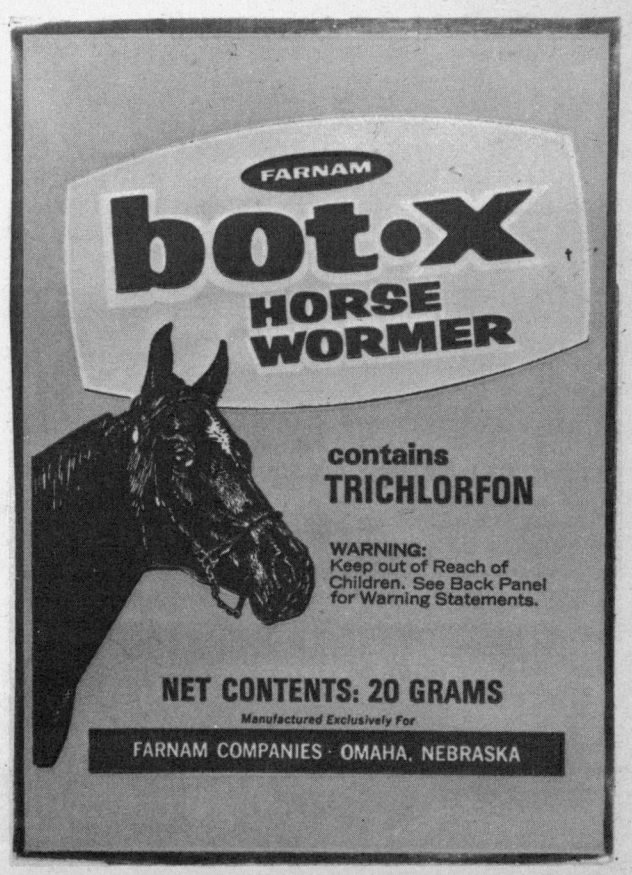

Most veterinarians feel young horses should be wormed at least quarterly for bots and older horses a minimum of twice per year. Because cold weather kills botflies, the horses should be wormed after the first killing frost. Larvae passed in the feces won't pupate and the anthelmintic gets most of the remaining number in the stomach. The worming routine should be repeated at least two months following the fall worming, which will kill the bots migrating from mouth to intestines. The horse then is virtually bot-free during Winter.

An additional word about bots: During peak botfly activity, a horseman should pay particular attention to grooming. Frequent and thorough grooming will remove many of the yellowish-colored eggs which are glued to body hairs. Bots can be artificially hatched by rubbing warm soap suds or warm mineral oil and water (over 105 degrees Fahrenheit) on the affected areas. Thus exposed to the environment, they die before reaching the horse's mouth and sanctuary.

And it's virtually impossible to prevent botflies from attacking horses, if botfly activity is present. Since botflies don't eat, they can't be attracted to poison baits. Insecticide works poorly at repelling the stubborn, bee-like insects.

As stated earlier, no reliable treatment has been found for either large or small stomach worms. Anthelmintics have virtually no effect, perhaps caused by the protection afforded through mucosal secretions. Hopefully, research being conducted into the behavioral patterns of these parasites will result in a therapy scheme.

While little is known about the tapeworm in horses, science has developed a compound that apparently kills it. The name is teinatol and this may have to be administered separately from commercial worming compounds since it may not be found in many.

Administration of anthelmintics is sound animal management for a horse infected with internal parasites, as nearly all are. But this is only one part of a parasite control program.

Horsemen should utilize a pasture rotation system, which entails moving horses from one pasture to another at regular intervals and running other species of livestock, primarily cattle or sheep, on the pasture formerly grazed by horses. Most equine parasites can't survive inside the body of another host species.

If it is impossible to graze another type of livestock on the pasture, that section should be clipped. This action not only promotes grass growth, but also exposes eggs and larvae to environmental conditions which kill them. If the pasture is severely contaminated, horses shouldn't be grazed on it for several months.

Many horsemen favor usage of temporary seeded pasture. Every three to five years this pasture is plowed and reseeded, which keeps concentrations of parasites from building to high levels. Before turning horses out on such a pasture, ensure they've been adequately wormed.

Since foals are born virtually parasite-free, every effort should be made to run them on uncontaminated pastures. Move them to other clean pastures at regular intervals, which will keep the parasite load at a low level.

If horses are kept in stalls or small paddocks, more work is required of the horseman. Manure should be removed daily and stored in an insulated pit for at least two weeks. Manure so stored generates heat which kills eggs and larvae. Even after a safe storage period, it is not recommended that the manure be spread on pastures; contact local residents who desire free fertilizer, or have it hauled away.

When feeding horses, never throw rations on the ground — they may become contaminated through contact with eggs or larvae in the feces. Use a manger or feedbox of some type.

Use care in the selection of bedding material. Don't use hay for bedding, since horses may eat it, including any eggs or worm larvae present. Always take a stall down completely once per week, replacing all bedding. If the stall floor is of clay or regular dirt, it should be dug up annually to a depth of six inches or so, then new flooring material deposited. This will remove all eggs or parasitic larvae existing in the soil.

Parasite eggs have the nasty habit of surviving in water. Therefore, if near a pond into which pasture drainage is possible, restrain a horse from drinking. He may imbibe parasite eggs which will hatch in his stomach.

Parasitism is a dirty subject, but one that too often is ignored. This lack of attention will manifest itself in dull-looking and performing horses. Worm him as needed.

Some wormers, like Equigel in paste form, are dispensed via a syringe-like arrangement. The paste is squirted on the horse's tongue and swallowed. Dichlorvos works well.

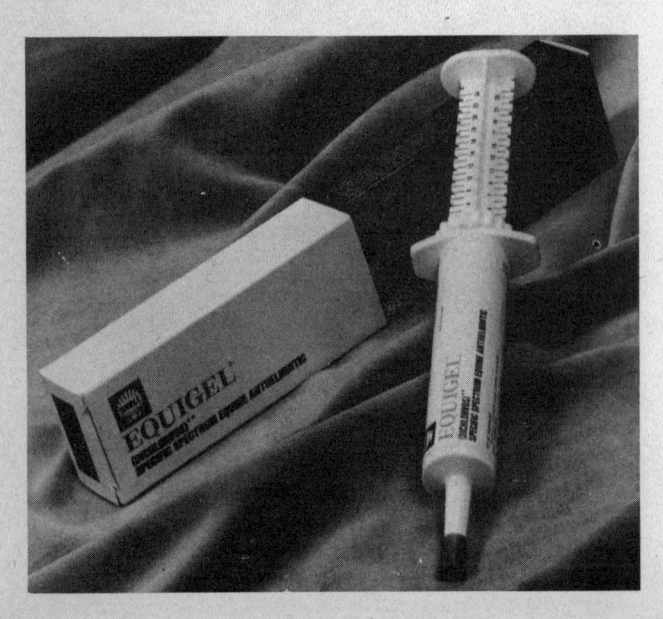

External

Just as man is bedeviled by external parasites, so is the horse. While man has at his disposal many chemicals and equipments to aid in his fight against "bugs," the horse only is equipped with an equine version of the flyswatter: his tail. He also has control of muscles underlying the skin which he will use in an effort to shake insects or parasites from the hide. Even so, he isn't a match for the pests attacking him externally.

The types of external parasites which will be discussed here are: mites, fleas, mosquitos, lice, gnats, ticks, ringworm, houseflies, stable flies, horseflies and blowflies. As with the section on internal parasites, treatment programs will be presented at the end of this classification.

MITES

So tiny they are invisible to the naked eye, results of mite infestation fall into four categories of contagious skin diseases: Sarcoptic mange, Chorioptic mange, Psoroptic mange and Demodectic mange.

Sarcoptic mange is perhaps the worst of the lot, usually chronic in nature once contracted. All four produce similar skin disorders, distinguished mainly by locations they prefer. After burrowing into the skin, the small mites produce lesions which exude a watery fluid that dries, forming scaly crusts. The hair falls out and the skin thickens. This process causes extreme itching and, in an effort to relieve it, a horse literally will rub the skin raw at infected locations.

Psoroptic mange usually affects areas protected by long hair — forelock, root of the tail and the mane — but spreads rapidly over the body. Sarcoptic mange doesn't favor areas covered with long hair, first becoming visible on the head, neck and shoulder regions. Chorioptic mange oftentimes is called leg mange, since the mites prefer the lower parts of the hind legs. In severe cases of involvement, the disorder spreads rapidly to the flanks, shoulders and neck. Demodectic mange, seldom seen in horses, generally confines its involvement to hair follicles and the sebaceous glands, particularly around the eyes and on the forehead. If unchecked, the entire body may become involved.

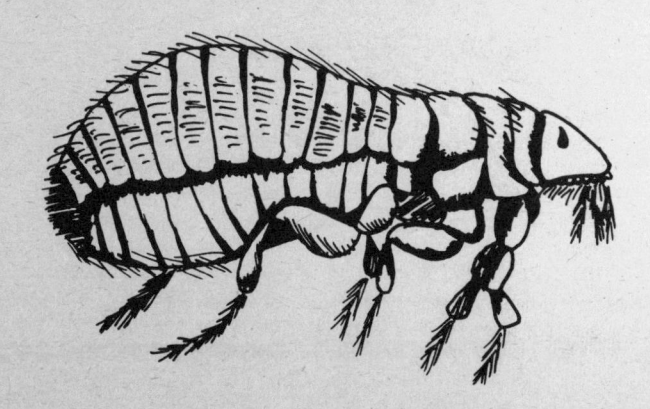

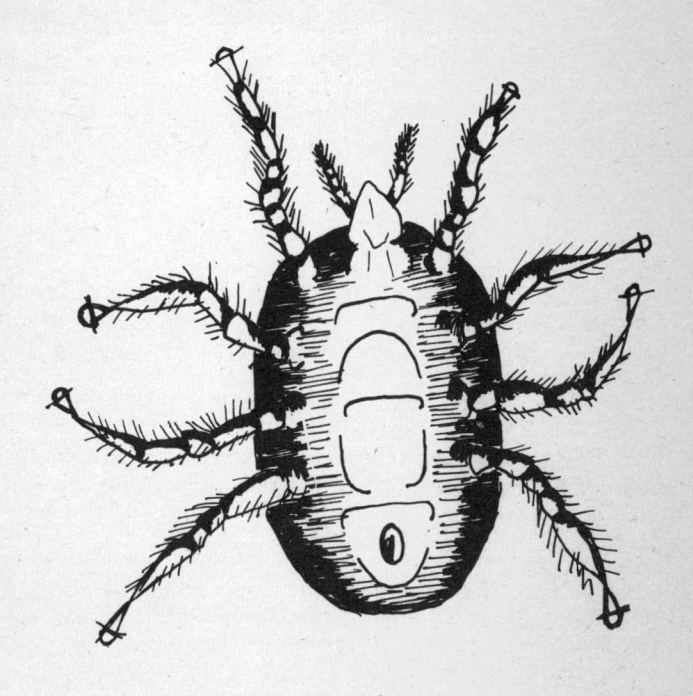

Mites are the cause of mange in horses and can be stubborn to treat. The itching they cause can lead to lost hair coat or such rubbing the skin is broken, leading to infection.

FLEAS

Tiny, dark brown or black critters, fleas bother dogs and cats more than horses. But a great many horsemen keep dogs or felines around their stables, so transferral of fleas from canine to equine occasionally occurs.

Fleas are bloodsuckers that cause intense itching and irritation for a horse. In his efforts to quell this itch, a horse will bite or rub the location of the flea activity, often to the point the spot becomes raw or sore. This behavior gives the horseowner indication of flea infestation.

The adult flea spends nearly its entire life on a horse, often laying its eggs on the coat. More frequently, however, the flea will disembark at egg-laying time and deposit eggs in a horse's bedding. After about five days of incubation, the young fleas emerge from the larval stage and jump onto the waiting host; thus, the life cycle begins anew.

Specific treatment, which will be given at the end of this section, can control fleas.

While fleas bother dogs and cats more than horses, occasionally the latter contract them. Like mites, fleas cause intense itching and can lead to problems.

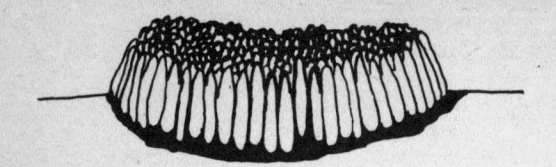

The life cycle of the mosquito is shown on this page, beginning with a raft of eggs laid on the surface of a quiet water source. Up to 400 eggs are laid at once.

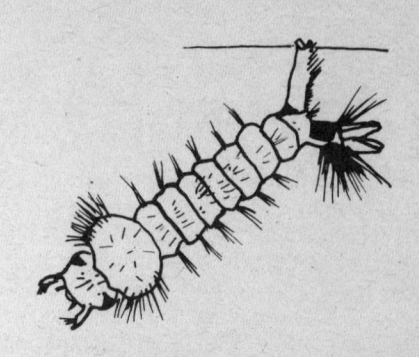

In the first of its larval stages, the mosquito breathes through a tube at the rear of the body. After moulting four times, the adult begins to take shape, seen below.

MOSQUITOS

Mosquitos are not only irritating, they are potentially dangerous to the health of a horse. Of the more than 140 species found in the United States, several are capable of transmitting debilitating or deadly diseases.

The life cycle of the mosquito begins when a female lays from one to four hundred eggs atop or near a water source. Common mosquitos lay their eggs directly on the water surface in a mass called a raft and the eggs hatch in a day or two.

In the larval stage, the mosquito comes to the surface and breathes through a tube called a siphon on the rear of its body. It moults or sheds its skin four times during rapid development to the pupal stage.

As a pupating mosquito, the insects cannot eat and only breathe through tubes on their backs. After about two days of development, the pupae breaks through its protective skin as a full-grown insect. It rests on the water surface until strong enough to fly away in search of a meal. The entire process can be accomplished in as little as seven days during warm weather.

Interestingly, only the female mosquito uses her proboscis for sucking blood from birds or mammals; the male exists solely on plant juices. Females can live up to three weeks during the Summer, laying rafts of eggs every second day of her adult life. She also survives quite well during Winter, laying her eggs again after the spring thaw.

Diseases are transmitted when the one of several species of mosquito bites an infected animal or human, itself becoming infected in the process. When it bites other mammals or birds, it then spreads the infective bacteria to the new animal, and so on. It therefore is possible to have quick and widespread outbreaks of diseases over entire states or countries, like the Venezuelan equine encephalomyelitis epizootic of late 1971. The outbreak began in Central America and was carried via the mosquito through Mexico and into the Southwest.

It takes lots of work to protect against this flying trash-can, which will be outlined later.

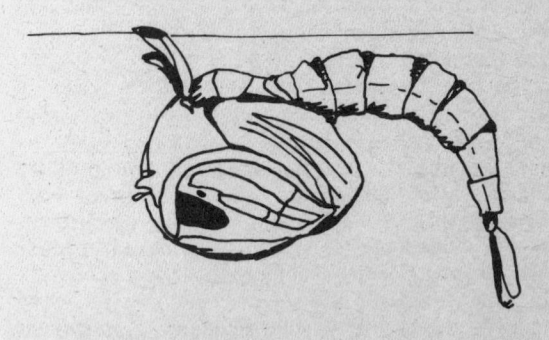

About two days after hatching, the mosquito pupates, breaking through its larval skin. It does not eat during pupation and breathes through tubes connected to back.

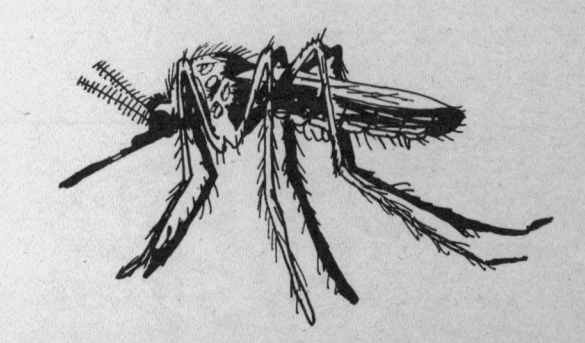

LICE

There are two types of lice which affect horses, usually during winter months. These are the common biting louse and the sucking louse. The former causes great itching as it bites the horse, as does the second when sucking. Both types seem to constantly be scurrying around and, if severe-

After shedding larval skin, the full-grown mosquito emerges and sits atop the water resting, until strong enough to fly off. Only female mosquitos suck blood.

Lice, active during the cooler months of the year, can drive a horse to distraction. The constant itching leads to rubbing against stationary objects with hair loss.

ly infested, a horse literally will be at wit's end, not knowing which spot to bite or rub next. He will appear restless and anxious, as would his owner if likewise infested.

As stated earlier, lice activity usually is present only through the winter months, subsiding with the arrival of Spring. Probably this is because more thorough grooming is possible during the warmer seasons.

It is possible to detect lice by separating the hairs and examining the skin at the roots under strong light. Sometimes lice will be found sucking or attached to the hair at the skin juncture. Lice can spread through a whole herd of horses in short order, passed from one to another. It is possible for eggs and larvae which have dropped to the ground to survive for up to three weeks in warm weather, simply waiting for a horse to amble by.

GNATS

Small in size but large in numbers and appetite for blood, gnats have been responsible for the death of vast herds of horses and cattle each year, primarily in the South and Midwest sections of the country. After spending the larval portions of their lives in swift-running streams or irrigation canals, innumerable numbers become airborne at once and resemble black clouds buzzing around livestock.

They exist by sucking blood from livestock, at the same time injecting a toxic material into the skin. In severe cases, this toxic substance builds to a level that causes death through hemorrhage. In cases of mild attack, horses usually will be restless, have poor coat condition, may be anemic, lose weight and go off their feed.

Preventing gnats is a costly, time-consuming and potentially dangerous chore. It behooves horsemen in areas of the country sustaining periodic attacks by gnats to review the treatment section following listing of parasites.

TICKS

A great deal is known about ticks and the damage they can do to livestock and man. There are two families of ticks in the United States, both of which act as disease carriers or can lead to secondary infection as the horse attempts to rid himself of the parasites: *Ixodidae,* or "hard" ticks, and *Argasidae,* or "soft" ticks.

Ticks have an interesting life cycle, either dependent upon a single host throughout its lifetime or three separate hosts, and all are bloodsuckers. Most "hard," three-host ticks mate on one host, which stimulates the female to faster feeding. About a week after mating, when her abdomen is engorged with blood, she drops from the host and spends another week feasting on the blood she has stored. Eggs then are laid under surface debris or in the soil.

If the weather is warm, eggs hatch in approximately two weeks and six-legged ticks emerge. These babies crawl up foliage and wait for passing horses for as long as eight months if conditions are suitable. When a to-be host contacts the tick-infested plant, the six-legged parasite transfers and crawls to a suitable spot, then begins to feed. It usually takes several days to become engorged with blood, whereupon the tick drops to the ground and moults, becoming a four-legged nymph. The new nymph crawls on vegetation and repeats the process of waiting for a host to pass by.

The successful nymphs that find hosts then spend a week or so filling up their self-contained tanks, then drop to the ground. After moulting for the last time, the nymphs emerge as adults and repeat the crawling-up/lying-in-wait procedure a last time.

The difference between three and one-host ticks naturally lies in the number of times a tick leaves the host. A one-host tick doesn't drop to the ground and go through the moulting stages; it's entire life is spent attached to one host.

Ticks have an interesting life cycle and many types can hurt horses. Besides sucking blood, the ticks pass all manner of diseases to horses, some resulting in death.

Should a horse's ear hair be clipped, some type of insect repellent should be used to protect the ear canal (left).

The "hard" ticks of importance, which will be discussed here, are the Lone Star tick, Gulf Coast tick, Rocky Mountain wood tick, American dog tick, Brown dog tick and the Winter tick. Some aren't often found on equines, thankfully.

The Lone Star tick is not named after the fair state of Texas, but derives it's name from a silvery-white spot resembling a star on the female's body. It is found mostly on a line from Oklahoma to Virginia and all states to the south, most active during early Spring, Summer and late Fall. A three-host tick, it is capable of transmitting Rocky Mountain spotted fever.

The Gulf Coast tick extends inward from the Mexican border in Texas some two hundred miles, then east to the Atlantic Ocean. A three-host tick, it affects cattle more than horses, primarily during late Summer or early Fall.

The Rocky Mountain wood tick, understandably, is found primarily in the Northwestern regions of the country. A three-host tick, it has a life cycle lasting as long as two years from egg to adult stages. Adult Rocky Mountain wood ticks are seen mostly during Spring and early Summer, attaching usually around the head and ears of a horse.

The American dog tick, also three-host in cycle, is almost totally confined to the Central and Eastern sections of the country and doesn't affect only dogs. Rather, it is the vector (scientific term for disease carrier that infects others) for most outbreaks of Rocky Mountain spotted fever in the East.

The Brown dog tick much favors a host of the canine species, only rarely attaching to livestock. With dogs around horses, transfer from canine to equine is a possibility and bears watching.

The Winter tick is a serious parasite of horses in open ranges from the Gulf Coast states to Canada. A one-host tick, it usually attacks horses during winter months or in the early Spring, making it unique from other tick species which winter on the ground.

On a host, ticks mate and the female spends the next several days gorging on blood. When to the bursting point, she drops from her host and spends the Winter on the ground. Eggs are laid in the Spring and young ticks emerge in three to six weeks. They remain clustered together throughout the Summer, becoming active in Fall's cool temperatures. They then attach to horses and, after about a month on the host, are adults. They then mate and the cycle continues.

The only "soft" tick of any importance to horsemen is the spinose ear tick, a member of *Argasidae* band. When larvae hatch from eggs deposited on the ground, they crawl

Mosquito-transmitted Venezuelan equine encephalomyelitis struck down this new foal. Erradicate mosquitos!

onto vegetation and await the close passing of a horse or other livestock, then attach to the host and make their way to the ears, crawling deeply inside and remaining there for one to seven months. After developing through the nymphal stages, the ticks drop out and, after finding a spot with some type of shelter, moult to adults. They then mate and the female deposits her eggs to start the cycle again.

Horses infested with spinose ear ticks show marked pain through anxious expression and restlessness. He may cock his head to the side and, if infestation is severe, may be slightly deaf in that ear. He usually will be hard to bridle and will rub his ear, trying to dislodge the parasites. Permanent hearing loss can result if treatment isn't effected soon.

RINGWORM

Ringworm is a disorder caused by a fungus rather than specific parasite, but is logically included in this classification. Extremely contagious, the fungus lives in damp, warm soil and usually appears as a circular lesion with scaly exterior. Little hair grows at the site and it usually appears on the head, neck, croup, base of the tail, shoulders or breast, but can strike anywhere. It spreads rapidly from small, half-dollar-sized rings to huge lesions, or many small rings that are yellow or gray in color. They may itch and a horse will rub the spot to relieve irritation, often spreading the fungi spores to other parts of the body.

HOUSEFLIES

There are many types of *Musca domestica*, the common housefly, which irritate horses and can lead to serious problems. The housefly loves nothing better than manure, on which it feeds and breeds. In the act of feeding, it can ingest the microscopic eggs of the roundworm or large stomach worm. When it then feeds on the body secretions of a horse, particularly around the eyes or at the muzzle, it re-deposits these roundworm eggs in its feces and the horse gets ascarid infestation. When feeding on blood from bites by stable flies, it deposits large stomach worm eggs which can lead to summer sores, noted earlier in this section. They also are suspected of transmitting various eye diseases, which makes their control of importance to the horseman.

STABLE FLIES

These insects seem to favor the legs of horses and their bites are the most painful of all biting flies. Eggs are laid in damp or fermenting vegetation, not necessarily manure, and timespan from egg to adult is as short as three weeks.

When they appear in large concentrations, they can seriously affect the overall health of a horse or other livestock. He is naturally restless and anxious, continually flicking or biting at the insects as they land on him. He may go off his feed, losing as much as ten to fifteen percent body weight. Severe attack can lead to an anemic condition through blood loss. As noted in the section on houseflies, blood left from the stable fly's bite is attractive to the former, which can lead to introduction of large stomach worm eggs or secondary infection.

While caused by a fungus, not an external parasite proper, ringworm is itchy and leads to hair loss, specifically around the eyes. The disorder can be treated effectively.

The housefly is a dwarf compared to the insidious stable fly (left). Houseflies can transmit parasitic eggs, while stable flies can cause anemia along with severe anxiety.

HORSEFLIES

These pests can literally drive a horse berserk. When present in fairly large numbers, they stimulate activity on the horse's part in his effort to escape from the buzzing clouds. By so doing, he spends less time feeding and consequently loses weight which, if coupled with numerous bites over a short period, can lead to anemia or death through blood loss, though death is rare.

More often, death comes through diseases the horsefly introduces. The most prevalent are equine infectious anemia or equine encephalomyelitis, which the horsefly passes through his biting behavior. It's possible for a whole herd to be infected with either of these diseases in a short period of heavy fly attack.

Like the stable fly, horseflies aren't overly fond of manure as an egg-laying spot. Rather, most horseflies lay their eggs in clusters near or projecting above a water source, which hatch in five to ten days. The larvae fall into the water and crawl ashore on a muddy bank where they feed on minute organisms. When ready to pupate, the larvae crawl to higher ground where they won't be submerged for extended periods, then emerge as winged insects after a short period. They then mate, the female lays her eggs and the cycle begins again.

Because of scattered egg-laying sites, it's difficult to control this insect. More will be said on this under the treatment segment.

BLOWFLIES

These insects have a fondness for laying eggs in carrion, manure and open wounds of horses. When the larvae deposited on a wound, called screwworms, hatch, they burrow into the wound and exist on the juices collecting at the site. The distinguishing difference between the screwworm fly and blowfly is that the former lays its eggs only in the wound of a living, warm-blooded host, while the blowfly will lay its eggs on a dead animal or in manure, etc.

In severe infestations, animal death has been reported. The blowfly larvae cause irritation. Blowflies bother horses when feeding on their blood and a good insect control program is necessary to control them.

TREATMENT

A mange condition in horses, and treatment of same, is dependent to a large degree on the time of year and environmental conditions present. Therapy calls for a warm, lime-sulfur "dip" — liberally applying a solution to the hair coat some four to six times at ten to twelve-day intervals. In cold parts of the country, care should be taken to assure the horse doesn't chill, which could lead to respiratory ailments.

Another solution which has proved effective in killing the parasites is a nicotine sulfate dip, used only once. But it sometimes is difficult to eradicate both Sarcoptic and Demodectic mange with killing agents, resulting in a chronic infestation. A veterinarian will prescribe the solution to use and rely on his judgment. At the same time, he will prescribe treatment for any sore spots caused by the horse's rubbing in attempt to rid himself of the itchy bugs; usually an antiseptic ointment application following thorough cleaning and disinfecting.

Treating fleas requires attention not only to the horse, but also his bedding. As noted in the segment dealing with fleas, adults lay their eggs on bits of debris in the stall, so treatment of the horse alone won't solve the problem; it's just a matter of time until the young reinfest the animal.

Commercially available powders and sprays containing

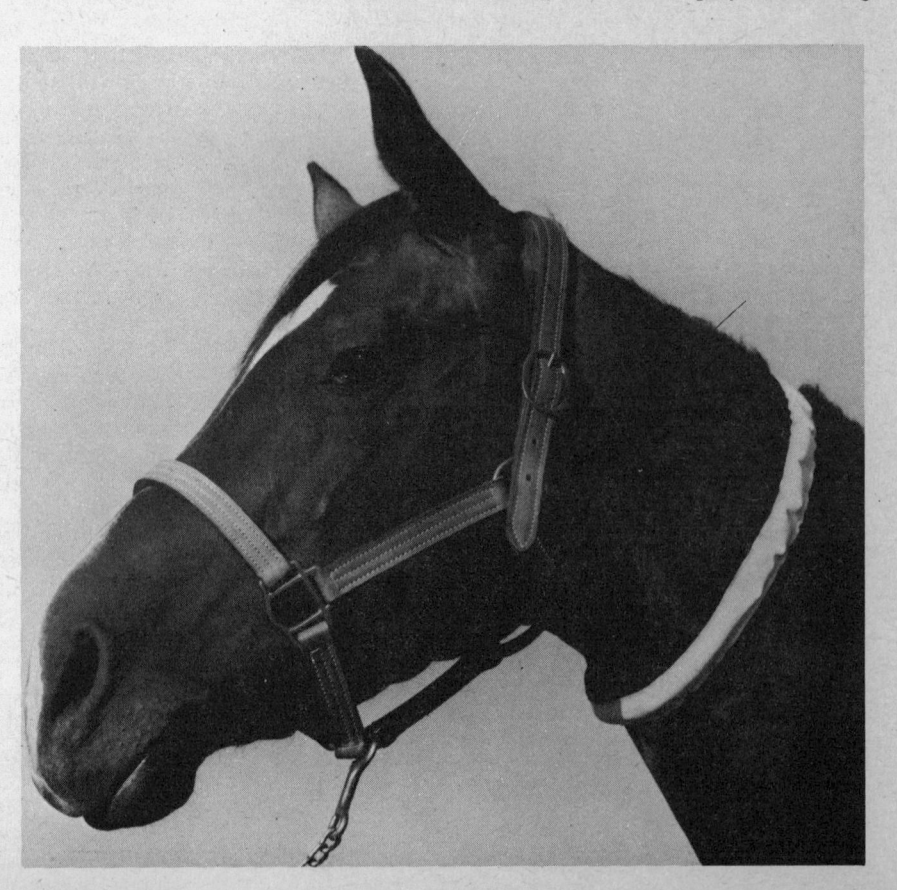

Some folks have been experimenting with the possibility of using fly collar for horses, similar to dog's flea collar.

During winter months, when lice become most active, it's usually impossible to shampoo a horse. This dry Top Form shampoo has helped in such circumstances.

pyrethrum, rotenone, lindane or malathion — used according to the manufacturer's recommendations — are effective in killing fleas on the horse. His bedding should be removed and burned, and before putting new bedding in a stall, the area should be dusted or sprayed with the compounds listed. DDT also is effective in killing larvae and adults, but many horseowners shy away from it...it also can kill horses!

When fleas have been removed, attention should be paid to any sores the horse might have acquired while trying to rid himself of the fleas. Disinfect the area and apply an antiseptic ointment. This will keep flies from the sore and lessen the chance of secondary infection — which could prove fatal.

Treatment of mites and fleas is within the grasp of the horseman, but most aren't equipped to do battle on a large scale against the mosquito. Each horseman can greatly reduce the mosquito population on his property through simple procedures, though.

Since relatively little water is needed for egg-laying, females often deposit rafts in water troughs, ornamental ponds, plastic wading pools, stock tanks, in scattered junk like tin cans, jars, bottles, tubs, barrels and old tires which have collected rainwater, and even under homes with leaky plumbing.

Because of this, horseowner should remove the trash on his property and store all buckets or barrels upside-down when not in use. Water troughs and wading pools should be cleaned at least weekly and faulty plumbing repaired.

Larger bodies of water or ornamental ponds call for the introduction of *Gambusia affinis,* better-known as the mosquito fish. This species has a positively voracious appetite for mosquito larvae, snapping them up as fast as they hatch. The two-inch fish require no care or supplemental feeding and perhaps can be secured free of charge from the nearest mosquito abatement office.

Draining swamps, spraying with DDT and other insecticides is best left to professionals or government agencies charged with direct responsibility. DDT is pretty tricky and will kill fish in streams or other life forms if not used properly.

Also, the horseowner can install fine-mesh screening on his stalls and barns, which cuts down considerably the number of mosquitos entering. Fogging the area with commercially available preparations will afford some protection, but must be repeated with regularity.

If horses are kept in pastures where screening or fogging is impossible, little can be done to protect a horse from mosquitos. Unfortunately, insect repellents don't afford lasting protection and usually must be reapplied every eight to twelve hours.

Since most lice infestation occurs during the winter months, treatment at those times is restricted usually to dusting with a commercially prepared lice powder containing rotenone, ronnel, Ciodrin, pyrethrins, malathion, lindane or similar compounds. Dipping at cold times could cause respiratory problems.

During the summer months, it's the usual practice to shampoo a horse vigorously, then spray, dip or dust the following day with one of the aforementioned chemicals in a lice powder. Once the horse has been treated, he should be moved to another stall for up to three weeks and his old stall thoroughly disinfected, the bedding burned. This protects against reinfestation, since eggs will hatch two to three weeks after being laid.

Efficient control of gnats, which mass in blood-sucking black hordes, is similar to the mosquito in scope and requirements. Since water again is involved, eradication is best left to authorities with experience in the matter.

The individual horseowner can, however, take certain measures to guard his horses from continual attack. Though temporary, some relief is available through combination of pyrethrum, synergist and repellent sprays. Cattlemen have long used smudge pots during times of heavy invasion and this also can work for the horseman. Cattle soon learned to crowd around the smudge for protection. If using this type

Using foggers like this from London is one of the most effective ways of checking insect numbers when used with regularity around stables during hot times of year.

Diseases like fistula of the withers — which may be caused by a parasite — have been discovered following outbreaks of bovine brucellosis, and vice versa. Therefore, keep close watch on herds of cattle and horses, segregating as necessary.

of arrangement, make sure no open flame is present or horses could be burned.

Careful attention should be given to the hair coat of the horse following attack by gnats. The small punctures are ideal entry spots for bacteria or other germs that could lead to bigger problems. Watch for eggs of the blowflies or screwworm flies, which will be removed with normal grooming that should be carried out daily.

Tick infestation requires attention to both horse and premises. If ticks are few in number, spray with a tick bomb or other tick killer. It is not advisable to pluck ticks from the skin, since often the heads or mouthparts break off and remain embedded, leading to infection or ulceration.

If tick infestation is severe, it is wise to dip the horse in lindane, toxaphene, malathion, ronnel or coumaphos. Dips or squirt-can application of these compounds into the ear is more effective than attempting to pick spinose ear ticks from the cavity. Follow directions listed on the package or can explicitly; these poisons could kill the horse if used in too strong concentrations. If the compounds are not pre-mixed, use a fresh batch with each application to assure efficacy.

Tick eradication in large pastures or open ranges is virtually impossible. Steps can be taken around the barn, however, using sprays or dusts of chlordane, diazinon, dichlorvos, dieldrin, lindane or malathion. These should be used only on limited areas and utensils, feeders, waterers or feed proper should not be treated. The horse should be kept isolated from the site until the chemicals have dried thoroughly. Remember: most of these compounds are poisonous to man, so use them with care at a veterinarian's direction.

Studies have shown that horses deficient in vitamin A tend to be more susceptible to ringworm than others, which means a good, balanced diet is a primary requirement in controlling this fungus disease. Washes and dips will effectively fight the condition, which a veterinarian will prescribe. As contaminated equipment can transfer the disease, disinfect all tack and grooming equipment coming in contact with the horse. His stall also should be cleaned and disinfected. Use rubber gloves when treating ringworm, since many types are contagious to man, also.

Treatment for houseflies rests with good stable management. They feed and breed in manure, so it should be collected daily and stored well away from the barn in a pit. Screened stalls will keep most houseflies out. An open-sided shelter with a roof for shade will allow breeze to enter and this keeps some flies away. Fly repellents also afford some relief but, because the housefly feeds on secretions from the mouth, nose and eyes, care needs to be taken when applying repellent to these areas. Follow label directions.

Stable flies only bother a horse at their dinnertime, which hampers effective treatment. Repellents are of little value in killing more than a few flies. Spraying the exterior of barns does provide some relief, as does fogging with synergized pyrethrum or dichlorvos.

Keeping horses in screened enclosures will give the best protection, turning them out at night when fly activity is at ebb. The horse gets enough exercise from this procedure to make it worth the time and effort on the horseman's part.

Horseflies are one of the most difficult insects to control and nearly any solution isn't fast-acting enough to keep flies from biting. The best results come from heavily wetting a horse's coat with synergized pyrethrins, which last for approximately three days, whereupon the procedure needs to be repeated.

Since water plays an important role in the development of this fly, control can be facilitated by professionals with

Probably the most effective way of keeping insects away from horses is spraying with repellents on the market.

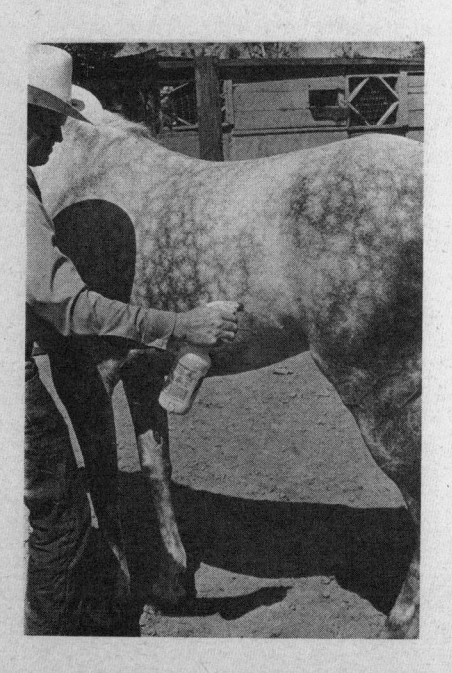

Shell Chemical Company has developed an off-shoot of their No-Pest Strips for home use, the Stable Strip. Charged with Vapona insecticide, it kills the bugs.

spraying equipment. A horseman can examine his irrigation system and, if it can be straightened or the water flow-rate increased, he should take these steps.

During a period of heavy fly activity, the wise horseowner watches his horses closely and grooms them regularly. This will remove eggs and lessen the possibility of bacterial invasion from fly-caused punctures.

Blowflies are tough customers that sometimes are repelled by such compounds as pine oil, but also respond well to poison baits. Since they lay eggs in manure, open wounds and carcasses of dead animals, the wise horseowner will store manure in a pit well away from the barn; treat all injuries and open lesions with disinfectants and antiseptic ointments to repel bacteria and flies; and deeply bury or burn all dead animals. These procedures will reduce the number of blowflies present and more protection can be had by stalling a horse in a screened enclosure. He may be turned out at night.

Parasitism is one of the most overlooked areas of equine health. Not all is yet known of the effects of parasitic involvement and a veterinarian will first get the word on new developments. Therefore, follow his recommendations and do your part to eliminate these freeloaders.

CHAPTER 7
PRACTICAL HORSE FEEDING

This Is A Complicated Subject, But One The Horseman Should Understand

Feeding horses seems a mysterious art, of which only nutrition experts have a sound knowledge. It needn't be this way; in fact, any horseman can learn the rudiments of equine nutrition, without learning to pronounce all the fourteen-syllable terms!

A horse has nutrition needs like any mammal, including man. These include vitamins, minerals, protein and energy. The horse receives these from his feed and water in most cases, or from compounds supplemented because the feed is lacking of those compounds.

Each horse has different nutritional requirements, due to weight, age, usage and individualism. Therefore, one diet cannot be outlined for, say, all roping horses. It's up to the individual horseman to prescribe the feed rations for his horses, a trial and error process. If the horses appear thin, their rations should be increased; if they look fat, cut back the feeds. The horse should receive only enough feed to keep him healthy and fit, neither skinny nor hog-fat.

The tables which follow can be used to set up a feeding program for individual horses without much fuss or bother. The keys to any formula are: the horse's requirements, the amount of essential nutrients in the hay being fed and the nutrients in the grain added to the feed.

Table 1 gives the required nutrients of growing horses, while Table 2 gives the same information for mature horses according to their usage and weight. These simply list some of the chemicals the horse needs for continued good health. Table 3 lists the nutritive components found in hay, while Table 4 lists the nutritive compounds found in grain. Table 5 does the same for pasture grasses and Table 6 lists components of supplements.

What the horseman does, therefore, is first determine the nutritional needs of his horse, dependent upon his usage and weight. He then checks to see which of those compounds, and the amounts, are found in the hay he's feeding. In most cases, the hay alone won't provide all the nutritional elements needed in the proper amounts, the reason grain is fed. The horseman then checks the nutritive components of the grain he's feeding to determine if the grain, when added to the nutritive components of the hay, provide all the needed elements. If it does, that's the ration his horse requires for good health.

If the combination of grain and hay does not provide all the needed compounds, he then must supplement with commercially prepared products that have the elements his horse's diet is lacking. Most horses can receive all the nutritive elements they need through hay and grain.

There is another course open to horseowners, aside from purchasing supplements. This is in the feeding of different hays or grains. Not all hays and grains have the same nutritive content, so by switching to a different hay/grain combination, the horseman might then provide all the requirements needed without supplementing.

Economics enters the picture at this point. Many horsemen have adopted the attitude that one specific type of hay or grain is best, the others suitable only for feeding to goats. In direct relation to the law of supply and demand, the price for this type of hay or grain has risen substantially, while less-popular hays and grains are considerably cheaper.

This attitude, according to internationally known nutritionist Dr. William K. Tyznik, is foolish. He advocates feeding the grains that are cheapest in the horseman's part of the country, meeting the nutritive requirements through other mineral supplements. He feels people should quit buying exotic supplements and additives to a great degree, using the money saved to purchase the best-quality hay affordable.

Rather than stoke the fires of controversy, we'll just say that the horse's nutritional needs must be met. Any of the methods outlined herein will work toward that end.

This is a sad example of owner negligence through insufficient quantity, compounded by inadequate types of feed. This horse was returned to health and strength.

QUANTITATIVE NUTRIENT REQUIREMENTS OF GROWING HORSES
(Daily Nutrients Per Animal)

EQUINE GROWING TO 450 POUNDS MATURE WEIGHT:

Body Weight (lbs.)	Daily Gain (lbs.)	Dig. Energy (calories)	Dig. Protein (lbs.)	Calcium (lbs.)	Phosphorus (lbs.)
100	1½	7400	.8426	.0383	.0240
200	1	8530	.6930	.0365	.0229
300	½	7950	.4532	.0264	.0165
350	¼	8080	.3982	.0229	.0143
450	0	8240	.3520	.0176	.0132

EQUINE GROWING TO 900 POUNDS MATURE WEIGHT:

Body Weight	Daily Gain	Dig. Energy	Dig. Protein	Calcium	Phosphorus
200	2¼	10,440	1.2166	.0574	.0361
400	1½	12,410	.9460	.0770	.0482
550	1	13,630	.8140	.0484	.0326
725	½	14,100	.7458	.0418	.0304
900	0	13,860	.5896	.0352	.0264

EQUINE GROWING TO 1100 POUNDS MATURE WEIGHT:

Body Weight	Daily Gain	Dig. Energy	Dig. Protein	Calcium	Phosphorus
250	2½	12,070	1.3596	.0671	.0420
500	1¾	15,400	1.1792	.1012	.0632
725	1¼	16,810	1.0384	.0572	.0383
900	¾	17,160	.9196	.0506	.0354
1100	0	16,390	.6974	.0440	.0330

EQUINE GROWING TO 1325 POUNDS MATURE WEIGHT:

Body Weight	Daily Gain	Dig. Energy	Dig. Protein	Calcium	Phosphorus
300	2¾	14,150	1.5510	.1144	.0708
600	2	17,210	1.2804	.1126	.0704
850	1¼	18,860	1.1528	.0724	.0453
1050	¾	19,200	1.0076	.0689	.0431
1325	0	18,790	.8008	.0528	.0396

TABLE 1
(Derived from "Nutrient Requirements of Horses," compiled and published by National Research Council, 1973.)

QUANTITATIVE NUTRIENT REQUIREMENTS OF MATURE HORSES
(Daily Nutrients Per Animal)

MATURE HORSE, IDLE

Body Weight (lbs.)	Dig. Energy (calories)	Dig. Protein (lbs.)	Calcium (lbs.)	Phosphorus (lbs.)
450	8240	.3520	.0176	.0132
900	13,860	.5896	.0352	.0264
1100	16,390	.6974	.0440	.0330
1325	18,790	.8008	.0528	.0396

MATURE HORSE, LIGHT WORK (2 hours per day):

450	10,440	.4444	.0176	.0132
900	18,360	.7810	.0352	.0264
1100	21,890	.9328	.0440	.0330
1325	25,390	1.0802	.0528	.0396

MATURE HORSE, MEDIUM WORK (2 hours per day):

450	13,160	.5610	.0202	.0154
900	23,800	1.0120	.0378	.0286
1100	28,690	1.2166	.0466	.0352
1325	33,550	1.4278	.0625	.0418

MARE, LAST 90 DAYS OF PREGNANCY:

450	8700	.4752	.0229	.0716
900	14,880	.8250	.0429	.0330
1100	17,350	.9548	.0528	.0396
1325	19,950	1.1044	.0616	.0462

MARE, PEAK OF LACTATION:

450	15,240	1.0560	.0748	.0515
900	24,390	1.6456	.0924	.0783
1100	27,620	1.8238	.1034	.0849
1325	30,020	1.9272	.1122	.0858

TABLE 2
(Derived from "Nutrient Requirements of Horses," compiled and published by National Research Council, 1973.)

NUTRIENTS IN COMMON HORSE FEEDS: HAY (ONE POUND)

TYPE	Dig. Protein (lbs.)	Dig. Energy (calories/lb.)	Calcium (lbs.)	Phosphorus (lbs.)
Alfalfa:				
Early Bloom	.1110	951	.0112	.0021
Mid-Bloom	.0981	911	.0120	.0020
Full Bloom	.0868	836	.0112	.0018
Mature	.0702	803	.0065	.0015
Dehydrated	.1470	1025	.0152	.0026
Timothy:				
Pre-Bloom	.0585	940	.0058	.0030
Mid-Bloom	.0318	778	.0036	.0017
Late Bloom	.0317	759	.0033	.0016
Clover:				
Alsike	unk	881	.0115	.0022
Crimson	unk	864	.0124	.0016
Ladino	.1351	unk	.0153	.0029
Red	.0748	883	.0131	.0021
Native	.3900	687	.0053	.0016
Oat	.3800	784	.0023	.0021

TABLE 3
(Derived from "Nutrient Requirements of Horses," compiled and published by National Research Council, 1973.)

NUTRIENTS IN COMMON HORSE FEEDS: CONCENTRATES (ONE POUND)

Grain	Dig. Protein (lbs.)	Dig. Energy (calories/lb.)	Calcium (lbs.)	Phosphorus (lbs.)
Barley	.0730	1477	.0006	.0049
Corn (yellow dent)	.0470	1618	.0002	.0027
Cottonseed meal	.3510	1374	.0016	.0120
Linseed meal	.2967	1473	.0044	.0089
Molasses:				
Beet	.0380	1369	.0017	.0003
Cane	.1356	74.1	.0041	.0004
Oats:				
Rolled	.1252	unk	.0008	.0043
34 lb./bushel	.0760	1275	.0008	.0030
Skim milk	.3350	1616	.0126	.0103
Soybean meal	.3980	1425	.0032	.0067
Wheat bran	.1148	1037	.0014	.0117
Yeast, brewers	.3841	1304	.0013	.0143

TABLE 4
(Derived from "Nutrient Requirements of Horses," compiled and published by National Research Council, 1973.)

NUTRIENTS IN COMMON HORSE FEEDS: PASTURE (ONE POUND)

Type	Dig. Protein (lbs.)	Dig. Energy (calories/lb.)	Calcium (lbs.)	Phosphorus (lbs.)
Bluegrass:				
Immature	.0370	337	.0017	.0014
Milk Stage	.0240	346	.0007	.0009
Brome	.0530	347	.0020	.0018
Fescue, Meadow	.0469	787	.0044	.0032
Orchardgrass:				
Immature	.0310	255	.0014	.0013
Mid-Bloom	.0130	282	unk	unk
Milk Stage	.0010	261	.0007	.0007
Prairie Hay	.0264	unk	.0032	.0013
Sudangrass	.0520	unk	.0036	.0027
Wheatgrass, Crested:				
Immature	.0540	330	.0014	.0011
Full Bloom	.0240	420	.0019	.0014
Overripe	0	566	.0022	.0006

TABLE 5
(Derived from "Nutrient Requirements of Horses," compiled and published by National Research Council, 1973.)

NUTRIENTS IN COMMON SUPPLEMENTS: (ONE POUND)		
Type	Calcium (lbs.)	Phosphorus (lbs.)
Dicalcium Phosphate	.0222	.0178
Oyster Shells	.0385	0
High Calcium Limestone	.0330	0
Defluorinated Phosphate	.0330	.0180
Monosodium Phosphate	0	.0217
Sodium Tripolyphosphate	0	.0216
Steamed Bone Meal	.0290	.0136

TABLE 6

(Derived from "Nutrient Requirements of Horses," compiled and published by National Research Council, 1973.)

POSSIBLE DAILY FEED RATIONS (POUNDS)							
HORSE	Legume hay*	Grass hay+	Oats	Barley	Wheat bran	Corn	Salt, Calcium, Vitamin Suppl.
400-pound weanling	3.5	3.5	3	2	1	0	Yes
	3.5	3.5	4	0	2	0	Yes
	3.5	3.5	5	0	1	0	Yes
1200-pound pleasure/show horse	0	14.0	5	0	0	0	Yes
	0	14.0	4	0	0	1	Yes
	0	14.0	4	1	0	0	Yes
1200-pound average work	0	14	11	0	0	0	Yes
	0	14	9	0	0	2	Yes
	0	14	8	0	0	3	Yes
1200-pound strenuous work	0	14	16	0	0	0	Yes
	0	14	11	2	0	3	Yes
	0	14	10	6	0	0	Yes
1200-pound brood mare or service stallion	4	9	8	0	2	0	Yes
	4	9	4	0	3	3	Yes
	4	9	11	0	0	0	Yes
1200-pound mare with foal at side	6	8	14	0	2	0	Yes
	6	8	9	4	3	0	Yes
	6	8	15	0	1	0	Yes

*alfalfa, clover hays
+timothy, prairie, brome, bermuda, Kentucky, orchard hays

TABLE 7

VITAMINS		
NAME	SOURCE	BENEFIT
A	Green leaf plants, manufactured bodily through most normal feed or supplements	Body metabolism growth, reproduction; necessary for reproductive, digestive and respiratory systems
D	Sunlight, supplements	Sound bones and teeth; assists assimilation of nutrient calcium and phosphorus
E	Prime hay, green leaf plants, supplements	Increased reproductive ability
B Complex	Green leafy feed, fresh or dry	Body metabolism

TABLE 8

MINERALS		
NAME	SOURCE	BENEFIT
Calcium	Supplements; basic feed	Development of bones; body metabolism
Cobalt	Basic feed	Necessary bacterial action of the digestive system
Copper	See Iron	See Iron
Iodine	Supplements — rarely in proper amounts in basic feed	Body metabolism
Iron	Supplements; basic feed	Oxygenation of circulatory system; required by the digestive system
Manganese	See Sulfur	See Sulfur
Magnesium	See Sulfur	See Sulfur
Phosphorus	See Calcium	See Calcium
Potassium	See Sulfur	See Sulfur
Salt	Supplement	Assimilation of nutrients in body metabolism; aids in elimination of waste materials
Sulfur	Basic feed	Body metabolism

TABLE 9

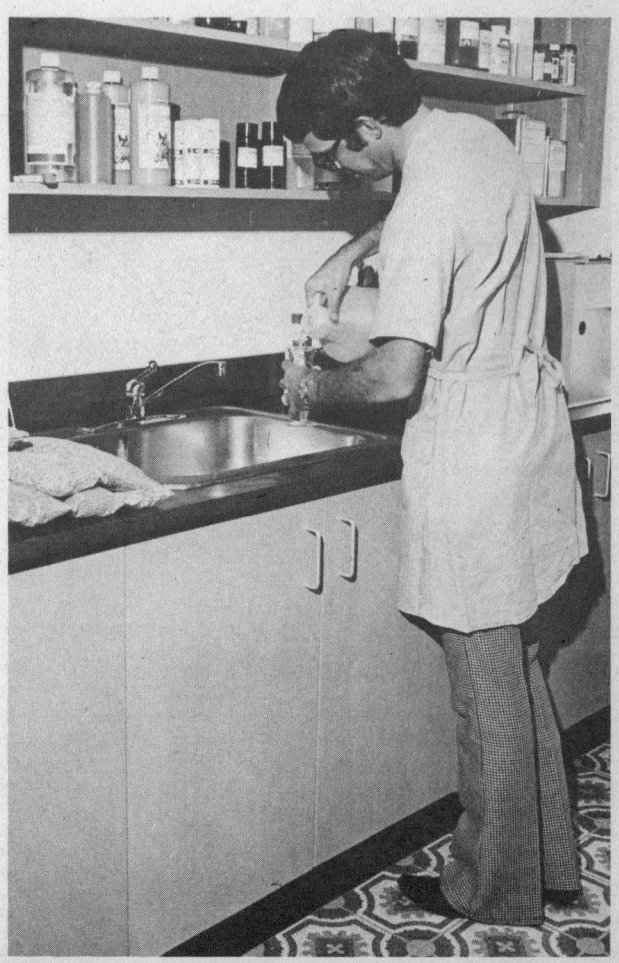

Many talented researchers are employed by horse feed companies that spend thousands annually in the search for the proper nutrients horses require, among others.

Proper exercise daily is compatible with a sound feeding program, to avoid some of the health hazards outlined in Chapter 4. A healthy horse is a happy individual.

Using these charts, it's easy to figure the horse's diet. As an example, suppose you own a mature horse weighing 900 pounds that is used at medium work for two hours per day (Table 2). This horse requires 23,800 calories, 1.0120 pounds of protein, .0378 pounds of calcuim and .0286 pounds of phosphorus per day.

He is being fed thirteen total pounds of hay, seven of early-bloom alfalfa, with six pounds of pre-bloom timothy (Table 3). In addition, he receives eight total pounds of grain, four each of corn and oats, the latter weighing 34 pounds per bushel (Table 4). He receives these nutrients total: digestible energy (calories), 23,864; digestible protein (pounds), 1.6200; calcium (pounds), .0472 and phosphorus (pounds), .0555. The formula for calculation of this ration is:

DIGESTIBLE ENERGY (CALORIES)
7 lbs. Early-Bloom Alfalfa @ 951 calories/lb.	= 6657 cal
6 lbs. Pre-Bloom Timothy @ 940 calories/lb.	= 5640 "
4 lbs. Corn @ 1618 calories/lb.	= 6427 "
4 lbs. Oats (34 lb./bushel) @ 1275 calories/lb.	= 5100 "
Total Digestive Energy	= 23,864 cal

DIGESTIBLE PROTEIN (POUNDS)
7 lbs. Early-Bloom Alfalfa @ .1110/lb.	= .7770 pounds
6 lbs. Pre-Bloom Timothy @ .0585/lb.	= .3510 "
4 lbs. Corn @ .0470/lb.	= .1880 "
4 lbs. Oats (34 lb./bushel) @ .0760/lb.	= .3040 "
Total Digestible Protein	= 1.6200 pounds

CALCIUM (POUNDS)
7 lbs. Early-Bloom Alfalfa @ .0112/lb.	= .0084 pounds
6 lbs. Pre-Bloom Timothy @ .0058/lb.	= .0348 "
4 lbs. Corn @ .0002/lb.	= .0008 "
4 lbs. Oats (34 lb./bushel) @ .0008/lb.	= .0032 "
Total Calcium	= .0472 pounds

7 lbs. Early-Bloom Alfalfa @ .0021/lb.	= .0147 pounds
6 lbs. Pre-Bloom Timothy @ .0030/lb.	= .0180 "
4 lbs. Corn @ .0027/lb.	= .0108 "
4 lbs. Oats (34 lb./bushel) @ .0030/lb.	= .0120 "
Total Phosphorus	= .0555 pounds

Of course, a ration is only as good as the feed used. If the horse is fed the best-quality hays and grains affordable, he will receive nearly all of the nutrients vital to his subsistence. A salt/mineral block can be put in his paddock or stall and he will take in the other minerals and compounds as needed.

Various feed facts have been provided throughout this book and they will be capsulated at this point:

Make any ration changes slowly, since the horse doesn't seem well-suited to rapid diet changes. These have led to many internal problems, among them colic.

The horse is able to better utilize nutrients in his feed if fed more than once per day. These feedings should be at the same times each day and always feed hay prior to grain. Since the grain is higher in nutrients, feeding it after the hay allows it to remain in the stomach longer before passing in the feces, leading to better utilization of the nutrients.

If the horse has a tendency to bolt his grain without thorough chewing, which leads to faster passage from the intestines, feed small amounts of grain often. Another solution is to put some smooth, flat stones in the grain bucket or manger, forcing the horse to eat more slowly and carefully.

Always buy the best-quality hay that's affordable, since there's more nutritive benefit in quality over quantity. Assure the feeds aren't moldy, dusty or spoiled and feed only what the horse requires to keep fit.

Provide cool, clean water at all times, even during the dead of Winter, since the horse derives nutrients from it. Never water a hot horse and don't water the horse after feeding grain. The bulk of the water will force passage of the grain before all the nutrients are utilized.

Keep a salt/mineral block available to the horse at all times. This free-choice aspect of supplementing allows the horse to take the minerals he requires when needed, and studies have shown the horse will use the salt/mineral block when needed.

Regular exercise is compatible with proper equine nutrition. As noted in Chapter 4, lack of exercise can lead to such problems as azoturia or tying-up.

Feed him right, exercise regularly and your horse will be serviceable for many years.

CHAPTER 8
FOCUSING ON FEET

A Fact-Finding Expedition Inside The Hoof Details Its Complexities, Which You'll Need To Know

Basic understanding of anatomy is important whether your interest in the animal is strictly for or eventually, a combination of profit and pleasure. Although medical science has advanced tremendously the past few years, enabling the veterinarian to control illness more proficiently, proper care of the horse is preventive medicine no horseowner should ignore.

The old saying, "No hoof, no horse," isn't an old wives' tale: it actually is a fact. Knowing the parts comprising the lower leg which includes the hoof along with their specific function, helps you practice proper leg and foot care just a little better. Once the question, "why" is answered, it will be easier to recognize the difference between proper care, adequate care or carelessness. The results of the care given will be quite apparent after a little time and experience.

Few potential horse purchasers bother to consult a veterinarian or horseshoer for advice concerning a horse they consider buying. Any unsoundness in the animal would be brought to their immediate attention and just might possibly affect the purchase. The present consideration is that a lame horse is more often than not a poor selection as a riding horse.

The horse with a perfect hoof need not have even wear on them. A competent horseshoer, through trimming and special shoeing if required, keeps each leg and hoof in proper position so the internal parts are functioning properly. When the hoof is neglected, the lower leg becomes involved in short time. There are many cases of the horseshoer being confronted with different hoof conditions on the same animal.

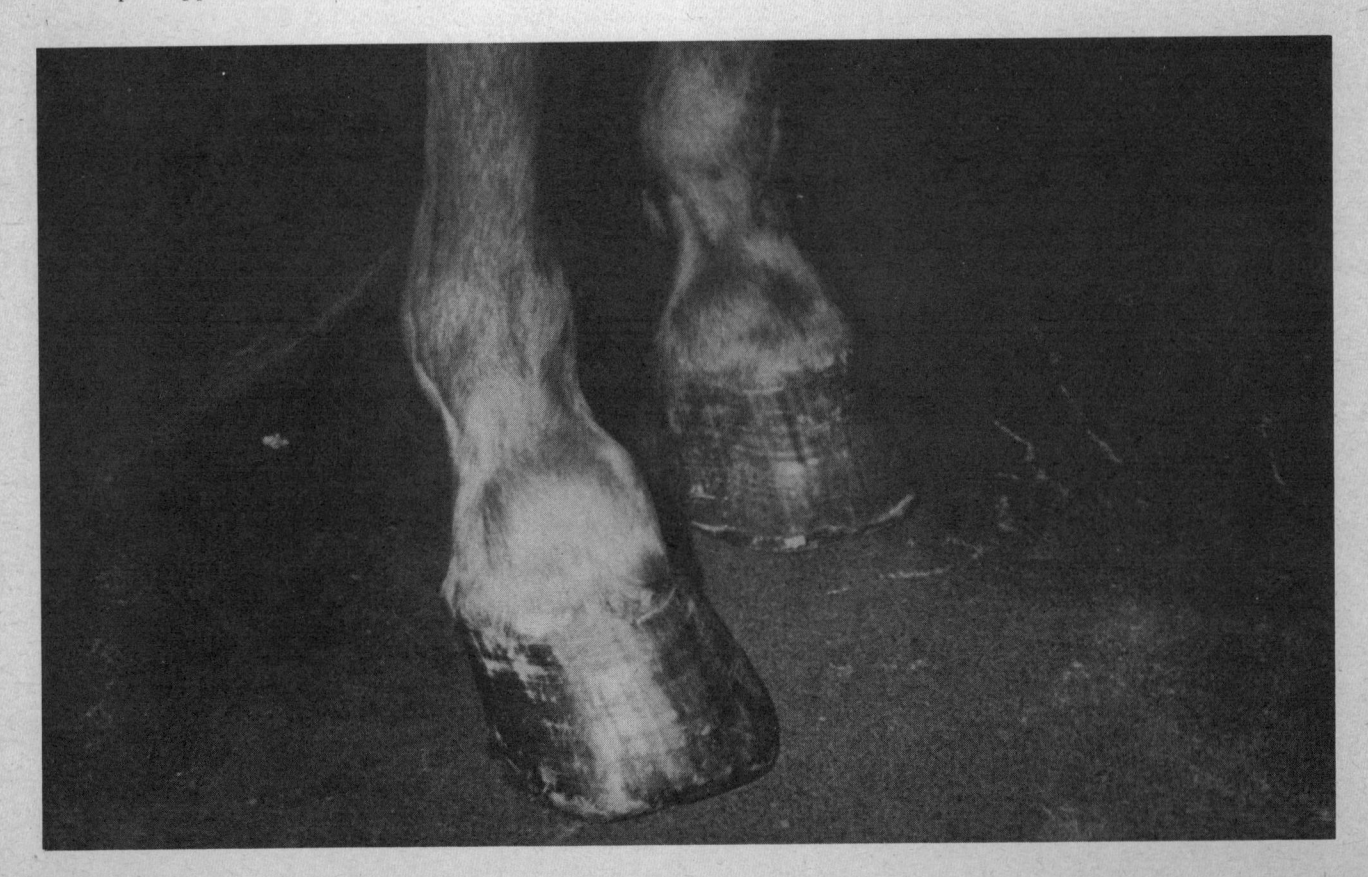

In the natural state, horses travel barefoot and nature seems most often to supply what is required to keep a healthy hoof. Unless man uses him on surfaces detrimental to hoof soundness, or the horse develops problems requiring corrective shoes, the great majority of horseshoers will tell you the shoe is not required or suggested.

Since there is little difference between the front and hind lower leg and hoof they are cared for in the same way. Each is composed of bones, tendons, and ligaments. The horse carries more weight on his front end than the rear, therefore the front hoof is slightly larger.

Bones of the lower leg are shown in the accompanying illustration. The cannon bone extends from the knee (or hock) to the fetlock. Although this bone is exposed to all sorts of injury, it rarely is broken because of its strength.

On each side, toward the rear of the cannon bone, there are two splint bones extending about three-quarters the length of the cannon. At the lower end of the splints, support and attachment to the cannon is by means of a strong ligament. Any excessive strain in this lower area results in damage referred to as splints.

Sesamoids are two triangular bones forming a part of each fetlock joint. They are covered with ligaments and cartilage, moving in conjunction with the action of the rear area of the cannon bone.

The navicular bone (distal sesamoid) is located in an opening to the rear of the coffin bone and moves with the action of the short pastern bone.

The two sesamoids and navicular bone have the deep flexor tendon toward the rear and covering the lower portion of the navicular bone. It is in this area that navicular problems are found.

Each end of the bones mentioned are parts of a moving joint and attached to each other by means of ligaments. Ligaments are strong, slightly elastic bands of connective tissue. The ends of the bones are covered with a smooth, protective covering called cartilage, and contained within a sac producing the liquid synovia for the lubrication of the joint. Synovia is produced as it is needed by the joint and when damage occurs to the joint, synovia production is increased.

An injury to a joint may result in an opening within the joint, thus increasing the normal production of synovia, which in turn seeps through the opening. The healing process is retarded considerably, subjects the area to infection, and last but by no means least, is painful to the horse. The result of this damage could be permanent disability.

In the upper leg, muscles are present that continue from the knee or hock as tendons. The common digital extensor muscle of the upper foreleg acts as an extensor to all joints below the elbow but flexes the elbow as well. Knee action is controlled by this extensor, which is located to the front of the knee and down to its attachment on the upper end of the cannon bone.

The superficial digital flexor is a muscle, continuing from the back of the knee as a tendon, and divides into two branches at the fetlock joint. The ends of these two branches continue on, attaching into each side of the short pastern bone upper end. It is located to the rear of the deep flexor tendon and performs the function which its name implies, that of flexing the knee, fetlock and pastern joints.

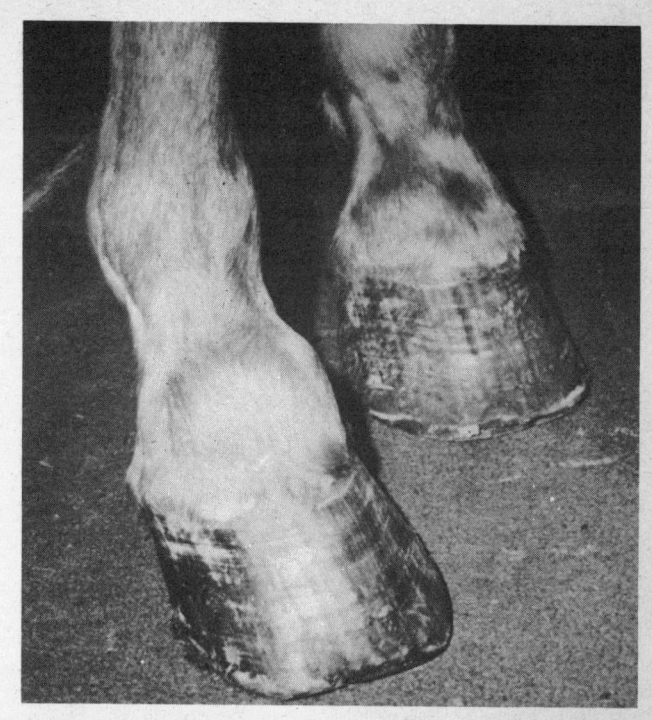

A key to hoof problems lies in formation of odd shapes, like this right front foot. The cause here was ringbone. Other hoof/leg ailments are outlined in accompanying text.

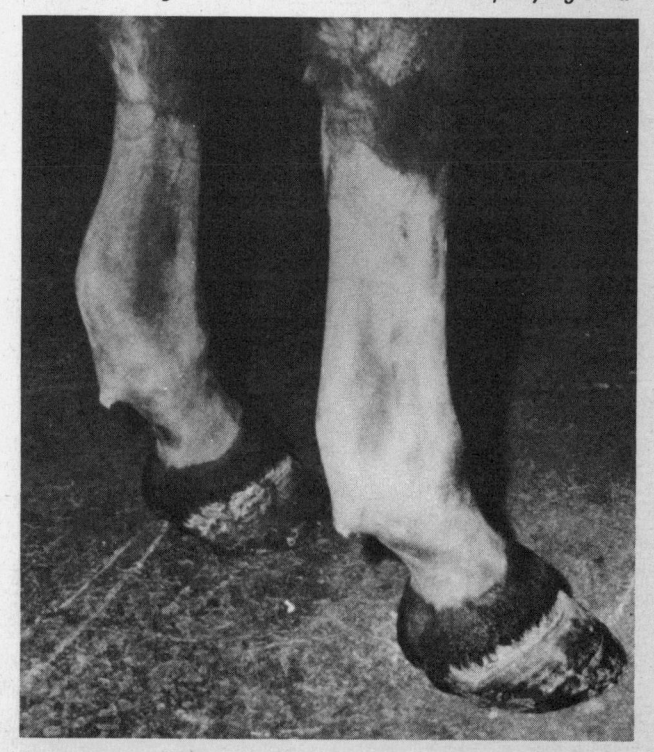

The classic example of a bowed tendon is shown on this left foreleg. The right foreleg, while almost normal, shows signs of having been bowed tendon victim, too. Horses with this condition require protracted vet care.

The deep flexor tendon is located to the front of the superficial flexor tendon, beginning in the upper leg as the deep digital flexor muscle. This tendon is the strongest in the lower leg and ends on the bottom of the coffin bone. These muscles and tendons act as shock absorbers for the leg as well as providing joint mobility.

Tendons in the foreleg, especially the cannon area, are subject to injury and strain far more often than the tendons in the hind leg. The deep flexor tendon is most often injured and inflamed, resulting in the impairment called bowed tendons or tendinitis.

If you visualize the tendons and ligaments as strong, heavy-duty rubber bands holding each of the bones in the proper place and relationship to each other, it is easier to understand just how much elasticity is required of them, and any damage done is extremely difficult to correct and impossible to replace. As good horsemen, the only recourse is to avoid damage or injury whenever and wherever we can.

The horse's foot consists of more than the hoof. It is comprised of the long pastern bone, short pastern bone, coffin bone, navicular bone, hoof, elastic parts, sensitive parts, and horny parts.

Hoof growth, being a continual process, varies slightly among different horses. All growth is in a downward and forward direction. Conditions under which the horse is kept must be taken into consideration when discussing hoof growth rates. Of the many practices involving horse maintenance, correct feeding, regular trimming and proper hoof moisture content are important to overall well-being. Surprising as it may seem, hoof growth definitely is affected by them. Dry, hot climates or surroundings will produce a hard, dry hoof; moist climates or surroundings will produce a soft, moist hoof.

Each condition mentioned requires the horseman to balance the situation correctively. Hoofs require a specific amount of moisture to remain healthy and if moisture does not come from the surrounding areas, it must be applied manually in the form of hoof dressings. When these dressings are applied, it is to the coronet (coronary band) area since this is the origin of all hoof growth. Many horsemen prefer using the wet soaking boots rather than the commercially prepared dressing compounds. How you accomplish the task of maintaining proper moisture in the hoof is not as important as being certain it is present.

Generally speaking, most hoof problems stem from improper care and some effects cannot be totally corrected. A prime example is a contracted heel developing from lack of proper moisture content. Once this condition is established, corrective shoes can help, but never will eliminate the actual problem.

The foot is a skillfully designed piece of living machinery performing many more functions than flexible support. You could compare the foot acting as shock absorbers to springs on a car. Can you imagine how uncomfortable it would be to ride in a car on uneven surfaces for long periods of time? Could you begin to estimate the extensive wear and tear on related automotive parts without these shock absorbers?

A great deal of pressure is exerted on the leg when the horse is in motion. As the horse travels faster, the pressure impact increases proportionally. Because of this pressure, the healthy hoof will expand to cushion the tremendous impact.

The frog is a V-shaped spongy, though horny, part first receiving the impact. Under pressure, it spreads out, forcing the bars outward. At the same time, the digital (plantar) cushion spreads and forces the lateral cartilages outward. The digital cushion is a wedge-shaped pliant cushion; the large lateral cartilages are between the upper wings of the coffin bone and the upper coronet. These are the highly elastic parts within the foot structure.

This is the main reason most horseshoers will advise against shoeing a horse unless it is absolutely required. The shoe is

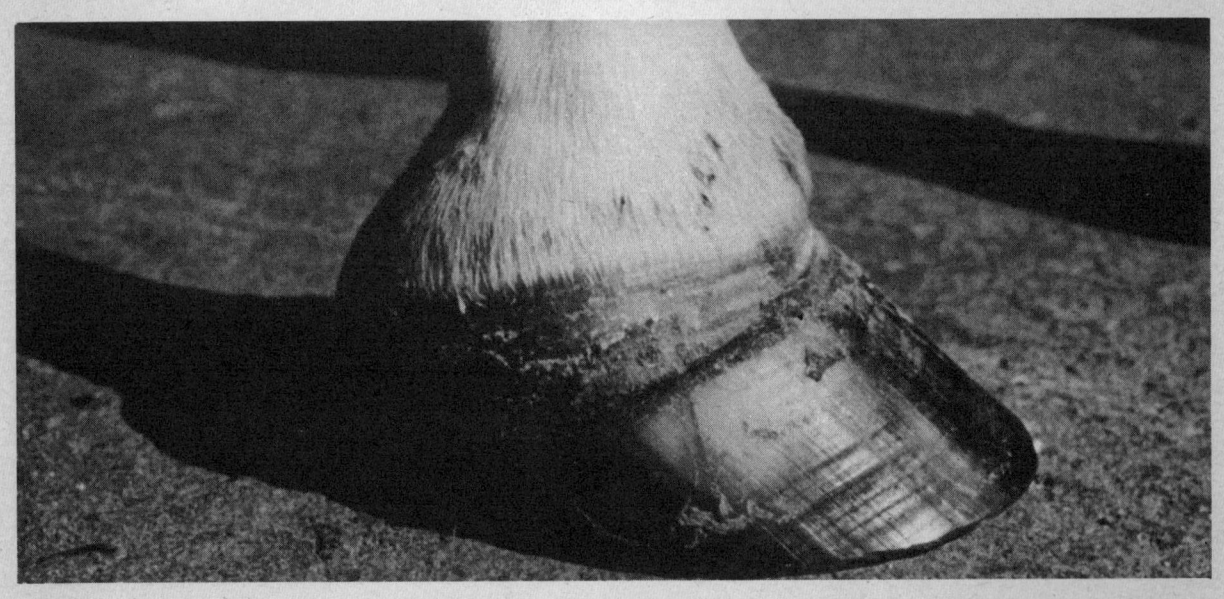

This is a super example of a horse suffering a ringbone condition. Following injury, the membranes of the pastern become inflamed, resulting in the formation of bony growth. If located where a tendon moves over bone, lameness can be end result.

metal and will not contract and expand with the hoof as it was designed, to cushion the pressure exerted upon it in motion.

Sensitive parts of the leg contain numerous veins, the healthy spongy frog contains proper moisture. When the horse is in motion, the natural expansion and contraction of the foot parts stimulate internal blood circulation.

As noted previously, all hoof growth originates in the sensitive parts of the foot. One sensitive part, the corium, covers the bones and elastic parts of the foot. The coronary band (coronet) circles the top of the hoof from one bulb to the other. It is a strong piece of flesh, approximately an inch wide, and contained in the coronary groove along the upper interior surface of the wall. From the papillae covering the surface of the coronary band, growth of the horny wall takes place. A thin band of flesh above the coronary band, the perioplic ring, produces the periople which is the glossy surface of the hoof wall retarding moisture evaporation.

In addition to the sensitive parts mentioned, there are sensitive coverings on the surfaces of the coffin bone and lateral cartilages. This develops into the horny laminae of the inside hoof wall. The sensitive sole covers the bottom surface of the coffin bone and develops, through papillae, into the horny sole. The sensitive frog covers the lower surface of the digital cushion and its papillae develop into the horny frog.

Because of wear upon the bearing surfaces of the hoof itself, nature has provided it with continual growth, as man has

As noted in the text, a horse's foot is a complex piece of animal engineering. This view shows hoof components.

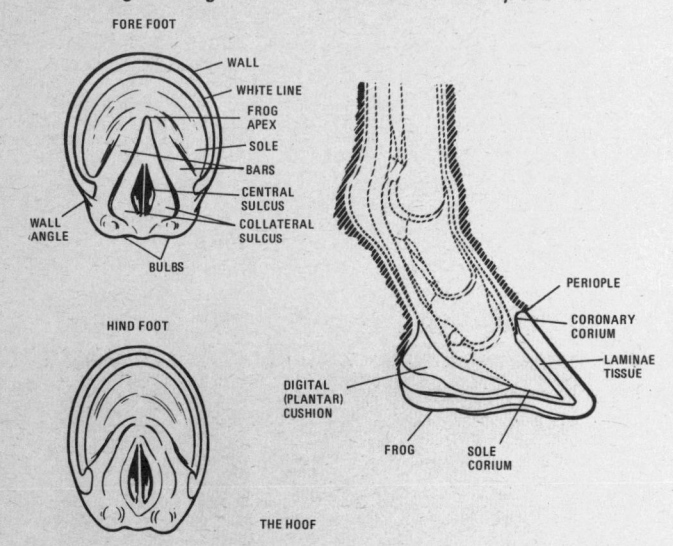

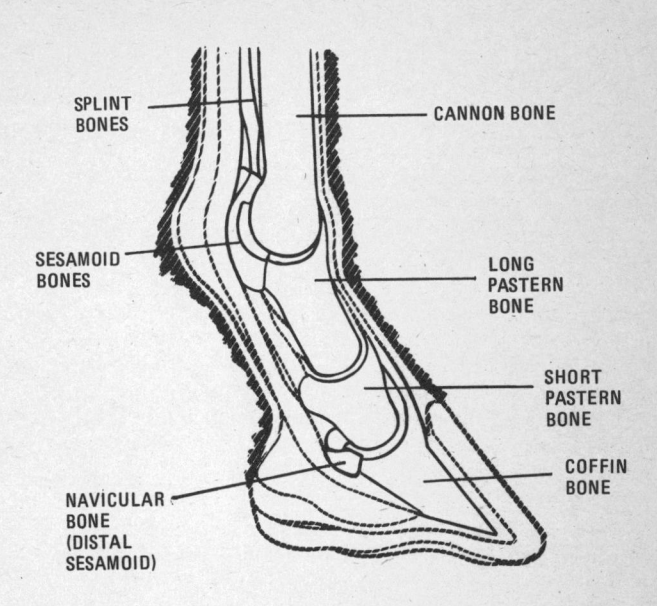

The bones of a horse's foot are highly complex and the accompanying text outlines some of the possible ailments.

fingernail growth. The hoof composition is tough and durable to withstand most hard use within reason. Hoof parts are the wall, the sole, and the frog. The wall is a sturdy protective wall for the sensitive portions within the hoof itself and is support for the animal's weight. At the front, or toe, the wall thickness is greater than it is at the back, or heel, since the heel area expands when weight is present. The top portion of the hoof is the corona and it is from this portion that the wall covers the entire outer surface of the hoof. The area falling halfway between the toe and heel is referred to as the quarters, and directly behind are the bars, which act as weight bearing surfaces and control hoof expansion.

The frog function has been discussed, but it is good to remember that although it is a tough, spongy part, it is located near tender portions above it and punctures or diseases of the frog can spread to them, causing infections and possible permanent disability through injury.

Enough horse leg anatomy has been covered to keep anyone but the anatomy-avid reader switching from text to illustration and back to text. It will require little memorization on your part to perceive that when an unknowing or careless horseman abuses the functions of the leg, he is asking for trouble. Each part of the leg was placed in specific relationship to another and the functions of each is clearly defined. When undue stress, strain, injury, lack of care are present, faults or impairment will be the result you have to live with.

It is certain that you know at least one "cowboy," no relation to the good old Western horseman by any loose definition. This guy or gal just gets on a horse and puts him through all the hot and fast motions he can think of, whether the horse is in balance for the move or not, whether the animal is trained for the maneuver or not. Another common failing in the would-be horseman is apparent when you see him pounding his mount on frozen ground. Then there is the poor horse who doesn't know how to pivot and is repeatedly abused in the leg area because the rider doesn't know how to train him to pivot properly.

The reason for pointing out faults in horsemen is for no other purpose than to restate a thoroughly sound practice when purchasing a trained and mature animal. If at all possible, consult your veterinarian and horseshoer prior to horse purchase if you are not as qualified as they are in spotting problem legs. Remember, once you purchase the unsound animal as a pleasure horse, the pleasure may end abruptly. Not one of us would expect the novice driver or one who doesn't drive at all, to purchase a used car without mechanical inspection first, so why not be as reasonable when buying a horse? Some horsemen have no idea how the horse was taken care of, or possibly abused, any more than the non-mechanic does about a "good buy used car" from Friendly Sam's lot number three!

One problem with the leg is extremely difficult to illustrate clearly and is primarily the product of unsanitary barns. It is a disease of the frog known as thrush. To anyone with half a nostril, the odor is unappetizingly overwhelming. Needless to say, with cleaning the hoof daily and sanitary stable practices, the disease should not be found in your barn. If the frog is extremely moist and infectious, with an fetid odor, call your horseshoer or vet; he'll tell you immediately what medication to use as a remedy for the problem.

A few of the more common areas to examine when trying to spot poor legs or poor conformation faults are shown in the accompanying illustrations with brief descriptions. No one is expected or encouraged to become a specialist overnight in the subject, but a more knowledgeable horseman can make it easier for the professional when called on a visit.

Sesamoiditis: The sesamoid bones — a part of the fetlock joint, are injured through concussion or joint abuse. A visual swelling is present and is hard to the touch. In this laming condition, new bone may be formed in an area where it interferes with ligaments and joint action.

Ringbone: Ringbone occurs in the bones of the pastern through injury or abuse. The membranes covering the bone/bones may become seriously inflamed, resulting in a production of bony growth. If the growth is located where a tendon moves over bone, lameness is the final effect.

Sidebone: Sidebones is a condition where the cartilage on either wing of the coffin bone becomes ossified. Since the cartilage is part of the leg shock absorbing system, heavy and repeated concussion causes them to lose resiliency. Lameness in the usual meaning of impaired motion is not a permanent effect.

Contracted Heel: In this condition, normal expansion and contraction of the heel does not take place. It is not a disease nor does it initially cause lameness. Many causes of this condition can be and are eliminated through correctly regulated hoof trimming by a qualified horseshoer. However, two causes of contracted heel can fall within the confines of good horse care — in that neglect of the owner to have the hoof properly trimmed at all times, and allowing the hoof to dry out excessively and remain in this condition. When the hoof reaches this radical stage of contracted heel, the horseshoer must resort to a corrective shoe, and the owner must make every effort to return moisture to the heel. In many radical cases, the heel is never returned to a normal condition, and the heel remains in a limited degree of contraction and expansion.

Sprained Tendons and Ligaments: Tendons, a portion of a muscle, are composed of strong strands of fiber but are far less able to contract and expand as the upper muscle tissues do. This limitation makes them subject to injurious sprains, the

Splints sometimes are hard to detect at the outset and, when seen plainly, usually indicate advanced condition. They aren't necessarily bothersome, but they can hamper performance.

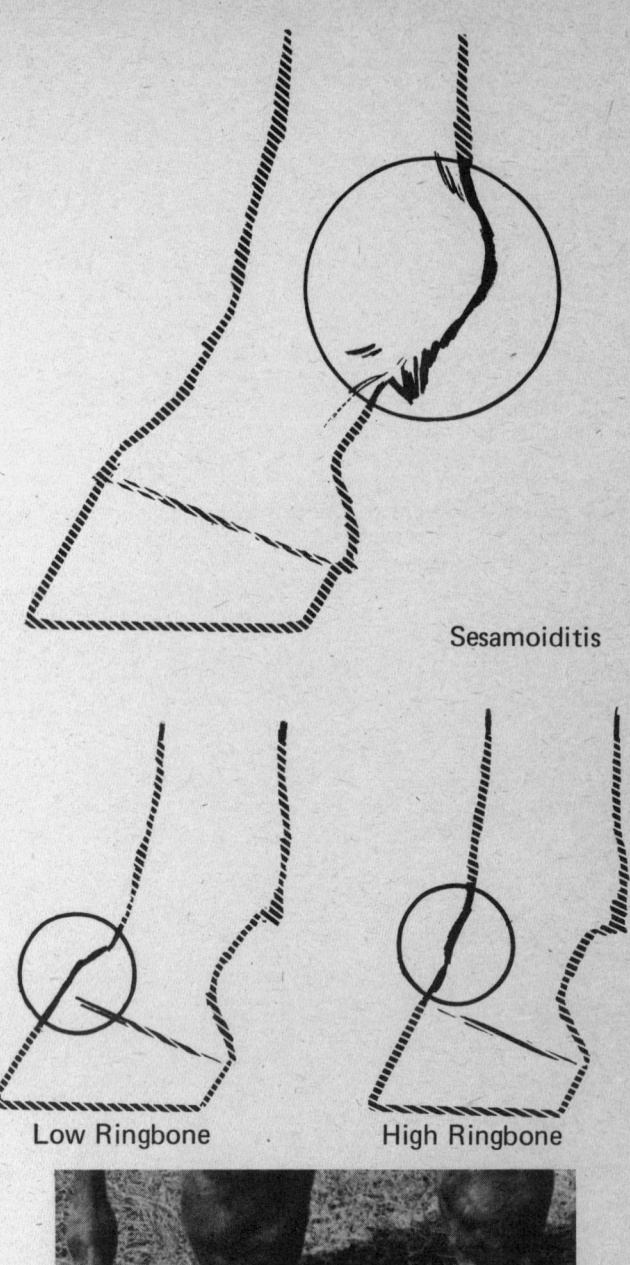

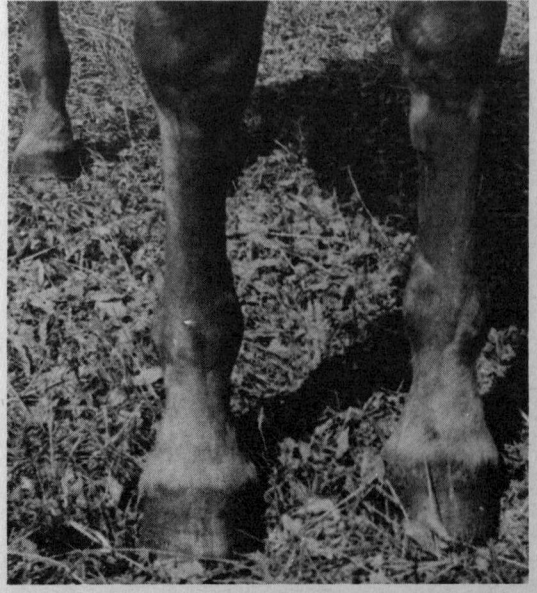

Sesamoiditis

Low Ringbone

High Ringbone

Sidebone   Contracted Heel

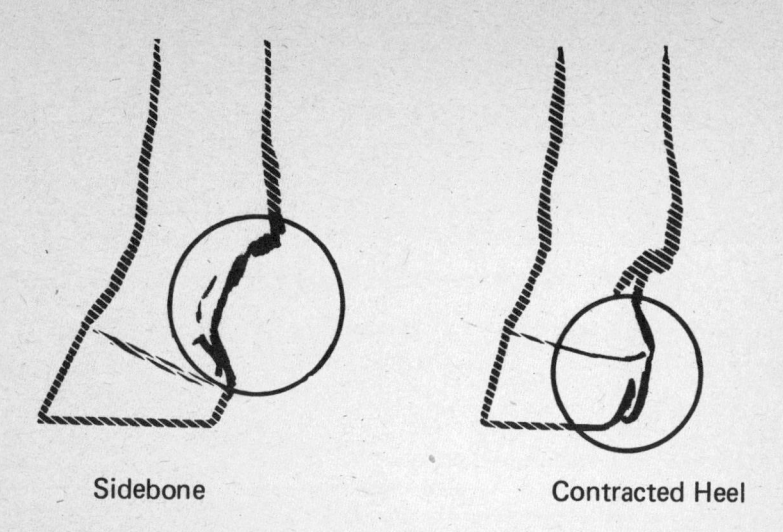

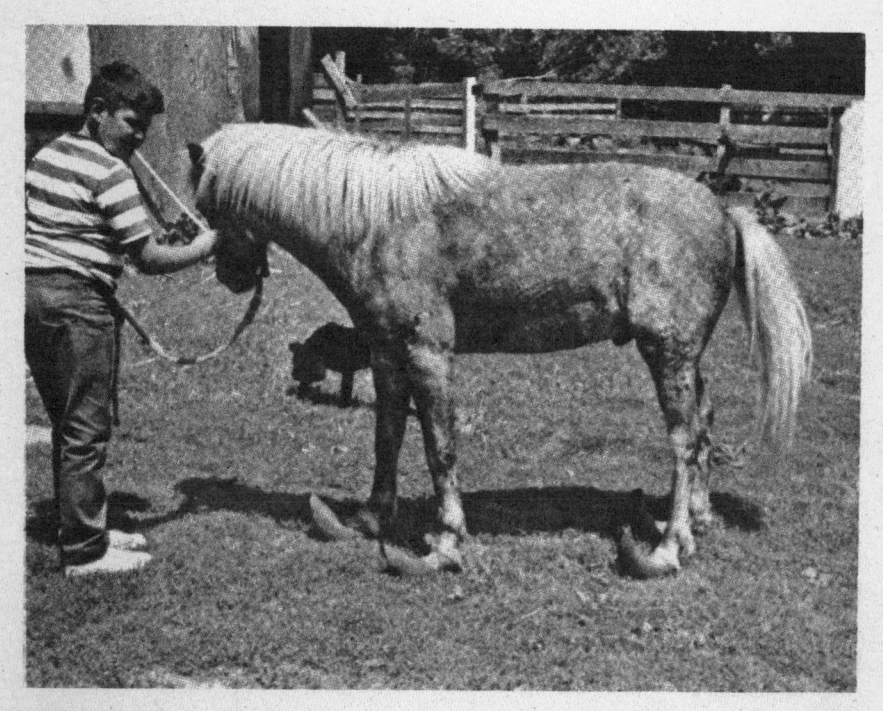

This is a sad example of how bad founder can become, the Shetland pony's feet having grown so long the horn is curving upward. Owner neglect was the cause.

cause of which are varied and numerous. Ligaments are similar to tendons in basic structure, but they are not a portion of elastic muscle. Their function is to hold one or more bones together or support joints. When the superficial tendon is slightly strained, a minor swelling may be seen and heat is generated. Although no apparent lameness is seen, the horse will flinch when slight pressure is applied to the affected tendon. In severe strains, the tendon fibers may rupture, causing a great degree of swelling along the entire tendon. The effect will be lameness and severe pain results when the area is touched. The suspensory ligament is attached to the top of the cannon bone, just behind the knee. It continues down the back of the cannon bone between the two splint bones to the sesamoid bones, where it divides into four strands. Two front strands wrap around the fetlock joint and merge with the extensor tendon, located to the front of the pastern bone; the rear two strands attach to the sesamoid bones. This ligament suspends the fetlock joint in its correct position and also acts as a tendon support. Generally, this ligament is not affected by strains unless a tendon ruptures as a result of hard, fast, and regular punishment from work on hard surfaces. When this condition occurs, the cause or area of trouble is difficult to

This out-of-condition horse may suffer leg ailments!

diagnose correctly at times due to the great amount of swelling present. If the leg is carefully examined, no "bow" will be present in a ruptured suspensory ligament as there will be in severe cases of ruptured tendons.

Founder: Founder is the common name given to laminitis, a serious disorder that causes excruciating pain to the afflicted horse. Essentially, it starts with inflammation of the interior of a horse's hoof. Since the hoof wall prohibits expansion, pressure on the nerves builds within the foot, causing pain.

Founder is caused by having the feet trimmed too closely, although more often through allowing a hot, sweating horse all the cold water he wants. Too, founder can be caused by ingestion of large amount of grain in one feeding, or eating too much grass at one time. A horse can be foundered, also, by working on hard ground, and mares have been foundered by retention of some afterbirth materials. Laminitis also has been linked to uterine infection in mares, or the strenous working of an out-of-condition horse. Usually only the forefeet are affected, but cases in which all four extremities were involved have been recorded.

Horses once foundered are prone to the condition in the future. Chronic cases are characterized by a dropped sole, the bone of the third phalanx extended downward farther than normal. Hoof growth will be speeded, resulting in telltale rings of growth. In extreme cases, the toe actually curves upward like a ram's horn.

Navicular Disease: The navicular bone is small, smooth and round, located at the rear of the cannon bone. Sometimes this bone may be fractured or drained of its lubricating fluid through a puncture of the frog, causing pain when the tendons controlling hoof movement slide over it. A horse with this incurable condition generally places weight on the toe of the affected foot, resulting in stumbling and making him unsafe for riding. It's difficult condition for a veterinarian to diagnose and an X-ray is the only sure method.

Thrush: This frog infection, characterized by dead sole and foul odor, is guaranteed to clear a horseman's sinuses! Caused by unsanitary conditions or failure to clean the horse's feet, it can involve the sensitive tissues of the foot and cause lameness. Sometimes an extremely thrush-riddled frog will be shed completely, a new frog growing in its place.

"No hoof, no horse" is valid, providing more is included in the old saying than hoof alone. The lower leg is the part of the horse referred to in the old axiom, the hoof being one part of the intricate system of animal engineering.

CHAPTER 9
SHOEING THE NORMAL FOOT

Few Horses Are Blessed With Perfect Feet And Legs, And All Need The Services Of A Good Farrier

Not all horses are blessed with perfect feet and legs. Sometimes, due to poor conformation or accident, a horse may have a defect. The seriousness of the abnormality will depend upon the degree to which the horse's gaits are affected. If the horse paddles slightly, his gait may be unsightly but he still can be a useful, dependable animal. But if the faulty foot conformation is such that the horse strikes himself or is not surefooted, his usefulness and even his safety as a riding animal may be limited. The horse is an athlete and his greatest usefulness is in being able to move with speed, agility, balance and safety. If he is limited in these aspects because of abnormal feet and legs, his value is drastically reduced.

Some abnormalities can be corrected or at least improved with proper trimming and shoeing of the horse's feet. Ideally, corrective trimming should begin shortly after foaling. Regular and frequent trimmings can help to straighten feet and legs as the young horse grows, often completely correcting minor faults and greatly improving ones more serious. Some faults never can be fully corrected, but proper trimming and shoeing can help to the extent that the horse still can be useful and sound.

Corrective work on a horse's feet always should be done gradually and with care. The object is to make the shape, level and the angle of the foot as nearly normal as possible so the horse will have a normal gait. Trimming never should be too drastic, because you may put strain on the bones of the leg. You cannot really change the bone structure once the horse is mature and to attempt it usually will make the

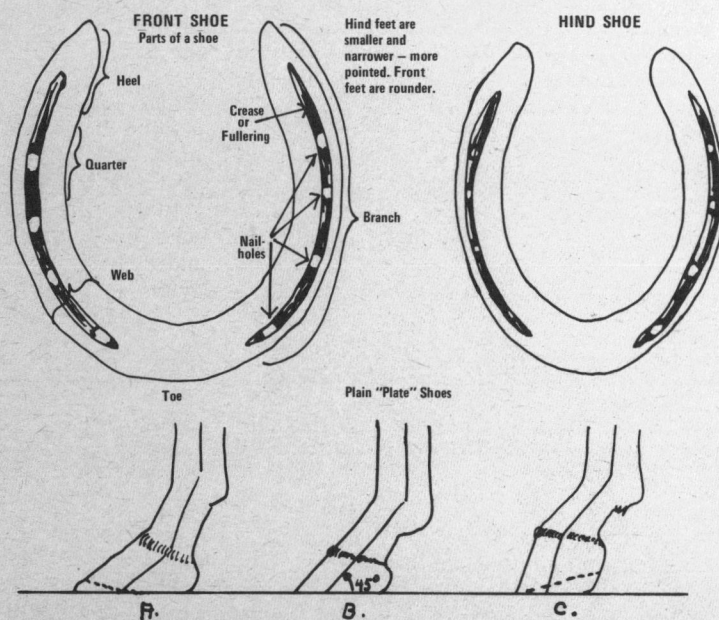

The horseshoe has come a long way since the first attempts using leather, et al. Plates today are of steel or aluminum, which are changed every four to six weeks.

A. Toe too long — foot and pastern angle broken backward. Dotted line shows how foot should be trimmed to straighten the foot angle.
B. Normal, balanced foot.
C. Stumpy foot with heels too long — angle broken forward. Heels and quarters should be trimmed.

75

horse lame and sore, or create problems worse than what you started with.

Faulty gaits in a mature horse cannot be totally corrected because any permanent changes in the conformation of the horse's feet and legs can't be made. But corrective trimming and shoeing can modify the horse's gait and way of going to improve it and perhaps make the horse more functionally agile in his traveling. Remember that this improvement is only temporary — the correction must be repeated with each trimming and shoeing.

Before describing in detail corrective trimming and shoeing, attention should be given to trimming and shoeing the normal foot. One always should have a good knowledge of a horse's feet, legs and gait — and horseshoeing in general — before attempting corrective trimming and shoeing.

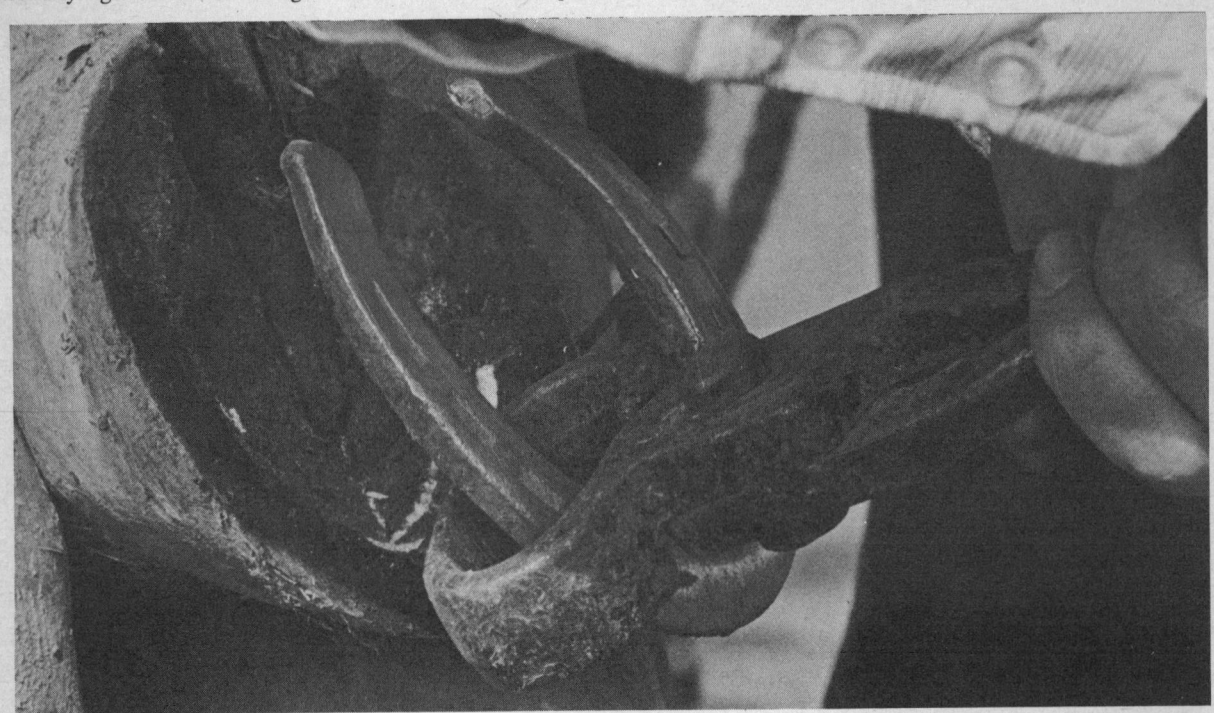

The first step for the farrier is to cut or straighten clinches and remove old shoe (above). A horseowner should not have applied hoof dressing, as this collects dirt on farrier's hands, apron, which isn't needed. With the shoe removed, frog is trimmed and shaped. The excess hoof wall then is nippered away. An owner need not express concern for the safety of his horse; the entire process is painless and farrier knows his job. He won't remove more than necessary.

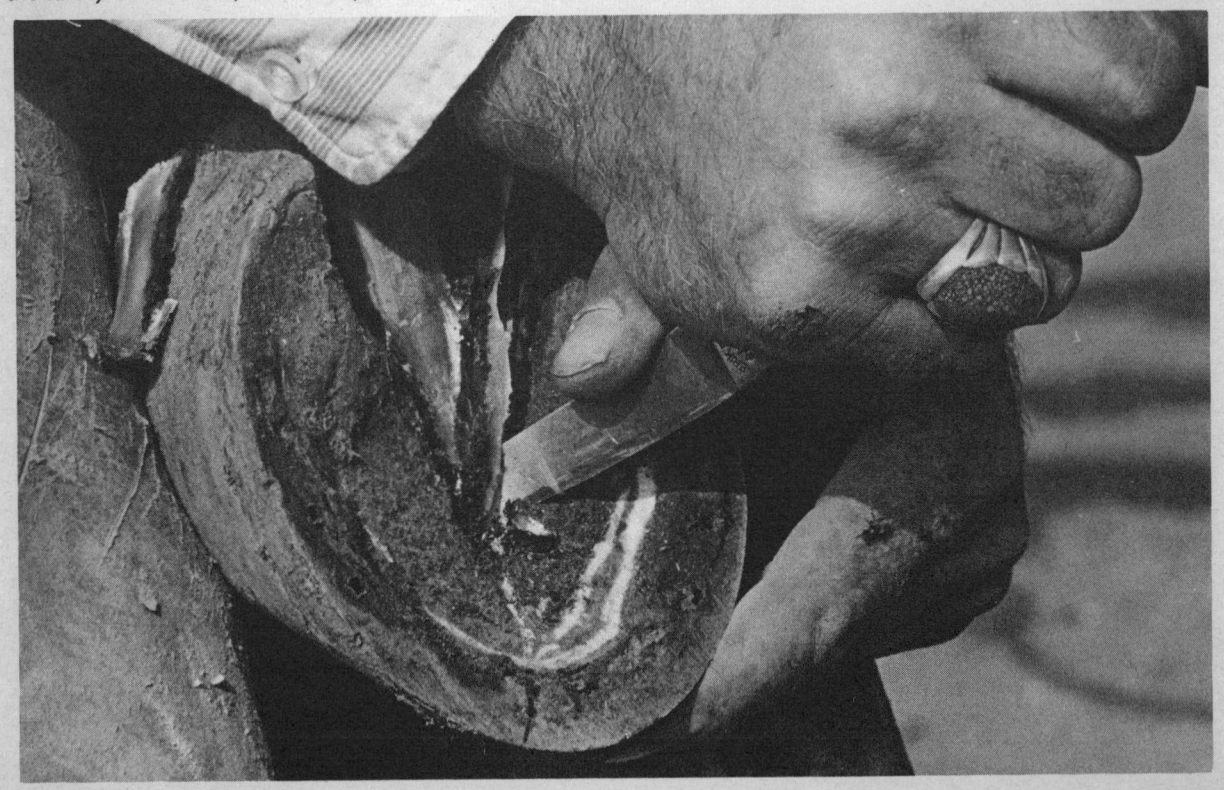

Once trimmed with nippers, hoof bottom is leveled and smoothed with rasp. Too much rasping weakens hoof.

Once the new shoe has been shaped to conform with the horse's foot, it is tacked to the hoof. Horseshoe nails have beveled edges to aid the farrier in identifying placement, as text notes. Nails, after being started, are driven sharply to cause curve.

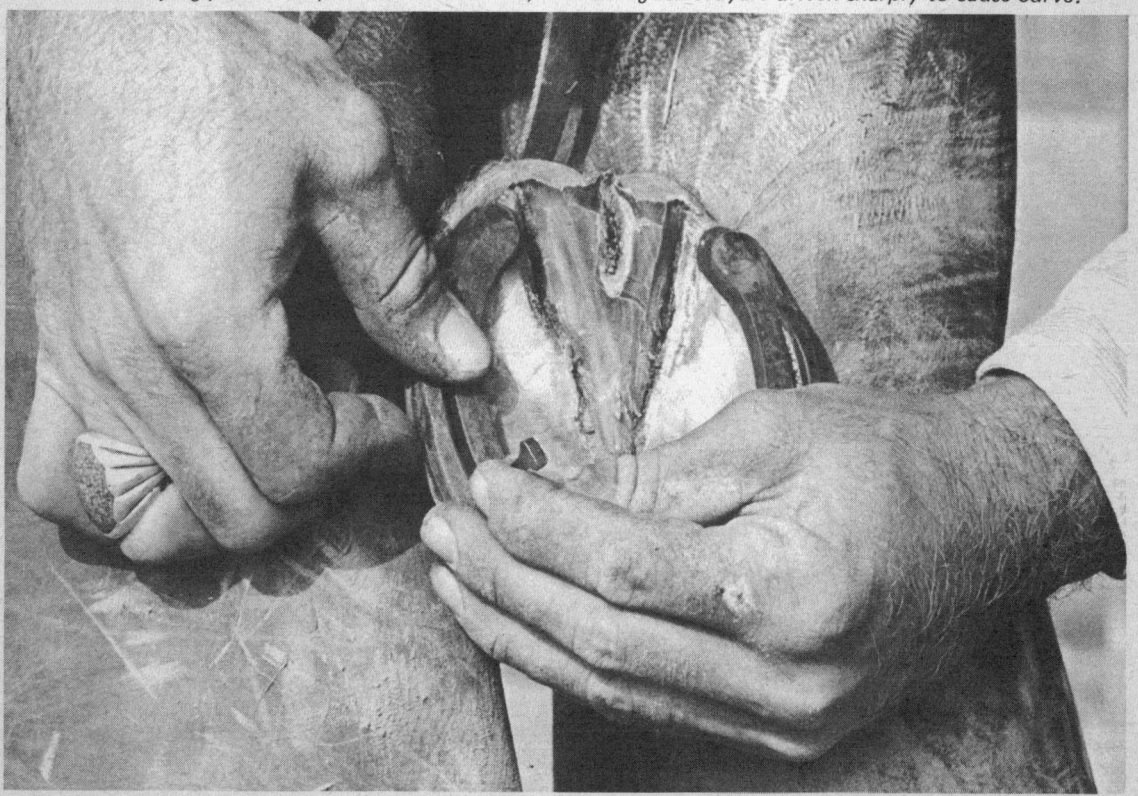

The horse's foot is a unique structure with an outside horny covering which grows continuously and protects the inner parts. In the natural state of running wild, the horse wore down his feet about as fast as they grew, thus his feet never were too long nor worn too short. The true wild horse seems to have been almost free of serious foot problems, but with domestication, confinement and use by man, trouble started. The horse was brought from soft ground and grassy prairies to hard roads; from light exercise to hard work; and from healthy, sanitary grasslands to confined and dirty housing in some cases. Today's domesticated horse sometimes is put in situations where his feet grow too long from lack of exercise, or is worked so regularly and steadily that the feet wear down faster than they grow.

If feet grow too long, they put a strain on the structures of the horse's legs — bones, tendons, ligaments and joints — and make the feet more subject to breaking and splitting. Besides lameness, long feet also can throw feet and legs out of balance by uneven wear on broken hoofs. This can result in strained joints, crooked legs or even a permanently crippled horse. At the other extreme — if feet wear down too far from excessive use, the horse loses the protective, insensitive outer covering, becoming lame and tenderfooted from walking on the sensitive tissues of his feet.

A domestic horse usually does much more traveling than a horse running wild and, unless the horse has unusually tough feet or is always traveling on soft ground like grassy sod, he needs some protection for his feet. Man discovered this fact quite early in his association with horses.

Several thousand years ago, horsemen tried to protect the feet of their horses using everything from socks to sandals attached with straps or thongs. The procedure of nailing iron shoes to the hoof wasn't introduced until about the Second Century B.C., and wasn't a common practice until the end of the Fifth Century A.D.

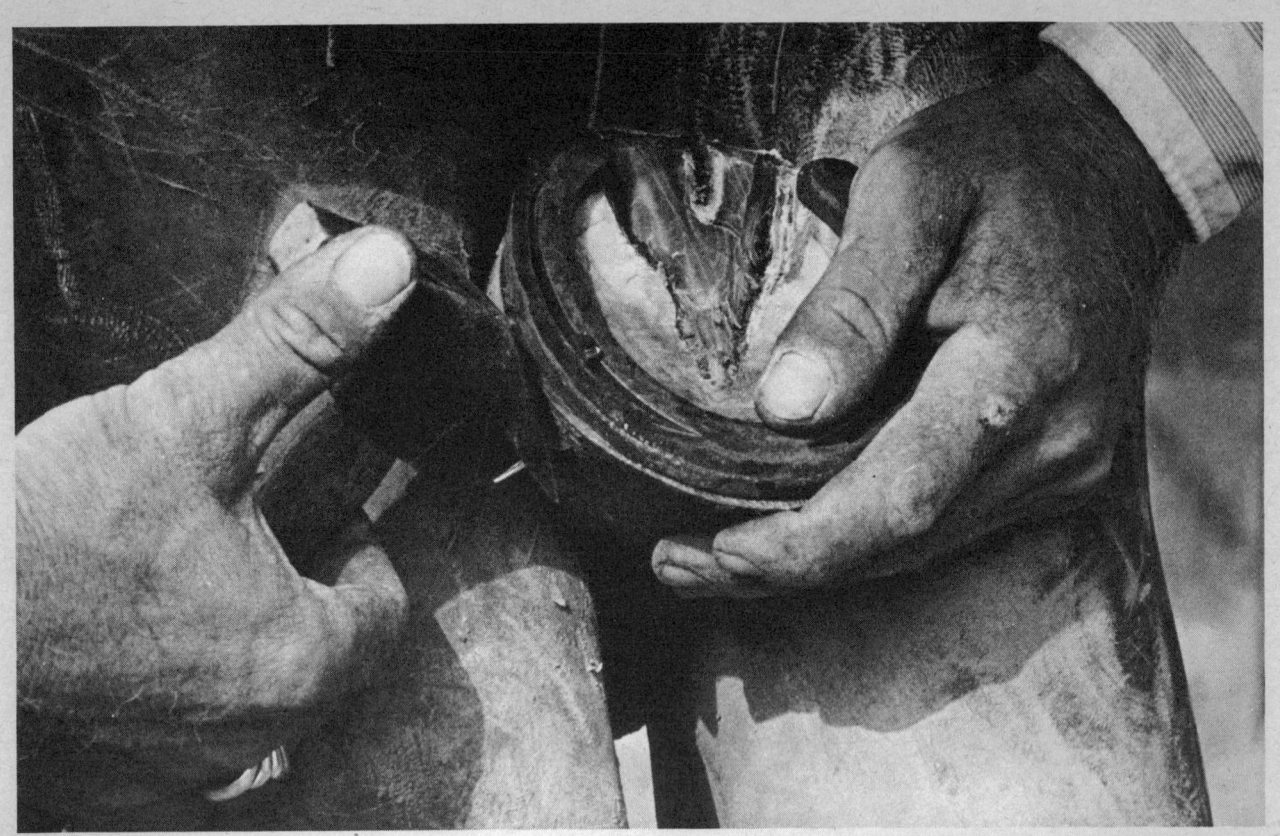

With the nail driven through hoof wall, excess is wrung off close to wall, for obvious reasons (above). The owner should attempt to keep horse calm, avoiding farrier injury. Once tips have been removed, a clinching block is used to tighten the shoe and turn the clinches. All that's left is rasping smooth the rough edges of the nails protruding from the hoof wall.

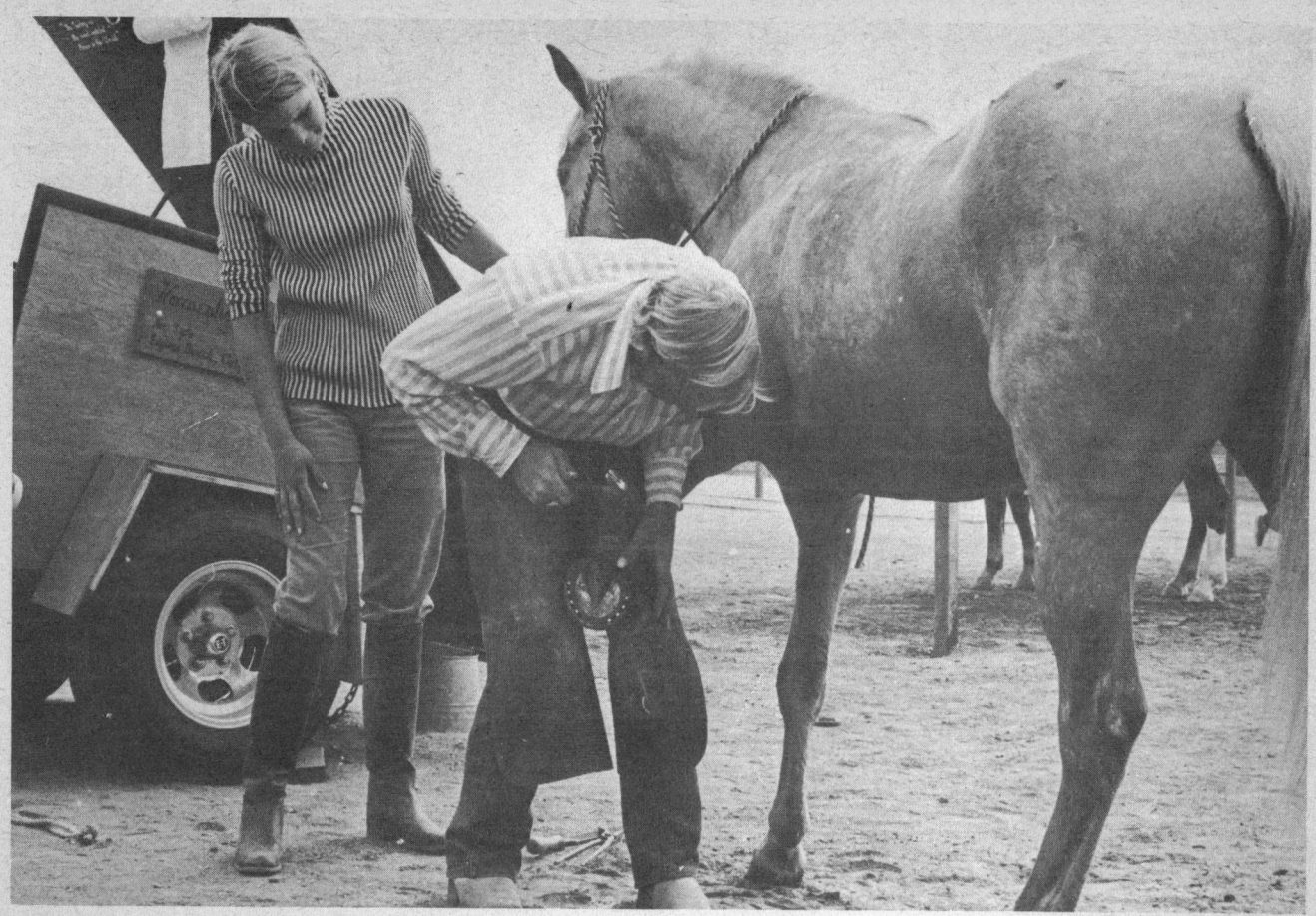

The task of a farrier is simplified greatly by owners cognizant of the problems facing the shoer, and attempting to keep them from happening. A horseowner should remain on the same side as the shoer and focus his attention on the animal, not man.

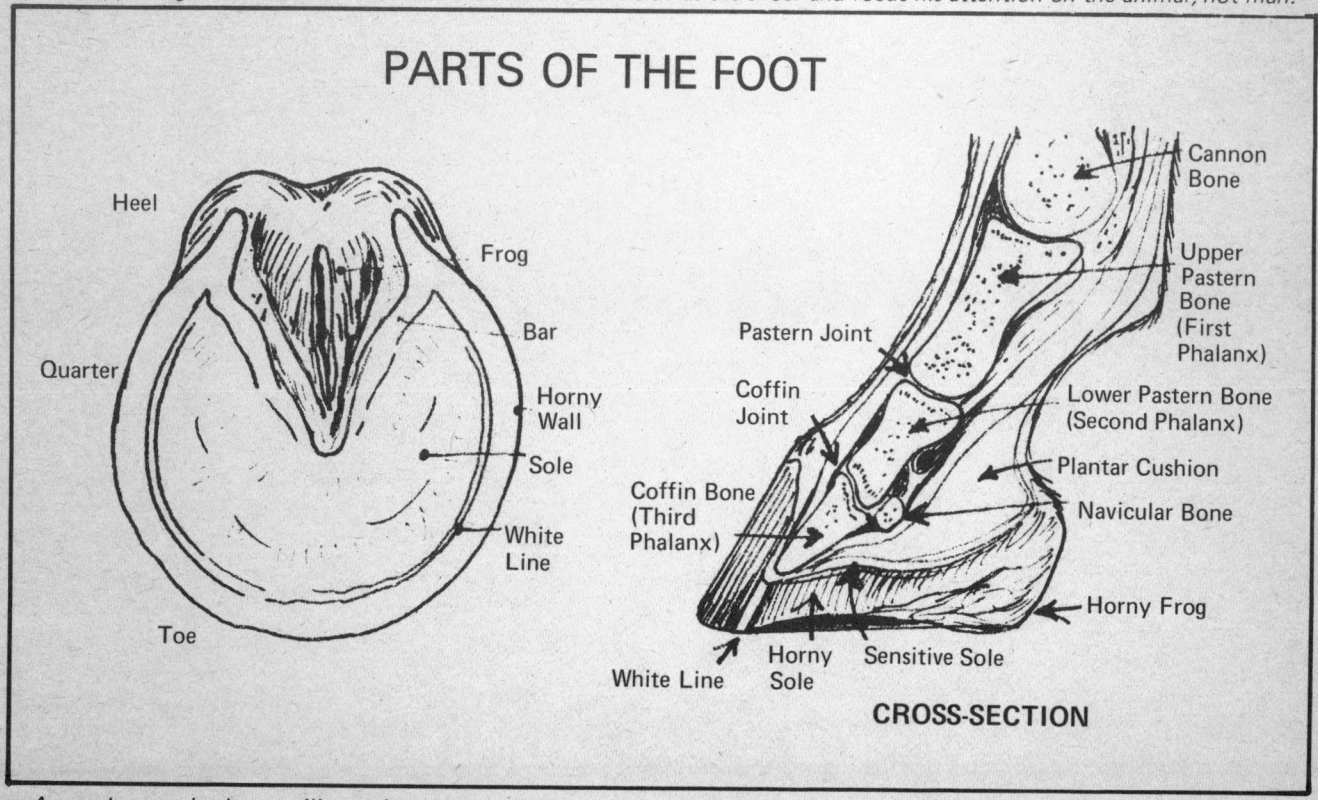

PARTS OF THE FOOT

Heel, Frog, Bar, Quarter, Horny Wall, Sole, White Line, Toe

Cannon Bone, Upper Pastern Bone (First Phalanx), Pastern Joint, Coffin Joint, Lower Pastern Bone (Second Phalanx), Plantar Cushion, Coffin Bone (Third Phalanx), Navicular Bone, Horny Frog, White Line, Horny Sole, Sensitive Sole

CROSS-SECTION

As can be seen in the two illustrations above, the foot of a horse is a complex structure that belies its outward appearance. Aspiring farriers require a sound, knowledge of the hoof's internal components and gaits, and here's a place to start!

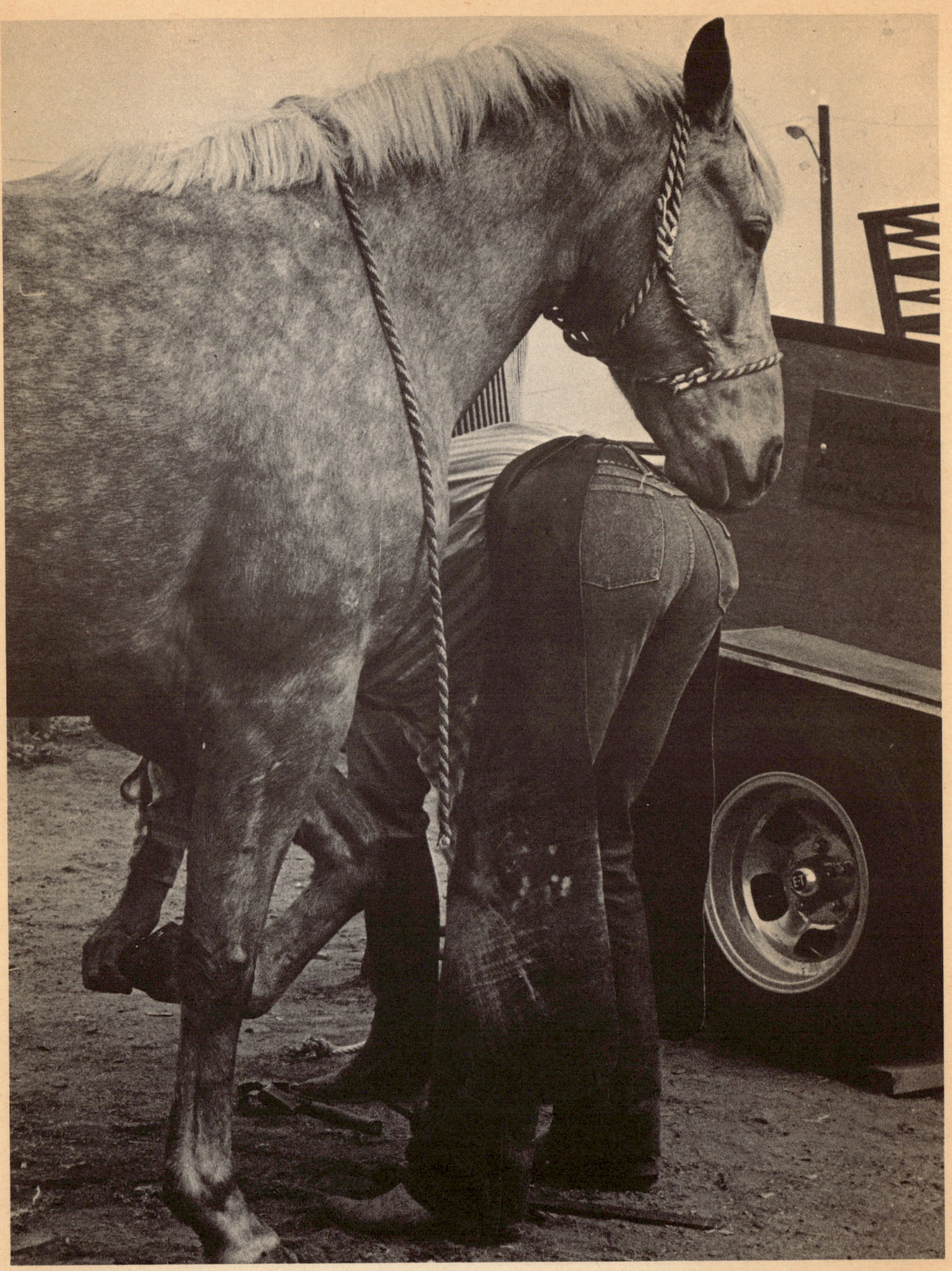

Unfortunately, not all horses faced by the farrier are as docile as this palomino. For this reason, it is imperative that the owner advise the shoer of behavioral quirks that could result in injury. Farriers aren't trainers; don't expect them to be.

WELL-SHOD HOOF

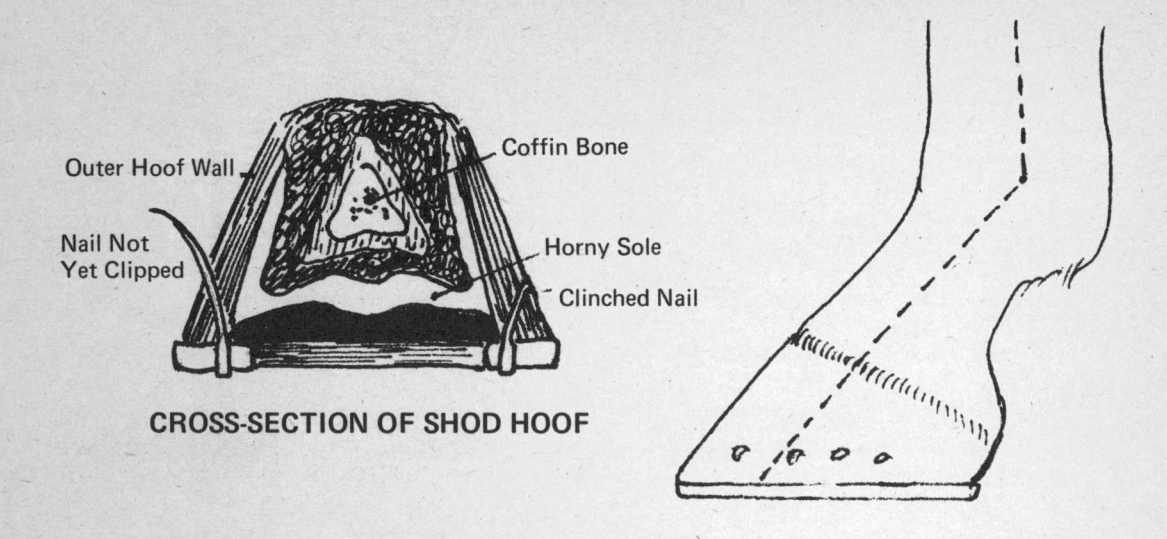

These two views show well-shod hoof the farrier strives for. The angle formed by the slope of the hoof's leading surface is complemented by attention to the bottom of the foot. The cross-section shows nail placement in wall.

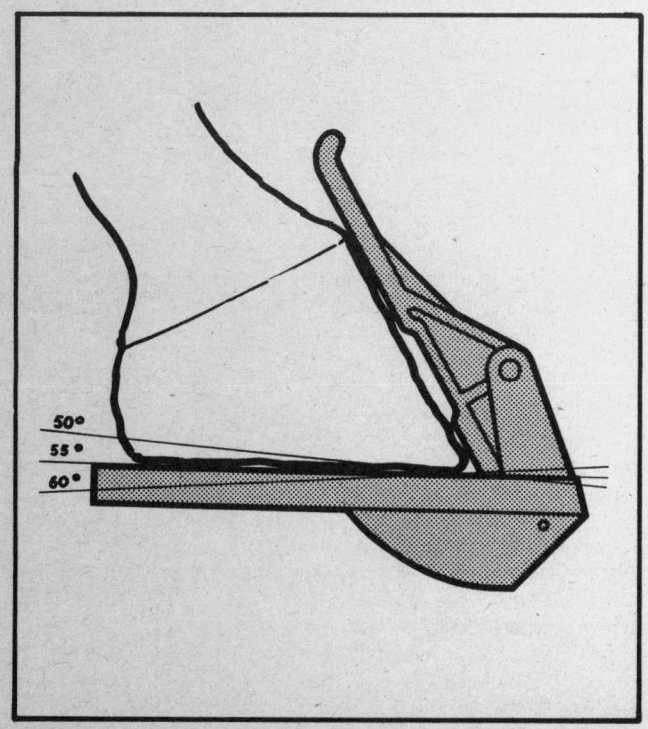

To aid farriers in determining the exact angle formed by bottom and face of hoof is this hoof gauge from Diamond Tool and Horseshoe. Like others on the market, it takes the guesswork out of most important angle determination.

The first step in any shoeing job is to carefully observe the position of the feet and legs when the horse is standing squarely and then observe him in action, at the walk and trot, to see the normal angles of his feet and to tell how he handles his feet — whether there is any paddling, winging or deviation from straightforward movement. Notice the point at which the foot breaks over and leaves the ground — whether the break-over point is at the toe where it should be, or off to one side. Uneven wear of the feet shows that the horse is not traveling straight but is breaking over crookedly and landing on one side of the foot instead of squarely. A horse that travels straight on sound, straight feet and legs will wear down the shoe evenly, with slightly more wear at the center of the toe.

When the horse is standing squarely there should be about a forty-five-degree angle in the slope of the hoof and pastern. Individual horses may vary somewhat from this; some have more sloping hoofs and pasterns, while others are more upright. Trimming never should be too drastic in an attempt to give the feet a perfect angle, because each horse has his own normal angle and radical changes may cause problems.

The foot always should be trimmed so that the pastern and hoof are of the same angle, forming an unbroken line. If you try to make a forty-five-degree angle on a horse that normally has less or more angle than forty-five degrees, you will be working against nature and the way the horse was put together; you'll be straining parts of the horse's legs.

The important thing is to trim the foot so that pastern and hoof are the same angle. If the horse's toes have grown too long, this angle line will be broken, putting strain on

The proper method of picking up a horse's front hoof is shown by noted equestrienne Heather Smith Thomas. In left photo, the right hand is run down the leg to the fetlock, while left hand pushes against the horse's shoulder, causing him to shift his weight off that leg. It then is picked up and cradled between the legs with the shoer's knees. If horse pulls, it comes away.

the legs. If the heel and hind parts of the hoof are too long, the angle line will be broken in the other direction. You will have to study the feet when the horse is standing squarely in order to judge how much hoof to remove to make the foot level at the proper angle. Some farriers use a special protractor to measure hoof angle and this can be helpful.

When you begin trimming the foot, first clean it thoroughly. A hoof pick or the blunt edge of a hoof knife is the best instrument for cleaning the dirt out of the hoof. Never use a sharp or pointed object for this cleaning; you could injure yourself or the horse if he happened to jerk his foot at the wrong time. When all dirt and debris are removed, trim any dead sole tissue with a hoof knife. All loose material should be scraped away, but don't trim much deeper — unless the horse has an abnormal buildup of dead material — for the horse needs this horny sole as protection for the inner tissues of his foot. After the frog is trimmed of loose tags, the outer hoof wall can be trimmed level with the sole, except at the quarters, with hoof cutters.

Trimming should be done from heel to toe or in a complete circle from heel to heel for a smooth, consistent cut. The hoof cutters should be held in such a way that they make a flat, level cut, to make a level seat for the shoe. In order to make a flat surface when trimming the hoof wall you must leave extra wall at the quarters, as the sole at the quarters is concave and slightly lower than at the heel or toe; if you cut this area level with the sole, you will have cut too much away and the wall won't meet the shoe in this place. If the bars need trimming, trim them level with the hoof wall at the heels.

After the excess horn of the foot is removed with hoof cutters, the trimmed hoof wall should be rasped smooth to make a level seat for the shoe. The rasp always should be held flat and level so that one side of the wall is not accidentally made lower than the other.

If the horse is to go barefoot, you should leave about one-fourth-inch of hoof wall projecting below the sole when trimming; don't remove all the extra hoof wall or he soon will become tenderfooted or sole-bruised from walking on the sole.

The outside edges of the wall, for a barefoot horse, should be smoothed and rounded with the rasp — leaving a sharp edge will make the hoof prone to split, crack or chip away. Rounding the edges also prevents injury to other horses in his pasture; wounds on lower legs can result from being stepped on or by running into the sharp snags of other horses' untrimmed hoofs.

If the horse is to be shod, trim the hoof wall level with the sole at the toe and as low as necessary at the heel to establish the proper foot angle. The shoe should be shaped to fit the foot, not vice versa, unless for the purpose of correction of some defect in gait. The shoe should fit evenly on the foot — the bottom of the hoof wall should rest flat down against the shoe. The heels of the shoe should not stick out excessively beyond the heel of the foot, especially on the front feet, or the horse may step on his front shoes when he travels. The shoe should fit the foot so that the outer edge of the shoe closely follows the outline of the trimmed hoof at the toe and around to the quarters. But at the quarters and heels the shoe should always be slightly wider than the hoof — except, again, in some instances of corrective shoeing for interference — and should extend slightly beyond the heels of the horse.

The heels and quarters of the horse's foot must rest on the shoe and have a little extra shoe width to allow for hoof expansion when weight is placed on the foot. If the shoe is too short or doesn't properly fit at the quarters and heel, it may cut into the foot as the hoof wall grows (the hoof may grow down around the outside of the shoe) or cause corns or other lameness. If the shoe is too narrow and short, the hoof tends to expand out over the shoe when weight is placed on it and the narrow shoe limits proper hoof expansion.

The shoe should be properly centered on the foot. For horses with good conformation and normal feet, the shoe can be centered by using the point of the frog as a guide, the frog dividing the bottom of the hoof into equal halves and pointing toward the toe. But in horses that are pigeon-toed or splay-footed, the frog usually points offcenter and cannot be used as a guide.

If a hoof is worn excessively on one side because of poor conformation or faulty gait, or if part of the hoof wall has been chipped, cracked or broken away, it might be impossible to make the foot level by trimming unless too much is removed on the opposite side. If one side of the foot is broken or exceptionally low, the branch of the shoe on the worn side can be shimmed with leather so that the foot will be level when the shoe is on.

When the shoe has been shaped properly to fit the trimmed foot, nails can be driven. Nails should be of the proper size for the hoof and the shoe, having heads that protrude slightly after they are driven. A nailhead that sinks too deeply into the crease of the shoe is too small and won't hold properly; the shoe may eventually work loose.

The nails should enter the hoof at the white line, the

Hind feet are held diagonally across the farrier's knees instead of between the legs. Should the horse pull on the leg, it is freed without damage to farrier's inside thigh.

The ball peen hammer and anivl still are the stock-in-trade of a farrier. Roger Erichsen shapes a new shoe.

area where the hoof wall and sole unite. In nailing on the shoe, hold the nail with thumb and index finger, resting your hand on the shoe to keep it in the proper position as you drive the nail. The location of the first nail doesn't matter greatly, as long as the shoe is properly centered and stays in position during the nailing. After the first two nails are driven, one on each side of the shoe, it will stay in place for the remaining nails.

Horseshoe nails are made with both straight and beveled sides so they will curve when driven. The beveled side of the nail point always should be toward the inside of the foot so that the nail will be directed outward as it is driven. The beveled side can easily be determined by the rough side of the nailhead; the bevel and rough side both are on the inside of the nail, thus the rule for horseshoe nails: Rough side inside. The rough edge being on one side, it's easy to tell which way to set the nail by feeling the head.

The nail should be held straight and aimed at the spot where it should emerge from the hoof wall. The nail should come out about three-quarters of an inch above the shoe, or about one-third or less of the way up the hoof wall. The actual distance will depend, of course, on size of the horse. A draft horse has much bigger feet than an Arabian, for instance; larger nails will be used in his shoes and the nails will come out higher in the hoof wall.

If a nail comes out too high or low, it should be pulled and redriven. If the nail is bent, use a new one. A high nail may press on the sensitive tissues inside the foot and make the horse lame. A low nail may break out of the hoof, not holding the shoe. Nails driven to a uniform height give the shod hoof a pleasing appearance, but if the nails come out somewhere near the proper position it is best to leave them; a nail pulled and redriven may weaken the hoof wall with the second perforation and eventually cause the shoe to loosen.

Because the foot — especially at the heel — should expand when weight is placed on it, nails never are driven into the hoof too far to the rear. The last nailhole of the shoe shouldn't be farther back than the bend of the quarter, or expansion of the hoof at the heel and quarters will be greatly limited.

Nails should be driven in the same direction as the hoof fibers, parallel with them, to minimize the cutting of these fibers and resultant weakening of the hoof wall. The fibers of the hoof grow parallel to each other and perpendicular to the coronary band. The driven nails should go into the outer portion of the hoof wall, never inside the white line that separates the wall from the sole, or they will puncture the sensitive part of the hoof.

A high nail is more apt to prick sensitive tissues or put pressure on them if it bends inward inside the hoof. If a horse ever flinches during the driving of a nail, the sensitive tissues may have been pricked or punctured. If this ever happens, the nail should be pulled out and iodine poured into the nail hole to prevent infection.

If you use light hammer taps when driving the nail, the point of the nail will travel parallel to the horny fibers of the hoof wall and won't sever them. Use light taps until the nail is about two-thirds the required distance, then strike one sharp blow to force the nail through the wall and finish its journey. The bevel on the nail point makes it curve outward and curves most when the nail is driven sharply and rapidly through the horny fibers.

Once a nail is driven and the head sunk into the shoe crease, twist off the sharp point with the hammer claws or cut off the end with nail cutters. The sharp nail tips should be cut off immediately: if the horse moves or tries to pull his foot away, the sharp tip could cut your leg. Keep track of those nail tips and discard them properly, so they won't cause a flat tire.

After all the nails have been driven and the tips cut off close to the hoof wall, cut a small notch underneath with the rasp. This notch will help keep the hoof wall from splitting when the nail end is turned over and clinched, and also will provide a place for the clinch. The nail end, when clinched, will be sunk into this little notch and leaves a smooth surface on the hoof wall. A clinch that is short and fairly well sunk into the hoof wall isn't apt to get knocked loose when the horse travels through rocks.

To clinch the nails, pound each nailhead tightly into the shoe crease while holding a piece of iron against the tip end, which bends the tip over into the notch you cut as it comes farther out of the hoof wall. Nails should be clinched alternately from one side to the other (two toe nails first, or the two heel nails, then working back or forward), rather than clinching all the nails on one side before nails on the other. Clinching alternately from one side to the other gives a more uniform seating of the shoe.

Nails should be clinched firmly, but not so tightly that the horse's foot becomes sore and nail-bound. If you clinch the nails too tightly, the horse may be lame for several days. Finish the clinch by bending the nails with the hammer, pounding the tips flat against the hoof wall into the notch cut. A short clinch holds better than a long one and looks nicer. A long clinch can be knocked and unbent in rocks or rough country and will work loose faster.

Nails always should take a short, thick hold on the hoof wall and should not be too high. Thus, they damage the least amount of hoof horn and the old nail holes can be removed with the natural growth of the hoof the next time the horse is shod. This is especially important if the horse is used steadily and will be wearing shoes out regularly, as when he is used as a ranch horse, in mountainous terrain, in training for endurance rides, etc. If the horse must be shod often, you'll want room in the hoof wall for the new nails for each succeeding set of shoes.

With the rasp, smooth the outside edge of the hoof where it meets the shoe, but be careful not to rasp the hoof wall too much. This horny wall is made up of tiny tubes — the horn fibers — and excessive rasping cuts and leaves them open, letting the hoof dry out. If the shoe was properly fitted and nailed on with no slipping, little or no rasping will be needed to smooth the hoof wall to the shoe.

After the horse is shod, have someone lead him for you at both the walk and the trot so you can observe the new shoes and the horse's feet in action, to determine if the shoes are set properly, aiding and not hindering his gait, and to be sure the horse is not lame or "ouchy" in any way from the shoes.

Shoes should always be as light as possible, taking into consideration the wear demanded of them, to interfere as little as possible with the normal flight of the horse's foot. The ground surface of the shoe is best plain, unless the horse needs extra traction. A plain plate will hinder and interfere least with his way of going. Toe and heel calks are not necessary, except for horses traveling in rocky or steep terrain, on ice, for draft horses that need extra traction for pulling, or for other special conditions when a certain amount and kind of traction is needed. Calks also are used on some corrective shoes in certain situations.

If a horse is used often and wears out many shoes, a hard-surfaced material like borium can be welded to the wearing surface of the shoe to make it last longer. Borium is the trade name for a material that comes as a steel tube impregnated with crystals of tungsten carbide that are very sharp and nearly as hard as diamonds. When this material is welded to an ordinary horseshoe, the steel melts and forms a bond with the shoe, while the tungsten carbide crystals retain their sharp edges. The rough surface that results will give good traction on rocks, concrete, ice, frozen ground, etc., and, with spots of borium added to toe and heels, may last many times longer than an ordinary shoe. This borium shoe will have to be reset periodically to allow for the growth of the horse's feet, but it will not wear out before the horse needs a reset, as some ordinary horseshoes do when a horse is used often.

Borium also can be added to shoes for a corrective effect, reinforcing wear points where a horse breaks over incorrectly and wears away the shoe on one side. Because the borium does not wear away, the shoe retains its original shape and keeps its corrective effect longer, helping the horse break-over more toward the center of the toe.

A horse's feet should be trimmed, or shoes reset or replaced every four to six weeks, depending on the individual horse's rate of hoof growth and the amount of wear on the feet if he is barefoot. A barefoot horse that gets some wear on his feet may not need to be trimmed this often.

All too often, shoes are left on a horse too long. Some people actually leave a horse's shoes on until they fall off of their own accord! A horse whose feet have grown too long because his shoes were left on may suffer leg wounds from striking himself with his long hoofs, strained legs, contracted feet, corns, or the like. Since the hoof wall grows perpendicular to the coronary band, the horse's base of support actually grows out from under him if his shoes are left on too long.

The farrier's tools are largely unchanged; they fit the bill, so why bother? Nippers, shown trimming away excess hoof wall, have been around for many decades.

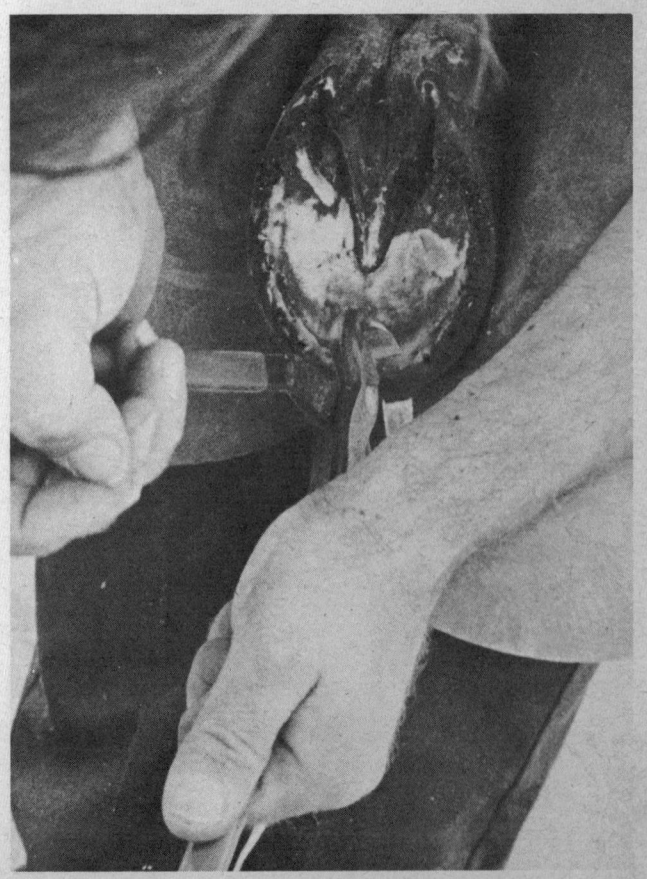

To remove a horseshoe, cut the clinched nails on the hoof wall with a clinch cutter or unbend them with old hoof nippers, then pick up the foot and use pulling pincers or old hoof nippers to pull the shoe. It is better to pull the shoe nail by nail than simply cut the nails, for cutting leaves nail pieces in the horse's hoof which will have to be removed after the shoe is off. Pulling nail pieces out is not easy and is more likely to break or crack the horse's hoof than removing the shoe properly with pulling pincers.

The pincers should be placed under the shoe, starting at one heel branch. Close the handle and push away from yourself to loosen the heel branch, pushing slightly toward the middle line of the foot. After that heel is loosened, the opposite heel should be. Each nail can be removed individually as it is loosened. As you pull the shoe, hold the foot securely and never twist the pincers or pull crookedly, and you will not injure the fetlock joint. Continue working down both branches alternately until the entire shoe is loosened.

This is the goal of every farrier: a well-shod hoof. If there are doubts about the ability of your shoer, bring in another who will give honest testimony about job done.

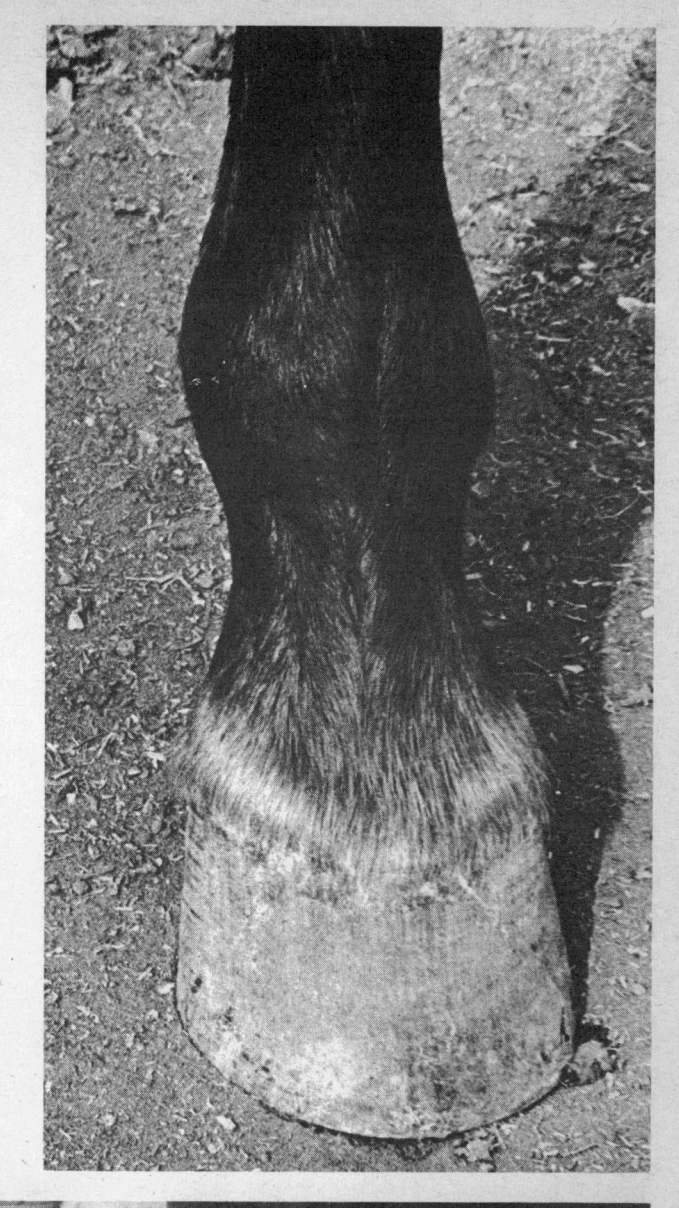

Shoeing a horse is not a casual task to be undertaken lightly by individual horsemen. It takes know-how in determining the proper amount of frog to pare away (below) and amount to be removed with a rasp. Unless you plan to do it right, don't bother. Leave feet alone.

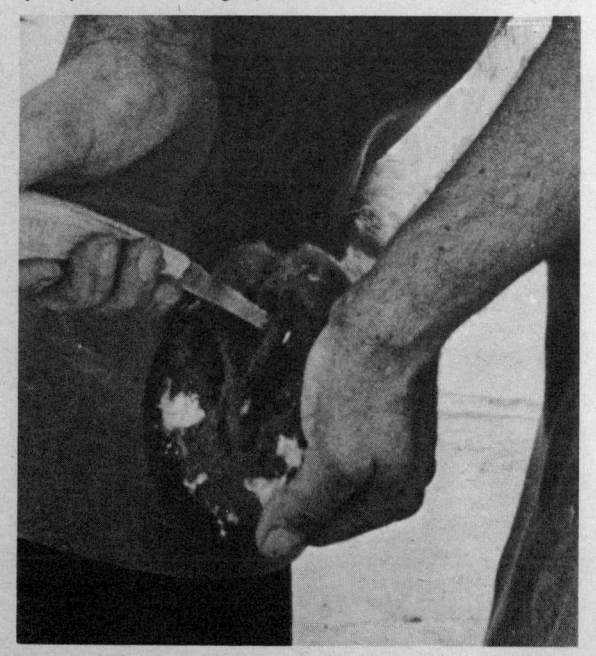

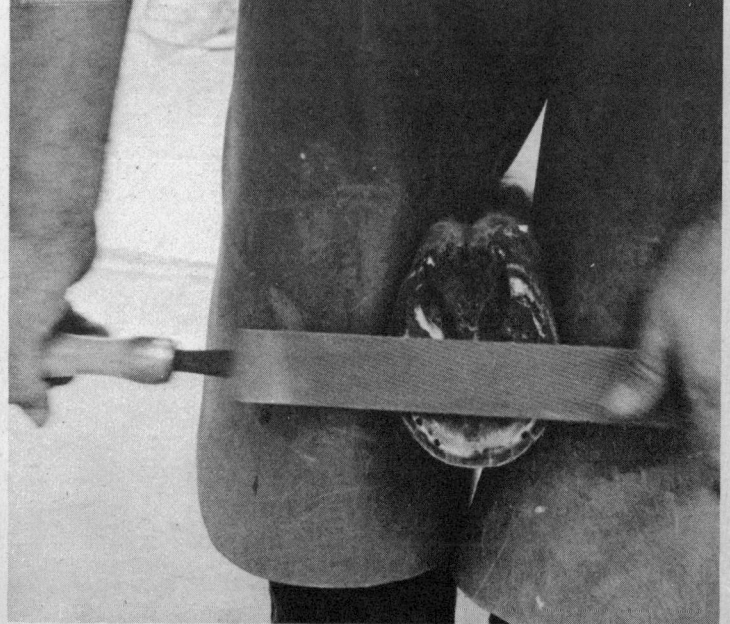

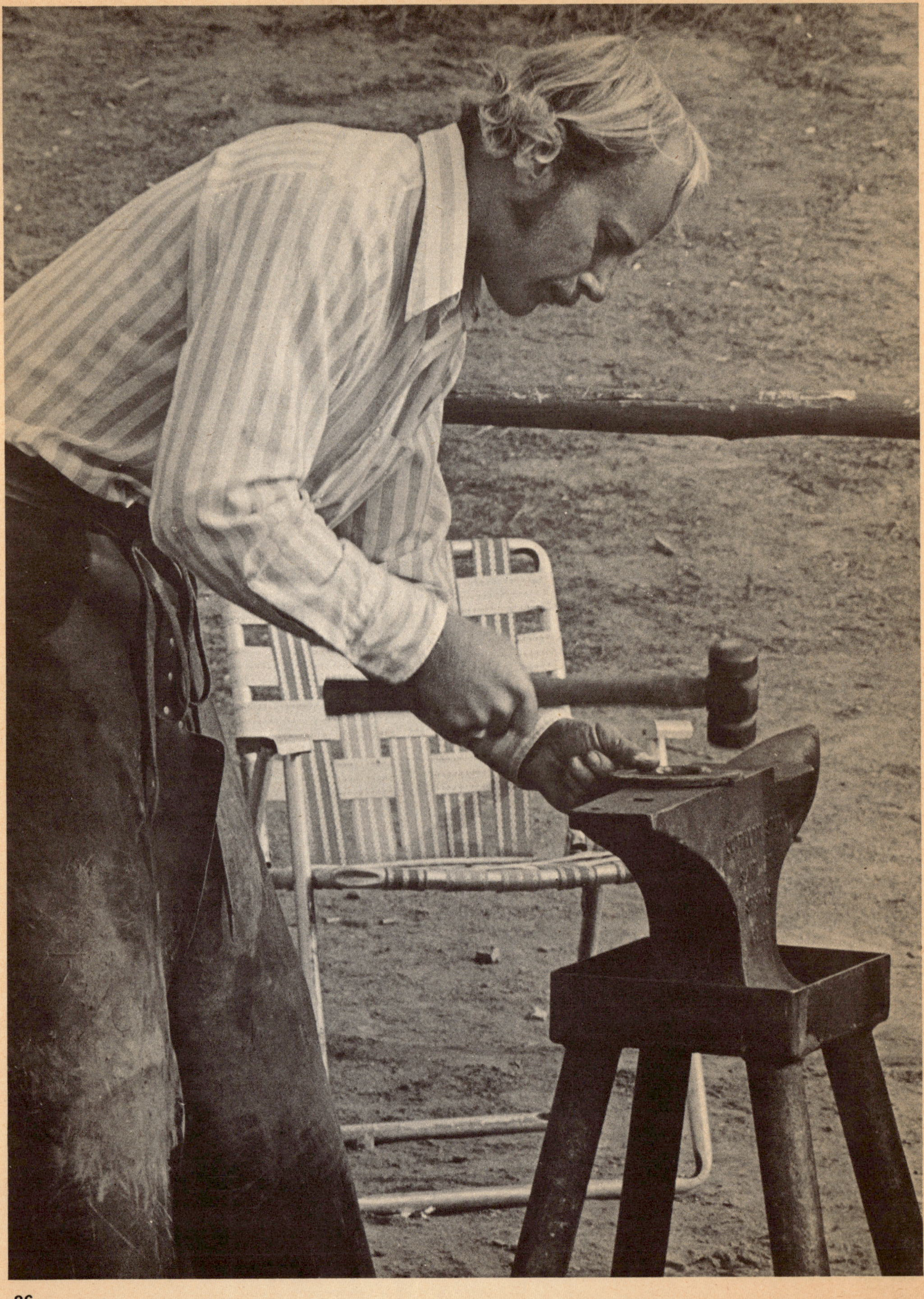

CHAPTER 10

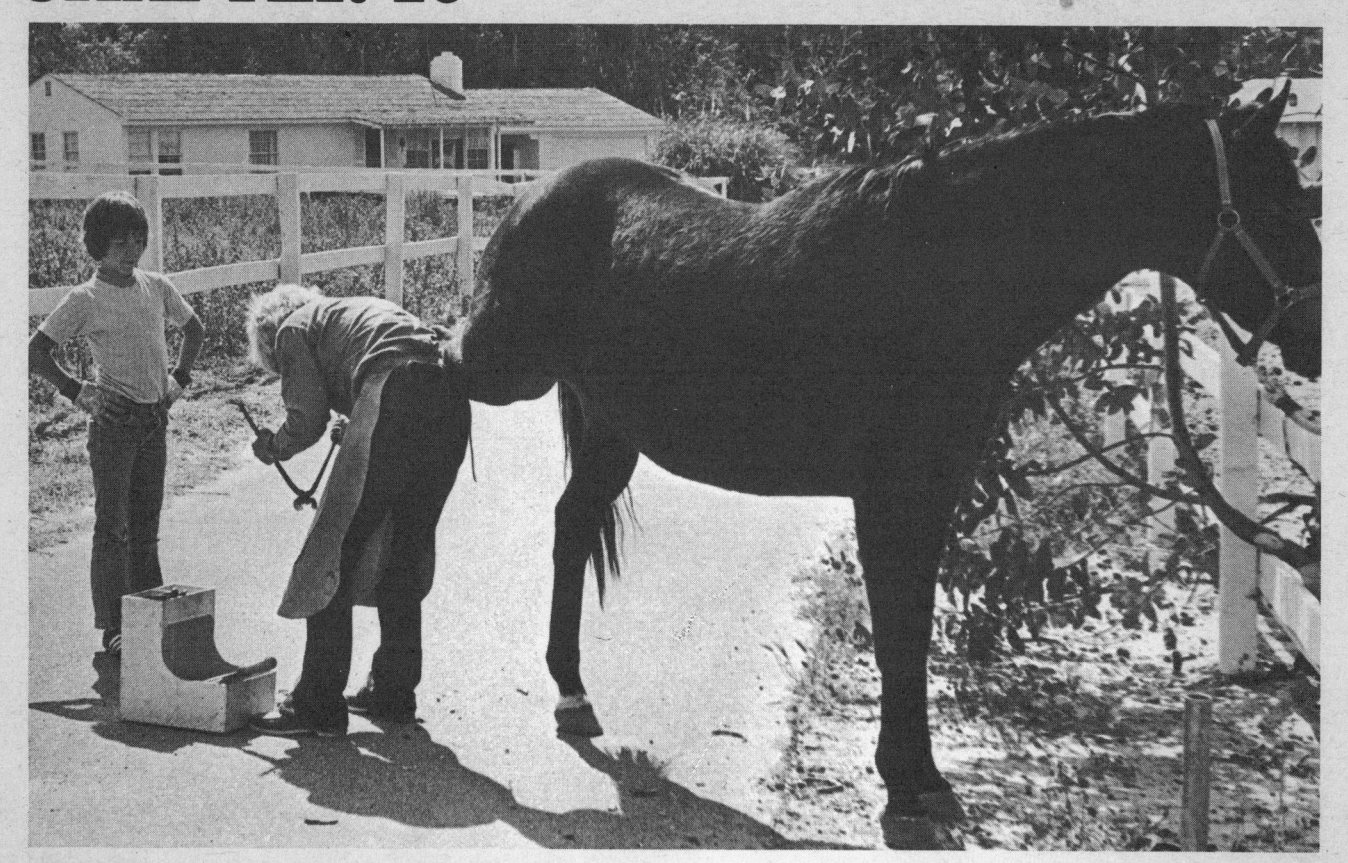

CORRECTIVE TRIMMING AND SHOEING

See What The Experienced — And Only The Experienced — Farrier Can Do To Alleviate Or Minimize Foot Problems

Corrective shoeing is done to improve or correct faults in the horse's gait that result from inherited conformation faults or injury, and also to relieve pain and encourage healing of certain diseases or injuries to the legs and feet.

There are many kinds of shoes used to correct foot problems in a horse. These new shoes can be made by a farrier or by welding additional pieces to, or cutting from, an ordinary horseshoe.

Many corrective shoes were designed in the days of the draft horse and were useful because they transformed a serious lameness into a mild lameness, allowing a horse still to be useful for work. But for today's horse, used under saddle, even a slight lameness or foot problem is too much. A shoe that reduces lameness isn't good enough, because the horse only is improved, not cured. Thus, a great number of the special shoes used in the past aren't satisfactory today.

A basic concept of horseshoeing is that weight in the form of horseshoes always reduces speed and decreases agility, no matter how it is added to the foot. Corrective shoes always should be as light as possible. The normal flight of the foot is a straightforward line. Any deviation from normal flight takes the form of an arc, either to the outside or the inside.

Adding weight through horseshoes will increase the arc because of the additional centrifugal force. Consequently, ordinary shoeing often will accentuate or increase a horse's defect in gait, the reason many horses overreach or interfere

87

only when shod. A horse that interferes — strikes one front limb against the other, or one hind limb against the other — or forges — strike a front foot with a hind foot — will do so even worse when shod. The added weight of the shoes makes his strides longer and arcs of foot-flight more pronounced.

Therefore, he must be correctively shod when he wears shoes, to prevent these problems if possible.

When attempting to correct a faulty gait, one must try to balance the foot both on the ground and during its flight through the air, producing a straighter way of going. One must fully understand the structures of a horse's feet and legs, and how a horse moves. Every horse must be considered individually when determining how best to correct his way of traveling, for no two horses move exactly alike. Though several may have the same fault or similar conformation that suggests a certain type of correction, it may require different shoeing methods to correct them.

A horse may indicate he needs one type of shoe when actually another will be better. For example, a horse that stands splay-footed, toes-out, usually will land on the inside of the hoof when he travels, wearing down the inside wall more than the outside. Occasionally, though, a horse will be splay-footed yet do just the opposite, wearing down the outside wall. One must study the horse carefully while standing and traveling to determine his way of going and shoe required.

After trying a corrective shoe, carefully observe the horse's movement again for improvement. Sometimes two or three methods must be tried before the best is found.

As a general rule, always try the least drastic method first, using a correction that will alter a horse's foot least. If this won't correct the gait enough to solve the horse's problems, more drastic methods may be needed. But remember: drastic changes can cause other problems.

Most horses need corrective trimming and shoeing to some degree because of faulty conformation. Few horses are blessed with perfectly straight feet and legs. Because of this, the hoofs wear unevenly. Since the foot is worn unevenly, it tends to grow unevenly and the problem can only get worse. The misshapen foot will continue forcing the horse's leg out of line even more, aggravating the problem.

When trimming uneven feet, the main objective is merely to trim away the areas that have grown too long due to uneven wear. The idea is to trim the foot more nearly level, so the horse will both pick it up and put it down straighter.

If the horse toes-in — pigeon-toed — the outside walls of his feet usually are worn down too much. When trimming, take off the excess hoof on the inside wall, from toe to heel, to help level the foot. Horses that toe-in or out usually don't break-over the center of the foot when it's picked up, but break-over to one side, causing more wear.

To help a horse pick his feet up straight, the toe can be squared somewhat, making the horse break-over the center.

If one side is flared out, he probably has a conformation fault in the leg, putting uneven distribution of weight on the foot as he travels. The cause may only be minor but the problem gets worse in time, making a weak hoof wall which breaks easily. By trimming and rasping the flared side of the hoof wall, one can help the foot regain its normal shape over a period of time.

Other problems can be helped by corrective trimming and shoeing. Consider the horse that toes-out, called splay-footed. In serious cases, the horse strikes himself as he travels because the foot swings inward as it flies through the air.

When a horse toes-out, his foot is not level because he wears down the inside wall. The foot breaks over the inside of the toe and lands on the inside toe and wall after an inward arc through the air. These feet should have the outside wall trimmed to help level the foot. If to be shod, special shoes can be used to help level the foot properly, made from ordinary shoes by cutting or welding additional pieces of iron to them.

If the foot is worn down exceptionally, a piece of leather can be used on that side between shoe and foot to level it.

Several corrective shoes can help a splay-footed horse. The purpose of them all is two-fold: to raise the inside wall to where the foot is more level, and to make the foot break-over the center of the toe.

A half-rim shoe has a rim on the outside edge of the side which will go on the inside wall of the foot. When this shoe is on the horse's foot, placed upon the ground, the shoe raises the inside of the foot. This interferes with the foot's breaking over the inside of the toe, forcing it to break-over more at the center.

A half-rim can be made from an ordinary shoe by welding a small rod to the edge of the shoe, from heel to the toe nailhole. A shoe of this type also can be used on a pigeon-toed horse, in the opposite manner, to raise the outside wall. This shoe is used to raise the low side of the foot and helps the horse break-over at the center.

Another shoe that can be used either for splay-footed or pigeon-toed horses has high inside rims and an open toe. This shoe is made by welding a rod about one-quarter-inch in diameter to the inside of the branches, leaving the toe

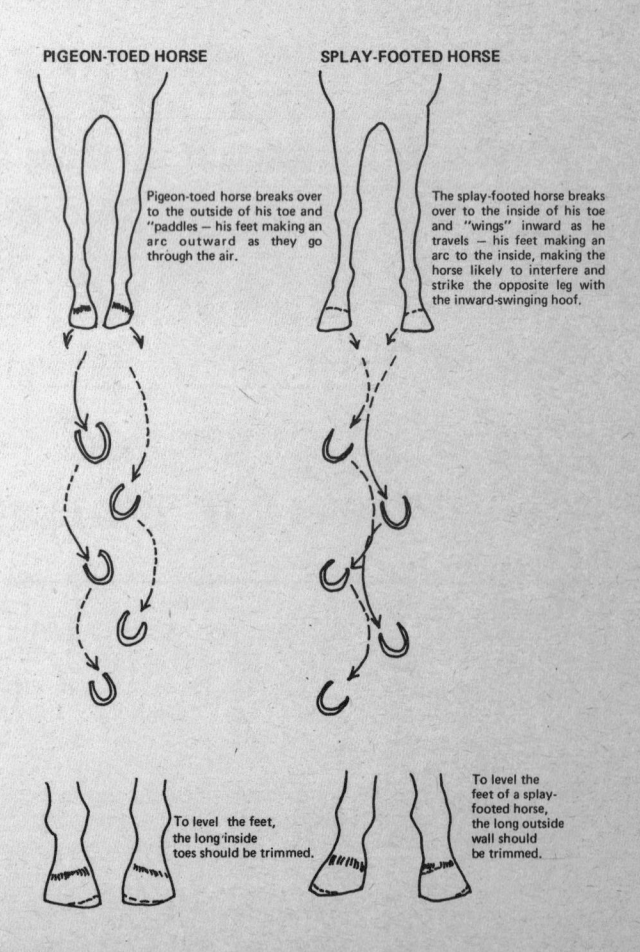

PIGEON-TOED HORSE — Pigeon-toed horse breaks over to the outside of his toe and "paddles" — his feet making an arc outward as they go through the air.

SPLAY-FOOTED HORSE — The splay-footed horse breaks over to the inside of his toe and "wings" inward as he travels — his feet making an arc to the inside, making the horse likely to interfere and strike the opposite leg with the inward-swinging hoof.

To level the feet, the long inside toes should be trimmed.

To level the feet of a splay-footed horse, the long outside wall should be trimmed.

On page 87, C.J. "Calamity Jane" Desrosiers, one of the few female farriers, shows proper hold for working on hind. Right: Gaits correctable with trimming and shoeing are pigeon-toed and splay-footed.

Side view of rocker-toe shoe, permitting easy and rapid break-over at the toe. The hoof at the toe must be dubbed and cut away to fit this shoe.

Rolled toe. Enables the horse to break-over easily at the toe.

Full roller motion shoe. The entire outside edge is ground away and smoothed to make break-over easier in any direction.

CORRECTIVE SHOES

Half-Rim Shoe (the rim on one side aids in leveling an uneven foot and helps the horse break-over center of toe)

High Inside Rims and Open Toe — Helps horse break-over center of toe

Calks (open toe) can also help force break-over at the center of the toe. Calks are about ½-inch high

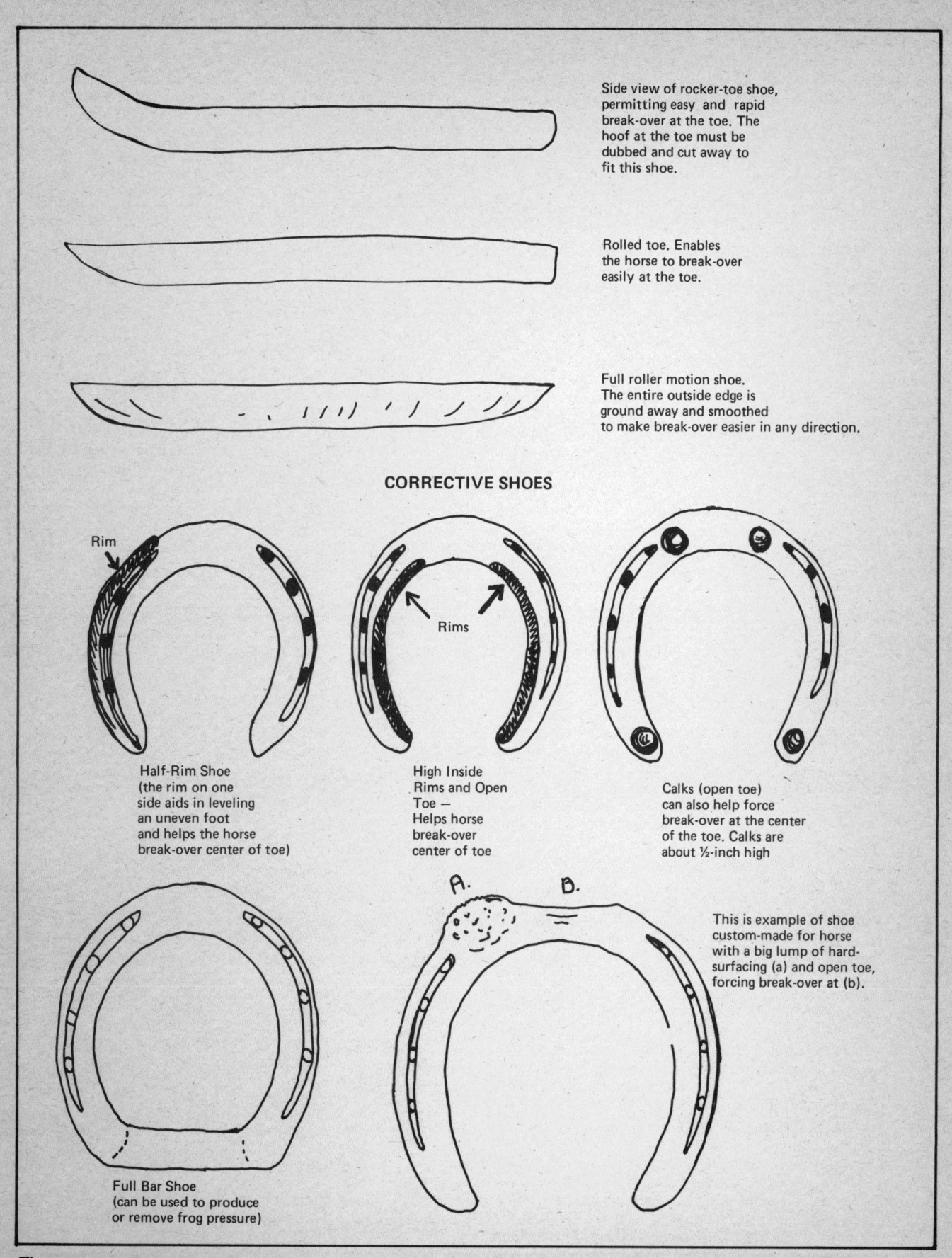

Full Bar Shoe (can be used to produce or remove frog pressure)

This is example of shoe custom-made for horse with a big lump of hard-surfacing (a) and open toe, forcing break-over at (b).

These are several examples of corrective shoes most frequently used by the skilled farrier. As noted in text, make all corrections gradually and employ the least severe first. More hoof can be removed if needed, but there's trouble if too much is removed initially. Corrective trimming and shoeing won't cure the gait defect, but it can restore usefulness.

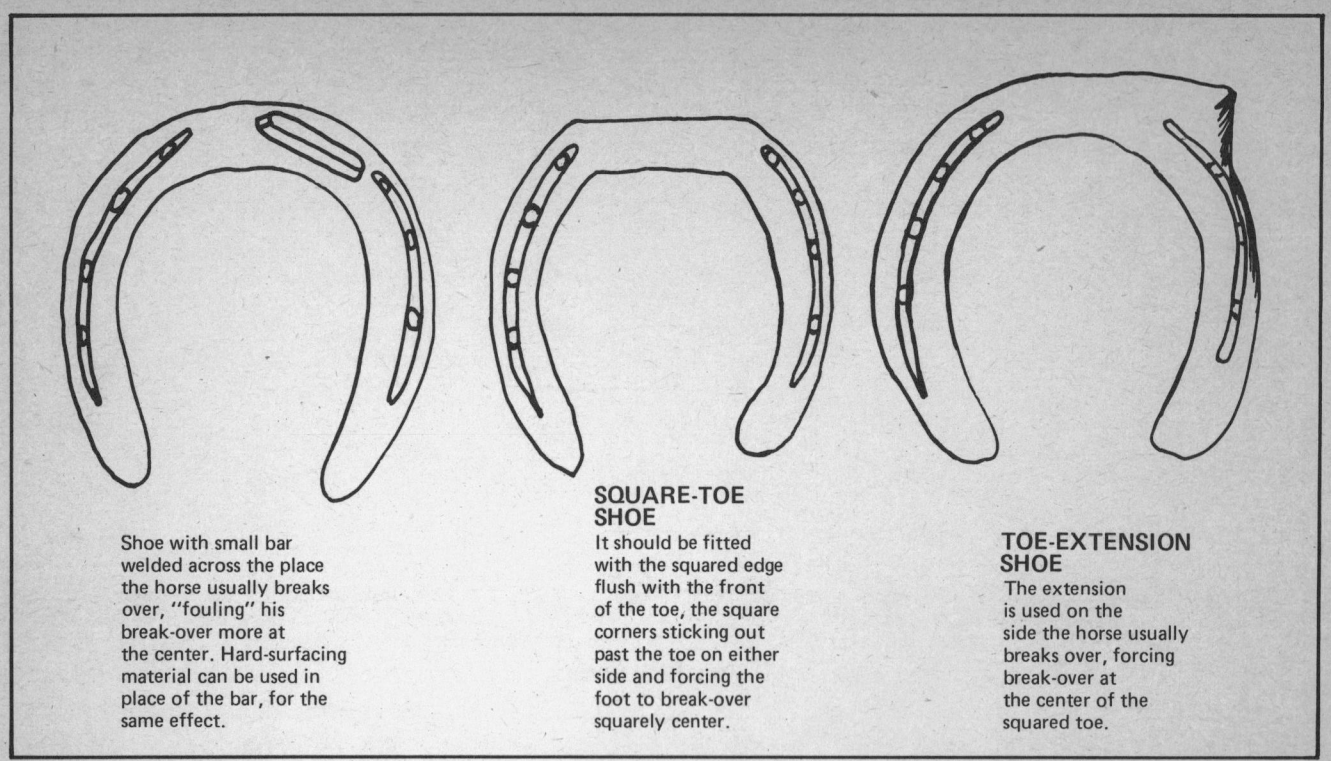

SQUARE-TOE SHOE
It should be fitted with the squared edge flush with the front of the toe, the square corners sticking out past the toe on either side and forcing the foot to break-over squarely center.

Shoe with small bar welded across the place the horse usually breaks over, "fouling" his break-over more at the center. Hard-surfacing material can be used in place of the bar, for the same effect.

TOE-EXTENSION SHOE
The extension is used on the side the horse usually breaks over, forcing break-over at the center of the squared toe.

Three examples of corrective shoes that help correct improper break-over, forcing the toe to break-over at the center, are illustrated above. A horseman first must discover the true nature of the gait defect, then apply the proper corrective shoe.

undisturbed. The rods on each side help make the horse break-over the center of the open toe. A shoe of this sort can be used if the foot is trimmed quite level initially.

Shoe calks sometimes can be used to create the same effect as the welded rod. The calks should be about one-half-inch high and are welded to the heels and to either side of the toe at the first nail position. Like the high inside rims, these calks help force break-over at the center of the toe.

Many mild cases of toe-in or toe-out are corrected by using square-toed shoes. The square toe makes the foot break-over straight. The foot should be trimmed level and the shoe placed so the toe of the foot is even with the toe of the shoe, the square portion sticking out on either side. Don't dub off the horse's toe.

A toe extension on the shoe serves the same purpose even more effectively. This shoe is made by welding an extension to the toe of the shoe, on the side over which the horse breaks. This extension thus interferes with the crooked break-over and helps the horse break-over straight.

Interference can be a serious problem. Sometimes it's only mild, if the horse merely brushes one leg against the other or does so only when tired or excited. But interference becomes serious if the horse does it consistently or forcefully enough to cause injury. Interference is most common in the hind legs and the fetlock joint is the most common site of injury. Trotters and pacers tend to interfere in front, striking the opposite knee.

Severe interference usually can be corrected by squaring the toe — or using a toe-extension shoe which forces the foot to break-over squarely at the center of the toe — then altering the shape of the hoof and shoe so it won't strike the opposite leg. This can be done by carefully determining the part of the foot or shoe doing the striking. This is done by using chalk or some other coloring substance, coating the opposite leg in the area the horse strikes, then observing where the telltale coloring is brushed onto the hoof or shoe

that does the striking. That portion of the hoof is then rasped and the shoe altered to fit. The offending foot then will not quite reach the opposite leg. Corrective shoes for a horse that interferes always should be extra-light.

Other problems that can occur when the horse travels are forging and cross-firing. Forging is a fairly common defect in which the toe of the hind foot or shoe strikes the heel or sole of the front foot on the same side and occurs

This is the appearance of a hoof that was surgically removed from a dead horse, with inside components removed. Note the thick edge at the coronary band.

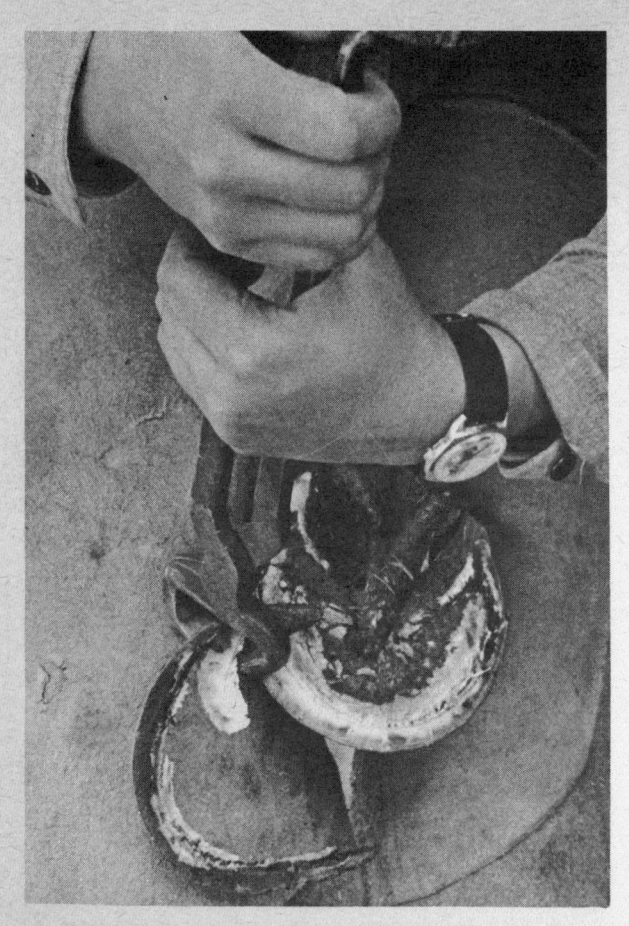

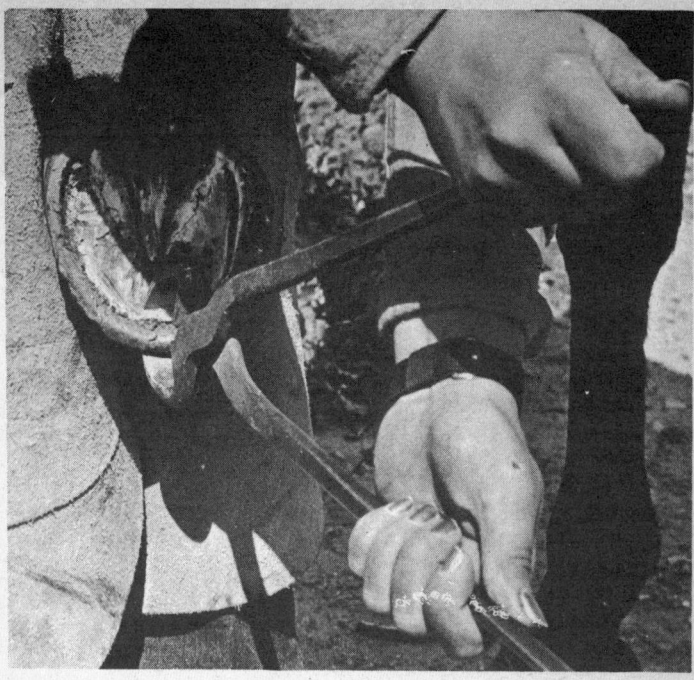

Removing shoe and trimming (left and above), Calamity Jane uses nippers. These are first two shoeing steps.

A heavy rasp then is employed to level hoof (left). When smooth, white line is easily distinguished (below). Nail inward no farther.

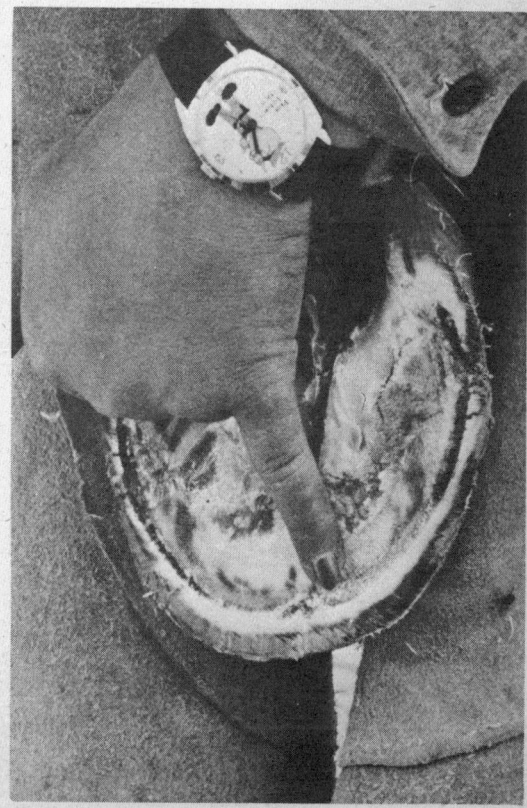

A farrier will shape a shoe to fit the hoof, not vice versa (right), as feet often don't comform exactly to shoe shape.

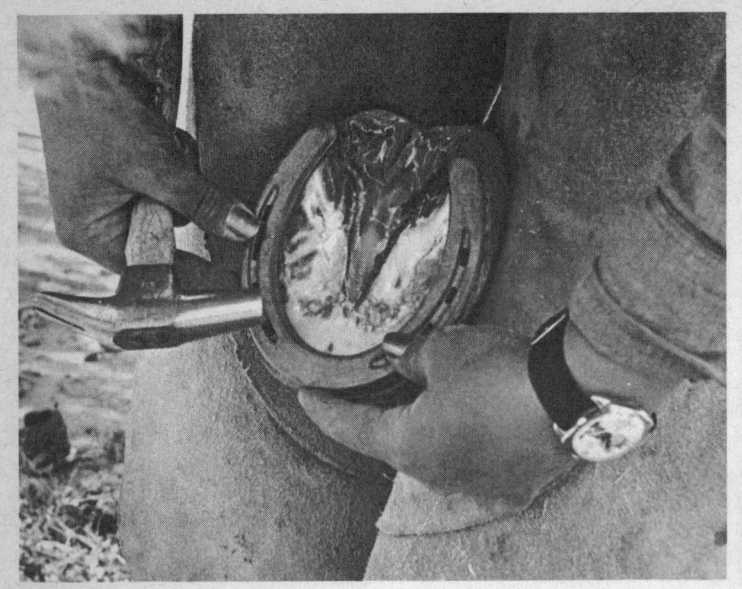

During shaping, the shoe continually is matched against the foot (above), until conforming perfectly. If necessary, a leather pad is cut from a large blank, then tacked on. This is common with horses used for endurance riding.

most commonly at the trot. Forging can be due to poor conformation: a horse that has hind legs too far underneath his body; sickle-hocked; from having a short back and long legs; or long hind legs and short front legs. It also can be caused by leaving too much heel on the front shoe.

In severe cases of forging, there is damage to the front foot from the continual striking, or the horse periodically pulls a front shoe by stepping on it with his hind foot, perhaps tripping in the process. In more common, milder forms of forging, the trot is simply a noisy gait because the front and hind shoes clack together.

To correct forging, keep in mind that the front foot must be encouraged to break-over and be lifted from the ground more quickly to get out of the way of the approaching hind feet. Too, the hind foot must take a slightly shorter stride so that it won't quite reach the front feet.

The horse should be ridden at the walk and trot as his leg action is observed to determine the rate of speed at which the forging is worst. Also, check the horse's conformation to see if the feet are properly balanced. If the horse is wearing shoes, check if they are properly fitted and of proper weight; a heavy shoe will aggravate the problem.

When shoeing a horse that forges, the heel of the front shoes and the toes of the hind shoes should be shortened so they will be less likely to meet. Lightweight shoes should be used, for weight increases the length of the horse's stride. A rocker or roller toe — or dubbing the front toes a little shorter — can be used on the front feet to encourage faster break-over and to come off the ground sooner. The hind feet should be left a little longer than normal so they won't break-over as quickly and shod with very light shoes. Shortening the toe of the hind foot too much in an attempt to keep it from hitting the front foot will usually make the problem worse, because the short toe will cause the foot to come off the ground faster. This makes it more apt to reach the front foot before it's moved out of the way.

The hind shoes can have slightly turned-out heels that extend one-half to three-fourths of an inch beyond the hoof, the extra heel tending to stop the hind foot as it is being put down, or can be shod with heel calks and a rocker toe to increase hock action, making the horse pick his foot up higher instead of swinging it so far forward. The heel calks tend to stop the hind foot before it hits the front foot.

Cross-firing is about the same as forging except it usually only occurs in pacers. The toe of the hind foot strikes the heel of the diagonal front foot. This problem is most likely to occur in a pacer that is splay-footed in front and pigeon-toed behind. The splay-footed front hoof moves inward during the first part of its stride and the pigeon-toed hind

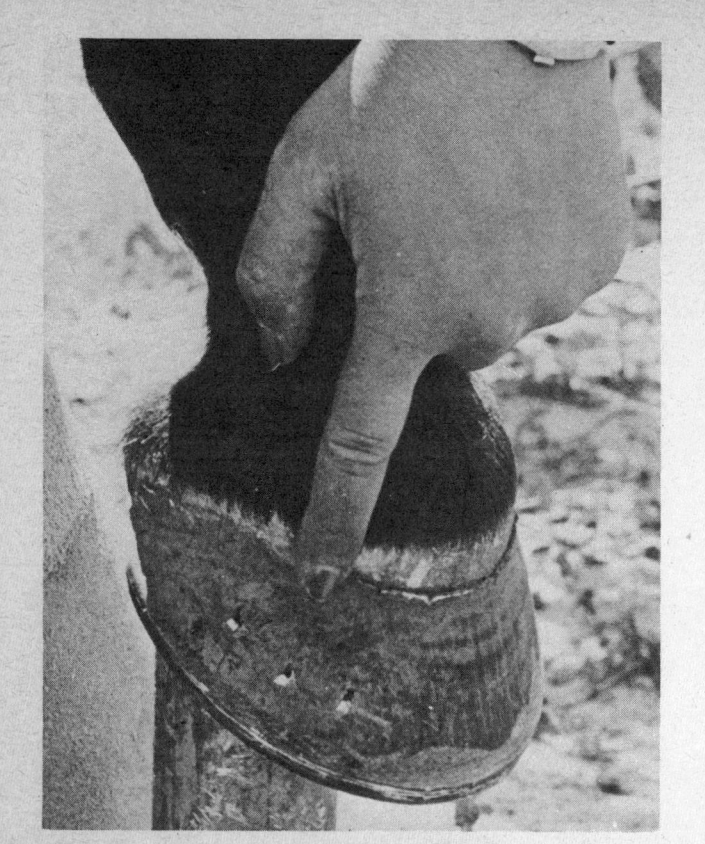

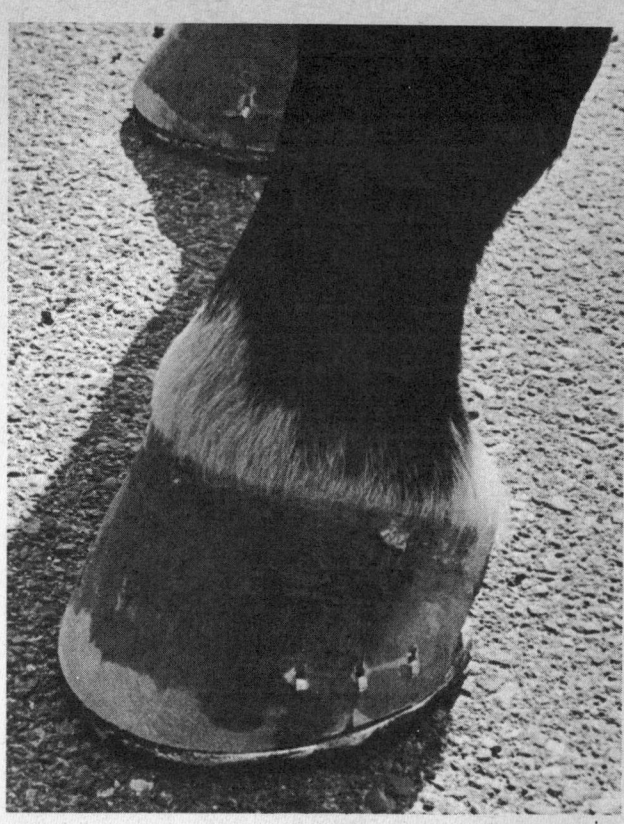

After the shoe has been nailed to hoof and the nail tips wrung off, they must be rasped to avoid horse cutting himself (left). The finished hoof, seen at right, is quite different than prior to shoeing. Farrier's attention is required again in a month.

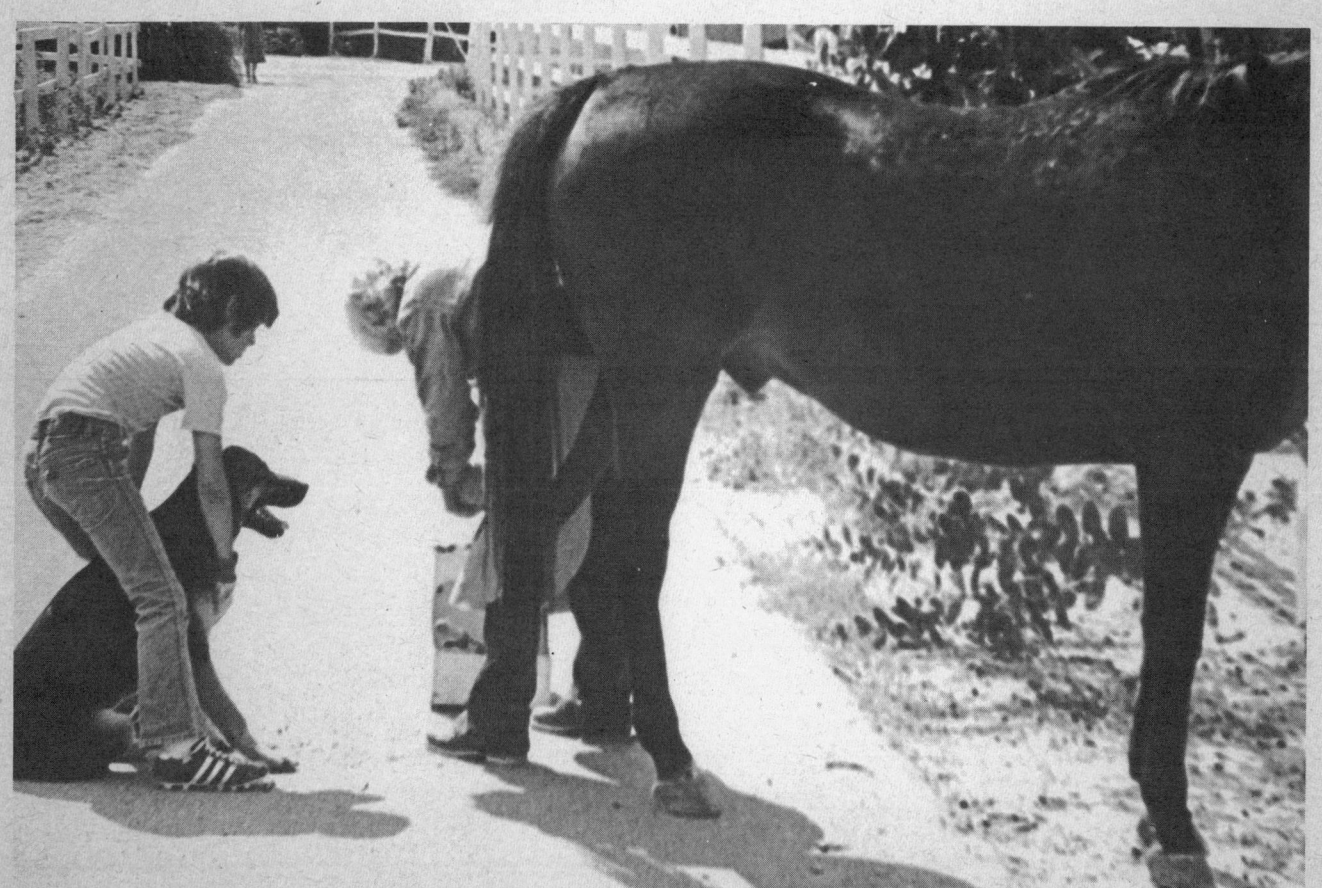

Spectators of all types gather when the farrier plies the trade. Unfortunately, not all horseowners know how to best ease the farrier's job. A horse that's jumping or pitching is difficult to shoe and many farriers will simply not attempt to do so.

During the rasping part of shoeing routine, Ms. Desrosiers utilizes a pipe and base implement. This is sturdy and a horse isn't likely to knock it over — especially when she stands on it! The inset photo shows the final rasping of the hoof.

foot moves inward during the last part of its stride, so diagonal feet meet. To correct this, both the fronts and hinds should be encouraged to move forward in straighter lines. The best way to accomplish this is to make the feet break-over the center of the toe and thus begin the stride in the proper direction — straight ahead.

Corrective shoeing also can be beneficial in treating certain types of injuries and abnormalities in the foot, such as flexor tendinitis, lameness from corns, chronic laminitis, contracted heels, ringbone, sidebone, cracked hoofs and wire cuts in the coronary band.

When shoeing a horse with contracted heels, remember that the frog must have pressure to help establish the normal functions of the foot and gradually spread the heels again. If possible, the horse should be allowed to go barefoot, since shoes tend to hinder normal expansion of the foot. If the horse can go barefoot, with his feet trimmed often, frog pressure and foot expansion will help correct the contracted condition.

If the horse must be shod, a tip shoe which just covers the toe area can be used if he isn't ridden much or in rocky areas. The tip shoe protects the toe from excessive wear but leaves the heel area unshod for greater frog pressure. A full-bar, half-bar or "T" shoe induces more frog pressure, the bar or "T" putting pressure on the frog when the horse puts weight on the foot. A slipper shoe lets the heels of the foot slide outward when weight is applied.

A contracted foot also can be helped by thinning the hoof wall at the quarters with a rasp. This thinning should start about half an inch below the coronary band in the area of the quarters and heels, gradually decreasing until the hoof wall at the ground surface is of normal thickness. This thinning helps the hoof wall expand when the horse puts weight on the foot. If the foot is thinned, it should also be shod with a pressure bar shoe which increases frog pressure and treated with hoof dressing daily to keep the thinned wall from cracking.

Corrective shoeing for a horse with ringbone calls for shortening the toe and putting on a full roller motion shoe. This shoe helps transfer action from the pastern and coffin joints to the bottom of the foot, the roller motion shoe making the foot break-over quickly and easily. The same type of shoe can help a horse with sidebones.

A horse with corns should go barefoot if possible. If he must be shod, the hoof wall and bar in the corn area should be cut away so there will be no pressure on the sole. A half or full-bar shoe can be used, fitted so the frog absorbs most of the concussion.

Cracks in the hoof wall sometimes require corrective shoeing. A shoe often will help keep the split hoof wall from cracking farther.

The foot should be trimmed so there will be no direct pressure on the split; in other words, that area of the hoof wall must not bear weight. This will allow the hoof wall to

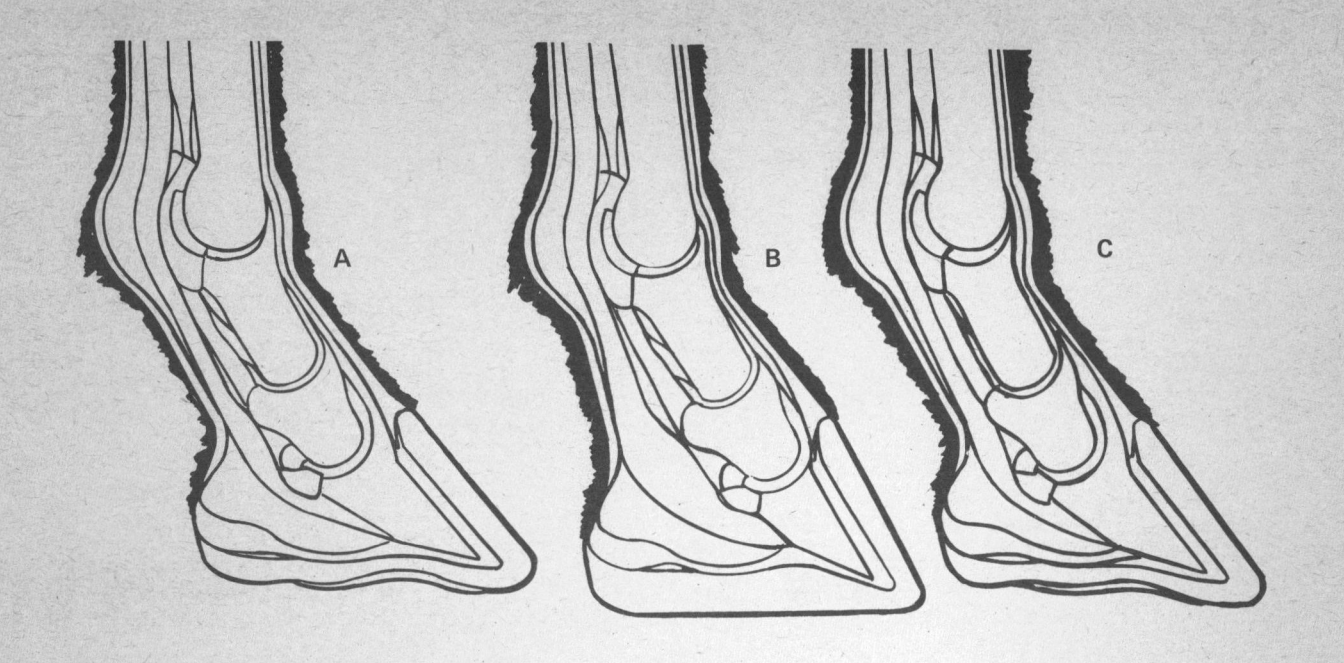

(A) The author's impression of the normal foot and lower leg of the horse. Note conformation of bones.

(B) In this instance, the hoof is not trimmed properly at the heel; internal parts are repositioned.

(C) This hoof has been improperly trimmed at the toe, rearranging the internal parts. Damage can result.

The above illustration shows the need for hoof knowledge. At left is normal foot, center is hoof with heel too long, and right is improperly trimmed toe. This shifts stress points within the foot and can cause serious lameness.

begin growing out without further widening of the crack.

The progress of the crack should be halted, if possible, by rasping a groove at the farthest point of the crack. If the crack penetrates into the sensitive tissues of the hoof, the horse will be lame because of infection. If this is the case, the crack should be thoroughly cleaned and disinfected with iodine, and the horse should be given a tetanus shot.

If the horse is left barefoot, the crack should be grooved and the bearing surface of the hoof wall in that area should be cut away so it doesn't bear weight and expand the crack. For a toe crack, the toe should be trimmed on either side of the crack. For a quarter crack, the hoof wall at the heel should be trimmed, from the crack on back, so the heel area will not take weight and spread the crack. Heel cracks are treated identically.

When shoeing a horse with a hoof crack, the foot is trimmed so the area around the crack does not touch the shoe and bear weight. Sometimes a clip on each side of the crack is helpful to keep the hoof wall from expanding, helping to support the hoof in that area. A half-bar shoe

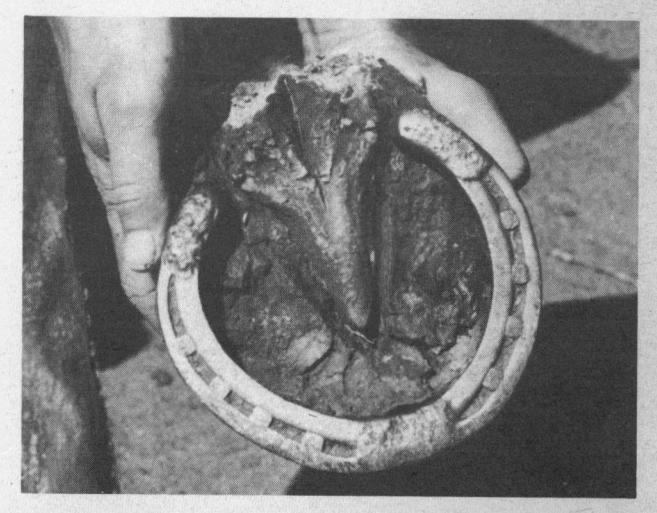

Borium is added to shoe (above right) to aid traction on slippery surfaces. Leather pads control loss of a hoof's moisture, necessary for healthy, normal frog (right).

sometimes is helpful for a quarter crack, producing frog pressure by allowing the frog to bear some of the weight that ordinarily would be borne by the hoof wall that has been trimmed away from the crack.

Part of the secret of growing out a hoof crack is to trim the foot often, so there will be little expansion pressure on the crack. If the hoof wall grows too long, the crack will tend to split farther. Careful grooving of the top of the crack and frequent trimming or corrective shoeing eventually will clear up a hoof crack that begins at the ground surface of the hoof wall.

If the crack is kept from widening or progressing, the normal hoof growth will eventually grow it out. But a hoof crack that originates in the coronary band from injury will be a more difficult and persistent problem. Corrective shoeing may be necessary for the rest of the horse's life, for a defect in the coronary band causes distorted and defective growth of the hoof in that area. The hoof wall in that place may have to be rasped every two weeks to keep the horn growth as nearly normal as possible, and the coronary band rubbed daily with olive oil or some other suitable softening agent if hard and dry.

Sometimes a severe hoof crack can be repaired with a strong glue. We saw this several years ago on a bad quarter crack in a 20-year-old mare's right front foot. She had a stubborn crack originating at the ground surface of the hoof, made worse by scar tissue at the coronary band above it, weakening the hoof wall in that place. Because of the weak strip in the hoof wall, this quarter crack spread upward rapidly in spite of conventional methods used to halt its progress. A strong, fast-drying glue was used to help hold the cracked area together and prevent further splitting as the hoof wall grew out. A glue used for this purpose must be strong or it won't hold the hoof wall solidly together when weight is placed upon it, expanding the hoof. The hoof wall must not expand in the area of the crack.

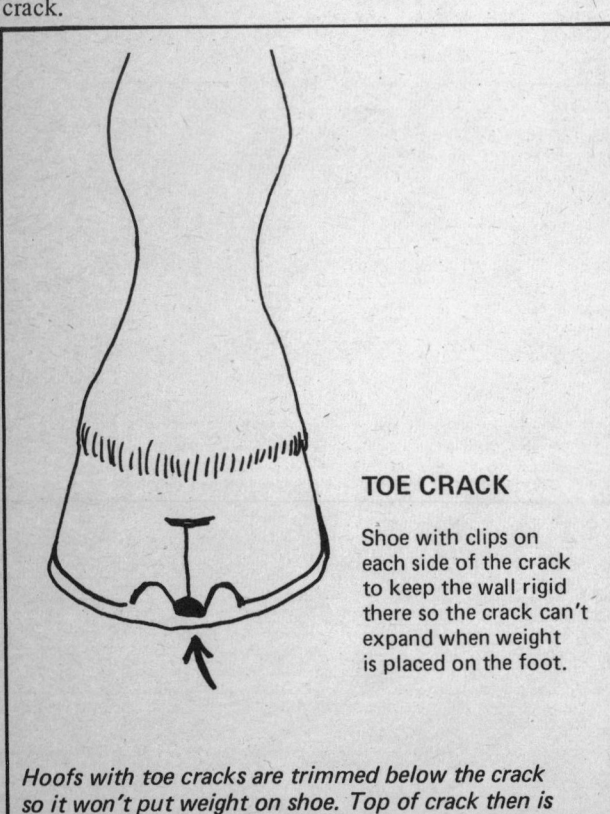

TOE CRACK

Shoe with clips on each side of the crack to keep the wall rigid there so the crack can't expand when weight is placed on the foot.

Hoofs with toe cracks are trimmed below the crack so it won't put weight on shoe. Top of crack then is rasped to help keep it from extending upwards farther.

First, the ground surface of the hoof wall was trimmed so the cracked area would not bear weight, then thoroughly cleaned to ensure there would be no dirt or foreign material to interfere with the adhesion of the glue to the hoof wall. A strip of strong fiberglass mesh was put over the crack area to add strength and the glue applied, thoroughly filling the crack. Her foot was held for twenty minutes so that the glue would have time to set before she placed weight on the foot. She was patient, even though the glue used produced some heat during its drying. After drying, it was solid enough to hold the crack and keep the area solid and unexpanding.

If done carefully and adequately, this is a procedure we would highly recommend for holding a stubborn hoof crack as the foot grows out. The foot still must be trimmed often, or the corrective shoes reset, and the glue may have to be replaced periodically until the crack has grown out sufficiently.

When shoeing a horse with flat feet, the sole should not be trimmed much, if any, and the frog shouldn't be trimmed. The wall should be trimmed only a little, enough to smooth it for the shoe. The shoe should cover the wall and white line and just barely touch upon the sole. If the shoe is seated merely on the hoof wall, the sole will tend to drop farther as the hoof wall grows and pushes outward. If the shoe is seated in such a way that there is too much bearing upon the sole — if the web of the shoe is too wide — sole pressure may cause bruising and lameness.

If a horse has chronic laminitis or founder, he sometimes can be helped by corrective trimming and shoeing. The foundered foot should be trimmed as closely as possible, more often than for a normal horse. Wide-webbed shoes may keep the sole from dropping farther. The heel can be trimmed as much as possible without making the horse tender to help correct and counteract the downward rotation of the third phalanx or coffin bone. The toe of the hoof wall can be trimmed and rasped back to a more nearly normal shape. The edge of the hoof wall at the toe should be shortened slightly so it doesn't bear on the shoe. The toe of the shoe should be rolled to help the foot break-over easily when in motion.

In a foundered horse, the pain is mostly in the toe area of the sole. Therefore, the best type of shoe for founder is designed to remove all pressure from the painful sole and transfer it to the wall and frog which are less sensitive. A wide-webbed shoe should have a concave upper surface so that when the horse bears weight on the foot, all pressure is upon the hoof wall and none upon the sole. The wide web is there to help keep the sole from dropping. It may also be necessary to protect the sole by using a rubber or leather pad under the shoe, or even a metal plate.

Corrective trimming and shoeing cannot always completely correct a fault or defect in a horse's way of going, or completely cure an injured or diseased foot. But corrective trimming and shoeing, carefully and conscientiously done, usually can help the problem to some degree, often making the horse more useful, or alleviating his pain so he can move more normally.

Corrective trimming and shoeing cannot produce miracles; in many cases an unsound horse will always be an unsound horse. But if the horse's feet or gaits are helped in any degree, it may lengthen the life of that particular animal as a pleasure horse or breeding animal, or enable him to fill whatever other role he may be used in.

In a very real sense, every farrier should be able to trim and shoe correctively, for few horses are perfect and most can be helped by proper trimming and shoeing methods that take even the minor defects into consideration.